Sport in the American West
Jorge Iber, series editor

Also in the series

Team picture of the 1962–63 NCAA champion Loyola Ramblers. Courtesy of the Loyola Sports Information Office.

BECOMING
IRON MEN

The Story of the **BECOMING**
1963 Loyola Ramblers **IRON MEN**

By Lew Freedman

Texas Tech University Press

This book is typeset in Perrywood. The paper used in this book meets the minimum
requirements of ANSI/NISO Z39.48-1992 (R1997). ∞

Designed by Kasey McBeath
Cover photographs courtesy of Loyola Sports Information Office and Paul Smulson.

Library of Congress Cataloging-in-Publication Data
Freedman, Lew.
    Becoming iron men : the story of the 1963 Loyola Ramblers / Lew Freedman.
        pages cm. — (Sport in the American west)
    Summary: "Details the 1963 NCAA championship run of the Loyola University's
    basketball team, with four African-American starters, a team of underdogs defying
    the ills of racial discrimination and prejudice."—Provided by publisher

    Includes bibliographical references and index.

    ISBN 978-0-89672-877-6 (hardback) — ISBN 978-0-89672-878-3 (e-book)
    1. Loyola University Chicago—Basketball—History—20th century. 2. Loyola
    Ramblers (Basketball team)—History—20th century. 3. Racism in sports—United
    States. I. Title.

    GV885.43.L67F74 2014

    796.323'630977311—dc23   2013050894

14 15 16 17 18 19 20 21 22 / 9 8 7 6 5 4 3 2 1

Texas Tech University Press
Box 41037 | Lubbock, Texas 79409-1037 USA
800.832.4042 | ttup@ttu.edu | www.ttupress.org

This book is dedicated to all of the African American athletes of the 1960s who made such a difference as pioneers in integrating college sport in the United States.

CONTENTS

Contents

ILLUSTRATIONS

BECOMING
IRON MEN

George Ireland, head coach of the Loyola Ramblers. Ireland had the foresight and willing-
ness to recruit African American players in the early 1960s when prejudice dominated
American society and almost no other coaches at NCAA Division I schools were doing so.
Courtesy of the Loyola Sports Information Office.

INTRODUCTION

oyola University of Chicago was ahead of its time during an uneasy American era, when racial matters were at the forefront of an impending and long-overdue revolution in civil rights. The Ramblers of the 1962–1963 NCAA college basketball season were basketball players first and pioneers second, though at times they didn't know they were pioneers at all.

Sociologists can make the case that one of the leading areas of breakthrough into mainstream American society for African Americans came on the playing fields of the nation's sports teams. Sometimes it was by design, sometimes by happenstance. But there is little doubt that doors were opened, even if just a crack, by sports teams, that the cause of brotherhood was advanced, and that the firm barriers of discrimination were chipped away by athletes sharing the concepts of teamwork.

With few exceptions, in any major sport it took until after World War II for Americans to accept integration on their playing fields. Heavyweight champion Joe Louis was one of the most famous people in the country— even before he won the crown in 1937—and was certainly the most prominent black American during his reign that lasted until 1949. This was at a time when possession of the heavyweight title represented the most prestigious individual honor in the sports world. In 1936, he was joined in a limited pantheon of black American sports heroes by Jesse Owens, the speedster from Ohio who won four gold medals in the Berlin Olympics.

In 1947, Jackie Robinson, formerly of the Kansas City Monarchs of the Negro Leagues and of UCLA's college football backfield, broke the twentieth-century Major League Baseball color barrier when he began playing for the Brooklyn Dodgers.

Before 1950, black players gained spots on professional football team rosters, and by mid-century the first African Americans were playing on teams in the National Basketball Association.

A milestone of integration in college basketball was achieved when Billy

Garrett became a star for the Indiana University Hoosiers in 1947. Garrett was the Big Ten Conference's first black starter.

All of these developments represented breakthroughs, but just because a single team made progress did not mean that African Americans were welcome on the rest of the teams in a league. It took until 1959 for the last Major League Baseball club to integrate. It took until the late 1960s for Southeastern Conference colleges to integrate their sports teams.

In the 2000s, it is routine and unremarked upon for a college basketball team to start five African Americans—indeed, to have a roster consisting of ten African Americans and two white players. That was not so in the early 1960s when the Reverend Martin Luther King, Jr., was still leading marches demanding basic civil rights and it took federal troops to integrate Southern schools.

At the Jesuit university on Chicago's near-north side along Lake Michigan, coach George Ireland was hung in effigy by hard-hearted local protestors for having the nerve to start multiple black players in his lineup. Few major college programs had three African Americans on the team at the time.

It took fortitude for Ireland to stick with his commitment to play the best players regardless of color when he started four African Americans at once, and it was risky for his future. He was aware he might face a firestorm—and he did receive hate mail—but Ireland did not back off. At one point during the school's landmark 1962–63 season, Ireland sent out a lineup in the middle of a game that was 100 percent African American. That represented the first time in the history of NCAA large-school basketball that any school had done that.

Until 1962, the only teams that as a matter of course featured five African Americans on the court at one time were the traditionally black schools of the South, such as Grambling, Florida A&M, Tennessee State, and their brethren. The University of Cincinnati defied tradition by starting three black players when capturing the 1962 NCAA title.

Texas Western University's milestone accomplishment, with five black starters in winning the 1965–66 crown, lay in the future. That victory gained far more attention than Loyola's accomplishment three years earlier. Loyola's triumphs have been overshadowed by Texas Western's defeat of an all-white Kentucky team, a circumstance exacerbated by production of the Hollywood movie *Glory Road*.

It seems like such a small thing now to witness four or five black basketball players on the court representing one school at one time, but basketball players of the sixties era understood that the college game was not that much different from society at large. There were limits; there were quotas. It was a big deal for a so-called white school to offer a scholarship to any black basketball player at that time.

Ireland was no calculating champion of integration in the vein of Branch Rickey, the general manager of the Brooklyn Dodgers who hired Jackie Robinson, and then several other black players such as Roy Campanella and Don Newcombe, to be the lightning-rod first African American major league competitors in the twentieth century. Rickey knew he was undertaking a monumental assignment. Meticulous planning and investigation predated his offer to sign Robinson. Ireland, conversely, was trying to build a better basketball program and win enough games to save his job.

One thing the two men had in common was that desire to win. Rickey knew that Robinson was a good enough player to uplift the fortunes of his team. And when Rickey hired still more African American players, the Dodgers became routine pennant contenders and regular winners.

Rickey held lofty ideals. He knew what he was doing was important and right for American society. Yet he also hungered for victory. Ireland, by instinct, if nothing more, also knew that being color blind in terms of offering scholarships would allow him to put the best possible team on the court. No one ever heard Ireland deliver major speeches on race relations. He was not that type of man. He was a basketball coach.

Yet what Ireland did, practicing what others hoped would become commonplace some time down the line (and it did), meant that he too was a pioneer. Throughout the civil rights movement's heyday, Dr. Martin Luther King, Jr., Ralph Abernathy, Andrew Young, and other black leaders said all they wanted was equal opportunity. In the tiny corner of the world that he could control—the Loyola basketball team—Ireland provided it.

If Ireland had recruited poorly and suited up four or five African Americans at one time and lost too many games, then he would have been kicked out of his job as surely as he would have been if he lost too often with white players. Nobody beyond the boundaries of Chicago would have heard of Loyola or Ireland. No, winning, and winning big, was what set this team apart and why its story is a special one. Not only was Loyola a champion of equal opportunity through its actions, but it set itself apart from all previous and future Loyola teams with its victories.

Results made the reward of doing the right thing as sweet as anyone could imagine. There was hardship and heartache along the way, though nothing as physically dangerous or dramatic as what was endured by those who confronted the vicious racism of the South head-on on the streets of Mississippi, Arkansas, and Alabama.

In a widely heralded game, Loyola, with its numerous African American players, met Mississippi State, with its all-white team, during the NCAA tournament. The situation shone a spotlight on Mississippi's antiquated laws preventing blacks and whites from competing on the same playing fields, and national scrutiny ensued when the Mississippi team had to defy government officials even to take part in the game.

In its own small way, by playing a game, the Ramblers contributed to racial harmony in this country. Ireland had many opportunities to retreat from his commitment to recruiting black players. He had many opportunities to retreat from playing the best men on his roster—and he received many threats warning him he better not play so many African Americans at once, that it would be bad for his health and theirs if he continued to do so. He continued to do so. The threats were loud, if hollow.

The early 1960s ushered in a time of change in the United States. The land of the free and the home of the brave was entering one of the most racially charged periods in American history as African Americans who had so long been discriminated against rose up and began a new and concentrated battle to attain the rights granted to them by the Constitution.

As it had been for about two decades, the sports world remained a leader in integration, helping pave the way for equality in society at large. Wherever a ball was thrown, kicked, or swung at with a bat, African Americans were getting long-overdue chances to participate in the most visible and most important collegiate and professional leagues. Barriers fell as if dynamited. An America sick with race hatred dating back to before the Civil War ended slavery, was awakening and gradually taking baby steps toward becoming a more just society.

Giant steps were being taken, too, but not all ills were cured overnight. Not all attitudes were transformed instantly. The premier black athletes of the late 1940s and right up to the early 1960s were grateful for opportunities denied their predecessors, but they were still resentful of slights that were common on their own teams, in their own leagues, and amongst spectators seemingly trapped in another time.

The college basketball season that played out over the winter of 1962–63 was, like Camelot, a magical time for the small Chicago school—for one brief, shining moment. It was the culmination of George Ireland's hopes and dreams. It was a morality play against the backdrop of the nation's angst about race. It was the coming together of a special team at the right time for an unheralded school. Those living talk of the closeness they shared on the ride to glory, how they came together as a unit and overcame some very serious obstacles to achieve triumph.

The Loyola squad endured much in order to conquer. Employing a dazzling fast-break style that had also served the professional Boston Celtics well, coupled with ego-crushing defensive full-court pressure, the Ramblers led the nation in scoring and frequently walloped teams by huge margins.

In December of 1962 the team competed in the venerable All-College Classic in Oklahoma City. In a game against Wyoming that was otherwise routine, the Ramblers became the first NCAA large-school team to ever have five African American players on the court at the same time.

During travels to away games against Southern schools, the Ramblers saw up close (and faced down) the raw, undisguised hatred of those who believed in white supremacy. The players dealt with segregation firsthand, contending with "colored" and "whites-only" water fountains, whites-only hotels and restaurants, even segregated taxicabs.

With the players already friends, and no discord internally because of differences in skin color, the tribulations of the road helped bond the whites and blacks of Loyola even more tightly. This made it a shock when the team was rent from inside in midseason. Two players did not make grades and were dismissed from school. A third, who did not play much, chose to depart. Neither of those lost to grades was a starter, but both were important cogs as the sixth and seventh men, the first two subs off the bench. Their departures could very well have disrupted the team's chemistry and ability to compete against the best opponents, particularly if a starter got into foul trouble. Yet the remarkable cohesiveness of this group helped them merely shrug off the loss of two integral players, doing whatever extra it might take to overcome their exits.

As the season wore on and the country took notice, Loyola rose higher and higher in the national rankings, reaching the number two spot in the polls. Then, when the NCAA tournament began in March, Loyola engaged in a series of games for the ages. Records were set, rivals faced, and one of the most famous and significant contests in college basketball playoff history played out in what accidentally became a model showcase for race relations. Nearly every time the Ramblers took the court, for a different reason, the game was unusual for its magnitude. At times Loyola was an iron man team, with the five starters playing the entire game. At a time when there was no college basketball on television, Loyola appeared on television.

Just about everything the Ramblers touched during the 1962–63 season was unique or ahead of its time. Right up to the final buzzer of the final game of the season, Loyola guaranteed excitement and suspense.

When a season of such drama unfolds, no one wants it to end, not the participants, not the witnesses. Inevitably the clock does run out and real life does go on. Frozen in minds but impossible to freeze in time, for Loyola, the most important basketball season in school history is never to be forgotten.

Players graduated from school, married, raised families. Some of them entered the business world. Some were lucky enough to play professional basketball. As time passed and as the men passed through middle age and came to retirement age—all those still living are around seventy now—their shared experience kept coming around on them. The biggest stars on the team had their jersey numbers retired by the school. The biggest stars on the team were inducted into Loyola's Sports Hall of Fame. Then, finally, the bench players were inducted into the hall. On the occasions of their special recognition, the players gathered for reunions in Chicago to both reflect on and relive their great accomplishments.

As the fiftieth anniversary of their greatest victories approached and passed, more of the world took notice. In 2013, the Loyola Ramblers became the first team inducted into the College Basketball Hall of Fame in Kansas City. Later that year, Loyola was inducted into the Chicagoland Sports Hall of Fame.

With each passing year, their own maturity no doubt playing a role in how they view the past, the more impressive their unique time together became. When they were young and fast and strong, the Ramblers were too busy chasing victories to attach any special meaning to what they did. Now, especially among the African American players, a deep satisfaction stems from the belief that they contributed in their own small way to the exceptional cause of the civil rights movement that reshaped America.

The entire journey, the adventure of the season, has bound tight for a lifetime the group of men who lived through it.

CHAPTER 1

THE SHOWDOWN WITH CINCINNATI

t was the opposite of the Robert Frost poem. Two roads diverged in the early season, before the snowy evenings of winter, but they intersected again at Freedom Hall in Louisville on the final night of the 1962–63 college basketball season. Neither the number one–ranked University of Cincinnati, playing in its fifth straight Final Four and chasing a third straight NCAA championship, nor Loyola, the hungry then-top-three rated team in the nation, would admit to any surprise at being there. By now the Bearcats, in their third championship game in a row, felt it was practically a birthright. For Loyola, the upstart, the comparative unknown on an unlikely journey, this was something fresh. But the Ramblers very much felt they had earned the chance to play for college basketball's biggest prize.

The distance between Cincinnati and Chicago is about three hundred miles by road. Yet the gulf between the basketball programs' histories might have been measured in light-years. In recent years, the Bearcats, the pride of the Queen City, had elevated the great Oscar Robertson to national prominence (or had he lifted them?). Twice Cincinnati had spoiled the dreams of powerhouse Ohio State, certainly among the greatest Buckeyes teams of all time.

Loyola was the new kid, little known outside the Windy City, in an era before college basketball filled the nightly viewing slots on seemingly every cable television channel between December and March. The basketball cognoscenti knew all about Loyola, though.

Coming off a 23–4 season in 1961–62, the Ramblers were ripe for a national breakthrough. Anyone who had seen them play recognized that they were going to be a dangerous team the next year, no pushover for anyone. Under coach George Ireland the Ramblers had developed two lethal and

Vic Rouse is perfectly positioned
to put in a basket after a rebound
in Loyola's NCAA championship
victory over Cincinnati, a dramatic
60–58 overtime game, in 1963.
Courtesy of the Loyola Sports
Information Office.

complementary areas of expertise. On defense, Loyola was indefatigable.
Playing full-court pressure defense was only a useful tactic if a team was
in tremendous shape. The Ramblers were. They never ran out of energy
and they harassed and annoyed teams that wished to bring the ball up-court
slowly and methodically. To those teams the Ramblers were like a swarming
plague of mosquitoes. It was maddening to try to run your stuff with someone in your face the entire time, challenging you, bugging you, disrupting
your thought process.

On offense Loyola was opportunistic, relentless in pushing the ball up
fast to score. Ireland showed no mercy. His men could be like a pack of
wolves on the hunt for dinner, never letting up, demoralizing teams with
their quickness, speed, running style, and jumping ability, playing so hard
for so long other teams gave out and gave up. That approach made Loyola
the highest-scoring team in the country during the regular season, averaging
ninety-plus points per game.

Still, the Ramblers played with one eye on Cincinnati. Cincinnati was
the kingpin. The Bearcats were ranked first in the land because of their
track record. Several members of the team figured to play professionally.

The Bearcats, and Coach Ed Jucker, were much-admired and respected. The Bearcats whipped everyone that stood in their way for three years running to reach this third straight championship final on March 23, 1963.

As a team in terms of style and preferred method of play, Cincinnati was the polar opposite of Loyola. Whereas Loyola loved to run, the Bearcats took their time dribbling the ball into the frontcourt and ran a patterned offense. Whereas Loyola sought the advantage by pressing all over the court, Cincinnati picked up men defensively after half-court. Teams didn't score easily on Cincinnati, the nation's leader in defense.

Loyola's offense resembled that of the Boston Celtics. During that period, from the late 1950s through the decade of the 1960s, the Celtics were the best basketball team ever assembled. They won eleven world championships in thirteen years, and offensively Boston, under genius coach Red Auerbach, thrived with the fast-break offense. The rudiments of Loyola's break were essentially the same as Boston's. A big man cleared the boards, then fired the outlet pass, and that middle man galloped into the frontcourt looking for an open man streaking down the sideline. Not everyone had the horses to operate in this way, but Loyola did.

Cincinnati's strength was controlling the tempo of a game, imposing its will on the foe. Cincinnati made teams play its way. The question was whether or not Cincinnati could slow down Loyola or Loyola could force the Bearcats into a running game. The team able to force the opposition out of its comfort zone and play in a manner it did not relish seemed the likely conqueror.

Early in the season Loyola and Cincinnati played on the same court on the same day against other foes as part of a doubleheader at Chicago Stadium. One team was coming off the court after a victory and another team was readying to take the court to warm up. This was a very confident Cincinnati bunch, with players like sharpshooter Ron Bonham, center George Wilson, and guard Tom Thacker, all of whom would soon be playing professionally.

"Cincinnati was on the same card," said Loyola guard Ron Miller. "I remember walking off the court and Tom Thacker was standing there. Thacker said, 'Nice game.' I said, 'I guess we'll see you guys in a while.'" That meant in March in the NCAA playoffs. Thacker's reply seemed a bit arrogant to Miller, though Cincinnati had earned the right. "We'll be there," Thacker said. "I don't know if you'll be there."[1]

That was a comment to remember. A little jibe. Championship teams come to the fight armed with that feeling of invincibility. It is one of the things that made them great. For two years, Oscar Robertson, the six-foot-five guard who some believe is the greatest basketball player who ever lived, was the cornerstone of the program. Robertson led Cincinnati to the Final Four twice, but the Bearcats did not win a title.

When Robertson graduated directly to the Cincinnati Royals, the NBA team that was the forerunner of the Sacramento Kings, there was considerable hand-wringing amongst Cincinnati fans because they lost a once-in-a-lifetime player. Yet Jucker assembled a fresh core that made up for Robertson's departure by spreading responsibility.

When the average basketball fan looks back and sees Cincinnati on the list of NCAA title teams in the early 1960s, the assumption is made that it was part of the Robertson era. It was not. The wonder of Cincinnati's achievements was that Robertson left and the team actually got better. Cincinnati won two crowns in a row without Robertson. As they breezed through the 1962–63 schedule, as Thacker insisted, there was an unshakeable belief that the Bearcats would be there in the end again, that Cincinnati would play for its third consecutive championship.

In the early 1960s, there was not a glut of preseason prognostication. Not every sports magazine, not every sportswriter, was a Nostradamus, gazing into the future to rate the nation's top twenty-five teams. The Associated Press and United Press International conducted polls. A select group of annual magazines such as the type that would later proliferate and clog newsstands each October were out there. Loyola had done enough to be noticed and ranked. Were those publications calling Loyola the best team in the country? No. The easy choice was Cincinnati. There was no sports talk radio, no Internet chat rooms, no bloggers to make Loyola a trendy pick. The Ramblers were ranked. Good enough. Cincinnati resided in the penthouse. Anyone who sought to serve an eviction notice knew that the seasoned, tough, savvy Bearcats would be waiting at the door.

"Cincinnati was the big gorilla in the neighborhood that year," Miller said. "You didn't even dare to think you could beat Cincinnati."[2]

Well, yes and no. By the time Loyola reached the NCAA tournament, a scaled-down version of the March Madness that dominates conversation across the United States for three weeks in March in the 2000s, Loyola did dare to think big.

However, by the time Loyola advanced to the championship game, any scouting report on its principal weapons would include a startling comment. George Ireland had demonstrated that he had become as miserly as Scrooge with minutes. His starting five had become his only five. In a virtually unprecedented approach to big-time basketball Ireland drifted into a pattern where he started five men, stuck with five men, and never substituted short of an emergency.

Les Hunter, Vic Rouse, and Jerry Harkness in the frontcourt, Johnny Egan and Ron Miller in the backcourt had become the Loyola Iron Men. Loyola got this far by riding the broad backs of this quintet. It was clear that Ireland was going to live and die with this crew.

By game time, when they were the last two teams standing, the proud Cincinnati Bearcats were confident of becoming the first college team to claim three NCAA championships in a row. Loyola, as Miller announced to Thacker months earlier, was seeing them there. Teams become cohesive units over time. They do so by fending off challenges—on and off the court. They do so by winning. The Ramblers had grown into its status.

"They were number one all year long," Miller said. "We were number two most of the year. It pretty much stayed like that."[3]

Cincinnati was the heavyweight champion. Loyola was the acknowledged, anointed top contender, though in some weeks it slipped to third in the ratings. At no time did Loyola fear Cincinnati. The Ramblers believed it was their turn.

The site of the championship was storied Freedom Hall, a neutral court that held more than nineteen thousand fans. One of the most prominent indoor arenas in the country, the Louisville building was a favored venue for college ball. A predetermined location for the 1963 championship, Freedom Hall was conveniently located a mere one hundred miles from Cincinnati and three hundred miles from Chicago. It was a place that the automobile-driving fan supporting either team could easily reach. Finding a ticket upon arrival was another issue. But when the game—the first nationally televised NCAA basketball title game—tipped off, Freedom Hall was loud and raucous with plenty of spectators rooting on both sides.

As hungry as Chicago was to follow the live action, residents were reduced to listening to play-by-play on WCFL-AM radio. The alternative was exercising inhuman patience and waiting for the game to be shown later in the evening on WGN-TV—on tape delay.

The jump-ball tap was smacked a few dozen feet away and it came into the hands of Cincinnati point guard Tony Yates. Beginning in textbook fashion Yates fed the ball into the low post where the six-foot-eight George Wilson gathered in the pass and slam-dunked for a 2–0 Cincinnati lead. It was a statement shot, the type of in-your-face basket that could set the tone for an entire game.

If the opening minutes of the game were a feeling-out process, again like heavyweights probing with their jabs, Cincinnati got the best of it. Yates was able to find Wilson open for inside shots. Ron Bonham, whose smooth jumpers could fill up the hoop in a hurry, found seams in the Loyola defense. Normally, the Ramblers' running game was jump-started by their big men, Hunter and Rouse, clearing the boards and zipping passes halfway up the court to Miller or team leader Harkness in hopes of catching the other team off-balance and vulnerable to quick, easy baskets. However, this was one time the bread-and-butter rebounders were stifled. Loyola's shooting was off. Outside jumpers and twisting layup attempts were either clanking off or rolling off the rim. The Bearcats seized the misses and prevented second attempts for Loyola.

Several patterns, all trending against Loyola, were established in the opening portion of the forty-minute game. Scrappy point guard John Egan missed a twenty-foot jump shot. Rouse missed an outside shot. Nothing was more shocking than the complete inability of Harkness to score.

By then Ireland had come to rely on five key players as his starters, a five that meshed perfectly. Egan, Miller, Hunter, Rouse, and Harkness each had his own role, but every team needs one player to count on in crunch time, when tension is high, the pressure is on, and there is a desperate need for a basket. For the Ramblers, that was Harkness.

Harkness stood six foot three and was a lithe, athletic, and rangy player who had the stamina of a long-distance runner, which he had once been. He never tired, and by his senior year he had blossomed into one of the finest players in the country. He was an All-American and the go-to guy in the lineup.

Now, for the first time, Harkness was not Harkness. He was a left-handed shooter, and in the opening minutes Harkness's shots were like darts being thrown at a board with him missing the bull's-eye every time. One shot hit hard off the rim and bounced harmlessly into the corner. Another shot was an air ball. Harkness, the steadiest of all Loyola players, was missing like a fastball pitcher throwing the ball over the batter's head. That was a terrible signal for Loyola's chances. On the bench, backup center Rich Rochelle watched Harkness's shooting with disbelief.

"Our team revolved around Jerry," Rochelle said. "As Jerry went, our team went."[4]

No player is a superman. Every player has a bad game. But money players, as they are called, come up big when the spotlight is bright. Harkness had always been a clutch player. He was the Loyola bellwether. He did not appear timid on the court. He did not appear out of sorts. But the same jump shots that for months so smoothly slid off his palm and swished through the net were off-target repeatedly.

About ten minutes into the game, Cincinnati led 12–5. One-fourth of the game had been played and it was apparent that the Bearcats were making Loyola play their way, not how the Ramblers wanted to play. The vaunted Loyola fast break was invisible. The Cincinnati guards shrugged off back-court defensive pressure. Usually, Loyola's full-court defense created traps forcing opposing guards to panic. Not Cincinnati's guards. They had lived with their own kind of pressure all season long—living up to their reputation.

A little more than halfway into the first half, Miller was on a wing as Cincinnati ran its regular offense. Loyola players were renowned for their quickness and they were ball-hawks, using their long arms to swipe careless passes. Miller sensed that a pass would head to Bonham. He gambled, lunging to tip it away. Only the pass was true, the ball nestled into Bonham's hands, and he swished a jump shot. That gave Cincinnati a 19–9 lead.

These were the types of plays Loyola always made. Not this night. Even worse, Hunter and Rouse were such reliable partners on the boards that most teams were outjumped, outhustled, and outpositioned. Not this night. Cincinnati was getting the majority of the rebounds. Radio broadcaster Red Rush, whose voice was sending the game back to Chicago, almost despaired.

"Cincinnati's getting the boards here tonight," he said.[5]

The minutes ticked by. Loyola, which averaged about ninety-six points a game, was sitting on ten points total. Harkness, who averaged about twenty points a game, had zero, not a single point.

"Can you believe it?" Rush commented after informing his listening audience of that surprising fact. "Harkness has yet to score in the ball game."[6]

Meanwhile, Bonham, who after college joined those perpetual champion Boston Celtics and earned two championship rings, was making his jumpers from the corner or from midrange just beyond the foul line. He had eleven points on his own by the time Loyola had eleven points as a team.

"His eleventh point," Rush noted after a Bonham score. "That's why he's an All-American."[7]

The Ramblers picked away at the lead, but missed shots were costly. If Rush repeated a theme during the disconcerting first half it was Bearcat rebounding. "They're getting the boards," Rush reminded his audience over and over. "There's no doubt about it."[8]

At this point in the season Loyola had a record of 28–2. Not only were losses as rare as diamonds discovered on the beach, but the number of close games Loyola had put up with was limited. The Ramblers had also disposed of four tournament teams on the way to the championship confrontation. They had seen it all, done it all, brushed aside just about anyone who believed they were vulnerable.

All year Loyola had burst from the starting gate, going on game-starting rampages, taking command early. On the biggest night of their college basketball careers the Ramblers came out passive and in retrospect were probably affected by nerves.

"I think our players were tight," Egan said, looking back.[9]

It was difficult to explain. Maybe wanting the title so much affected them all, he said.

"I think maybe sometimes you want something so badly, you just don't play as well as you are capable of," Egan said. "We were just sitting back and letting it happen. Maybe that was part of it. They rebounded so well we weren't getting a lot of decent shots. We weren't getting our layups. And we had not seen Jerry struggle the way he struggled."[10]

As the buzzer sounded to end the half, Loyola closed to 29–21. It was not an insurmountable lead, but Loyola rarely trailed at the intermission and the team had shown no sign whatsoever of seizing the momentum. The Ramblers had entered the contest wanting to show the nation what they could do. Instead, they had played their worst half of basketball the entire season. The players were upset and somewhat embarrassed.

"You see the score up there on the board," Egan said, "and you say, 'Oh, my God.' The feeling for me was we had come this far to play this poorly."[11]

The journey for Loyola had been a long and arduous one, really almost an unbelievable odyssey for the school hardly anyone in college sports knew about less than two years earlier. There had been hardship and so much had been endured by this special group that it seemed flat-out wrong to suddenly sense someone wielding a big crayon and rewriting what surely was the Ramblers' destiny.

This was their time. This was their season. Everyone knew how the biblical battle between David and Goliath was supposed to end. How could they lose? How could they fall apart at the last minute? They were on the cusp of greatness and it made no sense to be teetering over a precipice, all they accomplished jeopardized.

Yes, as Egan said, they had come so far. When tales of the greatest teams are told to grandchildren, the stories do not end with almosts. As they glumly trotted to their Freedom Hall locker room the Ramblers knew the next twenty minutes on the court would be the most important of their athletic lives. Their legacy was at stake.

Loyola point guard John Egan (11) and his backcourt partner Ron Miller (42) listen to sideline instructions from Ramblers coach George Ireland during a game. Courtesy of the Loyola Sports Information Office.

CHAPTER 2

THE COACH

I f anything summed up the way the average coach viewed Loyola filling its college basketball roster with African Americans in the early 1960s, it was a story that George Ireland heard secondhand about his efforts.

"A lot of these coaches hated the way I used so many blacks," Ireland once said. "They used to stand up there and say, 'George Ireland isn't with us tonight because he's in Africa—recruiting.'"[1]

That was one breed of coach's attempt at crude humor. That was mild talk during that era when the routine way to describe a black individual in the South was to call him or her "nigger." This was the era of separate but so-called equal in public education. A young black man might be lynched for looking at an attractive white woman with the wrong expression on his face. The bathrooms, the swimming pools, the water fountains were segregated.

America's greatest shame since the Republic was founded in 1776 was slavery. The fact that it took most of a century to eradicate it through the most powerful and embittering dispute the nation ever had—the Civil War—was astonishing. Worse, not even the bloodshed, the tearing at the fabric of the United States, the efforts to impose the principles of the Constitution and the Declaration of Independence at gunpoint, cured the sickness of the mind that lingered as racism in highly visible and demoralizing ways.

A hundred years after the conclusion of the Civil War, George Ireland was ridiculed for the simplest of actions he took during his tenure as Loyola University of Chicago's basketball coach. The mere act of seeking out black players for his team was still cause for comment, hatred, and derision.

There was some inner trait fueling Ireland's feistiness, his willingness to be different and step out on a limb when he welcomed black ballplayers to Loyola. In his small way, as those in the front lines of marches and demonstrations in violently inhospitable places spread across the South galvanized a nation, Ireland, too, displayed a type of courage.

It is wrong to assume that Ireland was a pure idealist, however. He did not reach out to black basketball players specifically to gain stature as a pioneer. In his most candid of moments the broad-shouldered Ireland, who had been an All-American basketball player at Notre Dame years earlier, would almost certainly admit that his primary focus was on winning the NCAA championship, not pleasing the NAACP.

That his interests meshed neatly with the National Association for the Advancement of Colored People's own cause and desires was not his aim, but a by-product of a broader goal. Ireland wanted to win and he wanted to win enough ball games to keep his job at the school in Chicago where he began coaching in 1951.

The simplistic denigration of Ireland by other coaches was ironic on more than one count. Ireland did not have to travel to Africa to recruit black players. He sometimes only had to travel to Chicago's neighborhoods, or more famously, to New York City. Plus, the shortsighted coaches making fun of him would never have believed that within the next twenty years their brethren would indeed be flying to African countries to seek out black talent for their college rosters.

Ireland was born on June 15, 1913, in Madison, Wisconsin. He grew into a broad-shouldered, dark-haired athlete who excelled in basketball and enrolled at Notre Dame in the early 1930s. He was an All-American during the 1934–35 season and earned his reputation as a hard-nosed player. He joked that Adolph Rupp, the legendary Kentucky coach who won 876 games and four national championships leading the Wildcats, called him "the dirtiest player in the game." Ireland liked to set up his listeners with that one, pausing after the Rupp description to add, "And just because I coldcocked one of his players right in front of his bench."[2]

One of Ireland's teammates with the Fighting Irish was Ray Meyer, two years behind Ireland in school. As a senior, Ireland was the squad's captain and Meyer was a sophomore. Although Meyer, who died in 2006, later eclipsed Ireland in fame and victories coaching his own talented teams at DePaul University, just a few miles down the road from Loyola between 1942 and 1984, he never won an NCAA crown. Still, Meyer's record of 724–354, with twenty-one postseason appearances, and induction into the Naismith Basketball Hall of Fame gave him more prominence than Ireland. That may have contributed to an ongoing rift between the two old teammates during their coaching days. Sometimes the air was so chilly between them that if they talked you could see their breath. The divide between the coaches also kept the nearby schools from scheduling one another every season.

Ireland moved into coaching almost immediately following his graduation from Notre Dame. His first job was at Marmion Military Academy in Aurora, Illinois, a community about twenty miles west of Chicago. Being a head coach suited him and he honed his skills and gained experience running a program during a lengthy stay in the job. From 1936 to 1951 Ireland ran the academy's hoops program and compiled a record of 262–87.

Such stability is rare at the high school level among coaches who wish to move up. Periodically a coach will find his niche and stay in one place for his entire career. But even more surprisingly, when Ireland did make a change, he was able to jump directly to a college head coaching role.

That type of change is unheard of in the modern basketball era. A coach moves from high school to college as a low-rung assistant, to chief assistant, and then after a number of years, if lucky, he gets the chance to grab a coveted college head job. The basketball world was a little simpler when Ireland was coaching. During World War II, Loyola's basketball program was placed on hiatus. For two seasons there was no dribbling. In the immediate post–World War II years, with the aim of rejuvenating the program, Loyola turned to Thomas Haggerty, a former DePaul coach whose own most recent life experience revolved around serving as a US Army officer for five years.

Haggerty was an extraordinary find, and for a brief time, Loyola was a basketball power. In Haggerty's first season, 1945–46, the Ramblers finished 23–4. A year later they went 20–9. Continuing the trend, they completed the 1947–48 season with a 26–9 mark and the 1948–49 season with a 25–6 record. That season Loyola conquered City College of New York, Kentucky, and Bradley before falling to San Francisco in the championship game of the National Invitational Tournament (NIT). At that time the NIT and NCAA were considered equals in prestige. Before Ireland, this Haggerty-led team recorded the Ramblers' best performance on the national stage.

After one more season at 17–13, Haggerty quit for another coaching job. He became the boss of the basketball program at Loyola of New Orleans. However, Haggerty's move was ill-fated. During the 1953–54 season he began experiencing serious health problems, and in 1956 he died of pneumonia. Haggerty was only fifty-one at the time.

Still another Notre Dame figure entered the picture at Loyola of Chicago. When Haggerty traded Loyolas, John Jordan, captain of the 1934–35 Fighting Irish team, took his place as head coach, signing a three-year deal. Jordan's 1950–51 club finished 15–14. But he surprised the administration after that season by asking out of the last two years of his contract. The top job at his alma mater had come open and Jordan wanted it. Loyola let him out of the bargain and he returned to South Bend, Indiana.

This coaching carousel was the backdrop for Ireland's arrival on campus for the 1951–52 season. Notre Dame men were particularly prized (if only because of the glories of the football program). When the Ramblers turned to Ireland they rented themselves another former Golden Domer. This one was a keeper, however. Ireland remained Loyola's head coach for twenty-four seasons.

For that short period in the late 1940s Haggerty had proven a brilliant leader, elevating Loyola to the program's greatest heights to date. It was only a matter of a few years, but briefly Loyola was recognized as being among the nation's best teams. Knowledge of that success, something going on just down the road from Marmion Academy, would have been a lure for Ireland.

Between the 1951–52 season (a solid debut for Ireland at 17–8) and the 1960–61 season, however, Loyola and Ireland more or less floundered. There were some average seasons, such as the 16–8 campaign of 1957–58, and some losing seasons. As Ireland honed his philosophy to emphasize the running game on offense and the full-court pressure approach on defense, he asked a lot of his players. Both of those styles are demanding, requiring players to be in superb shape with the skills to execute on the fly.

A decade was an eternity in college basketball, even in the slower-moving, less-demanding 1950s. Ireland may have sensed the administration growing weary of his running-in-place teams. He may have become frustrated being unable to recruit the kind of players needed to carry out his simple yet physically taxing philosophy of the game. Deep down he had to believe that if he could find the right guys he could make Loyola a big winner. There would be no what-ifs if he could blend his coaching instincts with the skills of the proper individuals.

In the 1950s, few coaches recruited African American ballplayers to schools that were not among the predominantly black universities of the South. Recruiting itself was in its infancy, really. Coaches did not travel to watch prospective players compete; they took the word of a trusted friend that an athlete was good enough to play for them. Word of mouth, not videotape, offered hints of capability. Chicago had its share of talented black basketball players, but no coach dared invite too many onto his roster at once in the touchy era. DePaul's Meyer was a little more aggressive than Ireland about doing so at the time—within reason. Ireland obtained his first black players in the late 1950s, and some, notably Clarence Red, performed admirably. The University of Illinois, in Champaign, and Bradley University, in Peoria, also made incursions into Chicago to recruit African American players.

Ron Miller thought one important reason that Ireland did not have much success recruiting Chicago kids was that they had too much familiarity with Loyola's on-campus facilities, particularly the bandbox of a gym that could hold only a few thousand fans and that seemed to be a poor relation to other schools' arenas. Alumni Gym opened in 1924 and Miller suggested that it was beyond middle age by the 1960s.

"We didn't really have a big-time gym to play in," Miller said. "Guys would see that and go somewhere else."[3]

Players being recruited from New York or Nashville didn't have any idea what the building was like that they would play in. A player from Chicago, however, could just drop by and look around. Usually, those players left unimpressed by the architecture.

In Chicago, perhaps more so than in other northern cities of its size, the barriers between blacks and whites seemed more rigid, and unwritten policy and attitude still prevailed for the most part. Young Americans in the 2000s, or for that matter those born in the 1980s and later, cannot imagine how harsh life was for African Americans in the 1950s and how it infected the sports world.

Clarence "Big House" Gaines was a coaching contemporary of Ireland's. A Hall of Fame coach who won 825 games over forty-seven seasons working for virtually all-black Winston-Salem State University, Gaines wrote an illuminating autobiography in which he discussed the social mores of the South and the limited opportunities for black players to acquire basketball scholarships.

"The social standards of the Old South were pretty rigid," said Gaines, who grew up in Paducah, Kentucky, and died in 2005. "Black adults who knew white people could greet them on the street and exchange pleasantries, but black people had to defer to whites. If the sidewalk was crowded, black people had to move into the street. No white acquaintance, no matter how well he knew the black, would ever dare to invite his black friend to eat at a lunch counter."[4]

When Gaines began coaching at Winston-Salem in the late 1940s, his team received almost no mention in the sports pages of the local newspaper. The only references to blacks were listed on a page headlined "Activities of Colored People." It took years of success, of his teams winning conference titles and advancing to the NAIA national tournament, for the Rams to receive more prominent sports coverage.

By the end of the 1950s, the black American athlete had made great inroads in penetrating previously white-only domains. Jackie Robinson had broken the Major League Baseball color line when he began playing for the Brooklyn Dodgers in 1947, and more and more black players were making their mark in baseball. Professional football and basketball were integrated.

In pro basketball, Ireland could watch the Boston Celtics implement his own offensive game style and win championships. The cornerstone of the great Celtics teams was a black man, Bill Russell. College basketball was both a regional and a national sport. While the NCAA and NIT were the organizations that drew teams from all over the land at the end of the regular season, the support and enthusiasm for college ball was not evenly distributed throughout the then forty-eight states. Pockets of popularity dotted the country.

Then, as now, the Kentucky Wildcats were a revered institution in the Bluegrass State. Under Adolph Rupp, Kentucky basically ruled the Southeastern Conference (SEC). The Big Ten was a powerhouse even then and had slowly and gradually integrated. Northern and western schools featured an African American player or two. If you were a black athlete from the South and you wanted to play college basketball you either had to attend a predominantly black school such as Grambling or Florida A&M, or you had to leave the area. The SEC was closed to black players.

New York was the biggest hotbed of basketball. That city produced so many talented high school players there was no room for all of them at the local colleges of St. John's, New York University, Manhattan, or Fordham. From the Bronx to Brooklyn, the boroughs bulged with high school talent.

Some of those players preferred to go far away anyway. They grew up in difficult circumstances, living in poverty in the world's most bustling city, and going somewhere else for a fresh start offered appeal. When New Yorker Frank McGuire transplanted himself to the South to first direct North Carolina's program (1952–61) and then South Carolina's (1964–80) he built terrific teams by scouring the New York City playgrounds and spiriting the players away to the South.

Those were white players, of course, but in the late 1950s and early 1960s, black players, in ever-greater numbers, were looking for the chance to go to college and play ball somewhere. Similarly, the black players of the South hoped to escape the worst excesses of discrimination by matriculating at a northern college. At the same time, unless a coach was like McGuire, with New York roots and background (he had played at St. John's), he might get lost trying to negotiate the proper channels, make the necessary contacts, discover how to bridge his out-of-town status, and convince good players to follow him elsewhere.

One coach Ireland competed with for New York talent was Gaines. Gaines said that as the competition his teams faced improved he had no choice but to recruit outside of North Carolina. Many of the athletic programs at black high schools were either lacking or absent. So he sought African American players in New York.

When New York's black players signed to come to North Carolina, Gaines said, their first culture shock occurred when they changed trains in Washington, DC. South of Washington, all of the black people were herded into the same cars. The players, he said, had no idea what was going on and were stunned to hear conductors tell them "it was the law in most Southern states that black people could not ride in the same train cars with whites." Some had played on integrated YMCA teams or grown accustomed to playing with white kids on playgrounds. Few had ever been out of New York, "but they were used to riding buses and subways side by side with white people, with neither race thinking much of it."[5]

One of Gaines's New York recruits was walking down the street with two Southern friends in Winston-Salem shortly after arriving from the North when a white police officer ordered them to get off the sidewalk. The Northern player did not think he heard correctly and did not move with the speed of his Southern brethren. So the policeman pulled a gun on him.

Even Northern schools couldn't guarantee equal treatment for blacks. Coaches needed outstanding recruiting skills to get wary African American players to attend their schools.

Essentially, a college basketball recruiter is a cross between a salesman (hopefully not snake oil) and a Pied Piper. Like the Pied Piper of story land, the coach had to play his tune, weave his magic spell and convince a basketball player he would be happy living a thousand miles away from home for the next four years.

Enter Walter November, to Ireland's benefit. Based in New York City, November, a white insurance salesman who was a basketball junkie before the phrase was invented, sought to provide capable African American basketball players with scholarships so they could further their schooling and careers. In modern vernacular November would probably be called a "street" agent and be a go-between individual whose role might be frowned upon by the NCAA and its policy enforcers.

November, who is deceased, stood about six foot two and was a burly man. He played a key role in making Loyola the improved program it became in the early 1960s. No one around can ascribe any motivation to him that was not pure. Some New York players November helped steer to Chicago said they hardly knew anything about him, never mind suspected him of gaining financially through his role.

By 1963, when Loyola was receiving widespread attention for its basketball success, Ireland was occasionally asked how he got so many good players from other cities, particularly from New York, but also from Nashville, to come to Loyola. He did not dance around his connection to November. In an Associated Press story that ran in the *Sarasota Herald-Tribune*, among other newspapers, Ireland spoke about November and his other sources.

"It's no secret in the recruiting world," Ireland said, "that I have a direct line into New York and Nashville. Walter November, an insurance broker, is a friend of mine in New York. I got acquainted with him several years ago when I was ferreting around for talent. He runs an amateur team as a hobby and he tipped me that [future All-American Jerry] Harkness would consider a tender."[6]

If any money changed hands between Ireland and November, none of the Loyola players knew a thing about it. If November benefited in any direct way from helping Ireland recruit New Yorkers, none of the Loyola players knew about that. Ron Miller, one of those players, said that November was friendly with his high school coach, Roy Rubin, and that Miller saw him at college basketball games at Madison Square Garden when Rubin took the team to watch them.

"He was just someone who was always there," Miller said. "He used to argue sports all of the time. He just talked basketball all the time."[7] Miller did not know November better than that.

November supervised a New York amateur team and he rounded up first-rate players for that squad. Miller said he never played for November. In the summer, Miller traveled to the Catskills resorts and played some ball, a common opportunity afforded New York high schoolers during that era.

"November was there, but he was always a spectator," Miller said. "I didn't know he had any influence. I guess he thought I could play college ball. He had a relationship with Ireland and he had a relationship with my high school coach. So that's why Ireland recruited me."[8]

Miller remembers November as a silver-haired man, always very pleasant, who could be seen at his high school games at times. Sometime later November might casually mention a play he saw Miller make. "He might say, 'I saw that game last week. Boy, you faked that guy out,'" Miller recalled.[9]

November befriended poor but talented black players and helped them relocate somewhere they might be appreciated for their basketball skills and yet would also be able to obtain a college education. He didn't give them money. He gave them opportunity. On the surface it sounds like a noble calling. While some Loyola players assumed November was paid by Ireland (perhaps out of cynicism engendered by later college basketball scandals), there was never any type of negative public attention focused on the November-Ireland connection or any evidence of cash exchanging hands.

Ireland got the chance to recruit players he might otherwise never have known about. At the least, November did a good deed. The player received a connection to a school that he might otherwise not be able to attend. This was a three-party arrangement and everyone benefited.

Jerry Harkness was the first New York high school player who benefited from the November-Ireland link. The big summer league in New York was the Rucker League and November coached in it. He got to know the best high school players in the best basketball-playing city on the planet. One of those players in 1959 was Jerry Harkness. Standing just six foot two to six three, Harkness played bigger. He was agile, he could leap, and he could score. He played forward rather than guard, unthinkable now at his height, but common a half century ago. November, his coach, believed in him.

Harkness, who was living in the Bronx, had so-so grades. He was a skilled basketball player, but his high school scholarship record made him a risky recruit for some schools. November contacted Ireland and told him he had a player who could blossom into a star. Ireland watched Harkness play and said, "He's not a bad player."[10]

Acting more on November's say-so and enthusiasm than being overwhelmed by what Harkness had shown, Ireland offered a scholarship. It was also likely that by heeding November's advice he made an influential friend.

"I hadn't even met him," Harkness said of Ireland. "He got in touch with me and I don't remember much of what he said, but he offered me a scholarship because of Walter November. Ireland knew there was a lot of talent in New York City. Here's a chance to make Walter November happy and get connected with Walter for future players because Walter always had good players on his teams. He didn't have the top players, but he had guys with potential like me, and it seemed as if Ireland could get some top players farther on down the line." [11]

Harkness remembered November as being a different kind of coach.

"He was a little different than a lot of other guys in that he tried to help you [while coaching]," Harkness said. "He tried to get more into your life. He helped a lot of guys go to college. He wrote George Ireland about me."[12]

Harkness played for November in the Rucker League, on Long Island, and in Forest Hills, showcasing his skills against the likes of Connie Hawkins, Roger Brown, Larry Brown, and others who became big names in the pros. "I had some real good games against some real good athletes," Harkness said.[13]

There were enough good New York players to go around, and many of November's recruits attended schools other than Loyola. Hawkins went to Iowa before becoming embroiled in a scandal that interrupted his career. Roger Brown had the same problem. Larry Brown went to North Carolina. According to Harkness, November also connected with such future pros as Hal Greer and Freddie Crawford. Those who did attend Loyola, Harkness included, were not even the cream of the New York crop.

After Harkness went West, November stayed in touch with Ireland, and he occasionally informed him of a player he might be able to woo to Loyola who fit his style of play and could be of value.

Sure enough, a year later Ron Miller was graduating from high school and showed potential. He also wanted to get away from New York. November stepped up again, contacting Ireland and informing him that Miller was a prospect he didn't want to miss out on. He thought Ireland should haul his butt to New York and recruit him.

One day Ireland came to Miller's house, accompanied by November. The smartest coaches learn early who has the ear of the player. Will the player make his own call on where he wants to go to school? Will his parents determine it? Will a friend of the family be the crucial link? It is imperative for the coach to figure this out or he may be wasting his time and the effort that might go into writing letters, making telephone calls, or in the present day, sending texts.

When Ireland went after Miller he was already beyond the first stage of pinpointing the very important people in the player's life. November got the door open and was on the scene when Ireland arrived. Miller said Ireland probably talked to him for about ten minutes during his home visit. The rest of the time Ireland focused on Miller's mother. She served cake and coffee and Ireland raved about that cake as if it was the first time in his life he had ever eaten such a sweet treat.

"He really sold my mom," Miller said. When Ireland told Miller's mother about the high percentage of graduates at Loyola, he had her on the hook. "He said, 'Everyone goes four years and graduates,'" Miller recalled. When he left, it was "George Ireland this and George Ireland that," he said.[14]

That was that.

One of the traits and skills of the profession that others admire in a college basketball coach is how well he "closes" in the living room. Ireland knew his stuff. He could ooze sincerity and he believed in his product, both his team and his school. He was not a naturally chatty man who could simply press a button and turn on the charm in the manner of the best fast-talkers of this era. But fifty or more years ago, selling slick was not going to play as well as it might in a later era where everyone, unless they have been sequestered in a Himalayan cave for decades, has been bombarded with public relations and advertising hype most of their lives.

"He was a very good recruiter," Miller said of Ireland.[15]

Today's college coaches might cozy up to recruits, acting as if they will be their big brother once they hit campus. Not Ireland. That was not part of his personality. He was the boss, the adult in the group, and he made sure his players understood it. He was not a touchy-feely coach, one who would go around hugging all of the guys at the end of practice. He was the stern dad figure and he didn't waver from that model.

Indeed, Ireland was not even that buddy-buddy with his own children, so he wasn't going to be a big softy with other people's kids. "He wasn't our friend, he was our father," said Judy Ireland Van Dyck, one of Ireland's two daughters and three children, who graduated from Loyola and became a nurse. "He treated our basketball players like he treated us."[16]

In this what-have-you-done-for-me-lately, reach-the-NCAA-tournament-at-all-costs environment of the 2000s, Ireland would long before have been fired after the up-and-down coaching records he posted during the first years of his tenure in the 1950s. The arrival of Jerry Harkness, Les Hunter, Vic Rouse, Ron Miller, Pablo Robertson, Rich Rochelle, and Billy Smith, all African American players at Loyola, was the culmination of a process. He had recruited and was playing a couple of black ballplayers by then, but the Ramblers hadn't made much of a breakthrough in the win column.

Branch Rickey called his efforts to integrate Major League Baseball "a great experiment." Ireland did not say much of anything about his efforts publicly and nobody really asked what it all meant in the late 1950s. Yet Ireland had chosen a controversial path when he decided to recruit African Americans, and it didn't take long for someone (exact blame has never been apportioned) to indicate what he or she thought.

One day Ireland arrived for work only to be greeted by a dummy of what was supposed to be him—colored black—hung in effigy. It was as if the Ku Klux Klan had made a road trip to Chicago. That was Harkness's freshman year, the 1959–60 season when the Ramblers finished 10–12.

"They hung my dad in effigy," Van Dyck said of people on campus, "and painted the whole thing black. It just hit me hard."[17]

So not only was Ireland recruiting black players, but he wasn't even winning games. That seemed to be the message from . . . from who?

"The students," Harkness said. "White students. And they're upset with the guy."[18] Upset with the guy for losing games, apparently, but also upset with the guy because he was bringing in black players and still losing. Chicago was not going to fall in love with George Ireland or his dark-skinned players so easily.

Harkness believes that the shameful incident was a galvanizing event for Ireland, something that made him more color blind than he already may have been prior to the incident. "He was hurt," Harkness said. "He was losing. He was hung in effigy. I think he said, 'Forget it, I'm going after the best ballplayers whatever color they are and I don't care about anything else.'"[19]

In theory Ireland should have been able to recruit black players from Chicago to join him at Loyola, rather than going all the way to New York, but he had only mixed success at that. Rich Rochelle, a backup on the great 1962–63 team, was from the area. Floyd Bosley was from Milwaukee and played one year, but he didn't last. Ireland pursued Chicago native Emmette Bryant, an African American high school star guard who eventually won an NBA championship ring with the Boston Celtics, but so did DePaul.

"Loyola did try to get me to go there," Bryant said recently, but he chose the Blue Demons because he had closer ties to an assistant coach there.[20]

While a handful of black men who believed they were at Loyola solely to play basketball may have been contributing to the changing tide of American society by their mere presence, review of the daily newspapers and perusal of the television evening news kept them informed that not too far away their fellow Americans, their fellow black brothers, were in turmoil.

In 1955 and 1956, during the years when Loyola's future black basketball players were in high school and junior high, the Montgomery bus boycott was taking place. One day an older black woman named Rosa Parks refused to trek to the back of the bus, where all good Negroes were supposed to sit, and she ignited a tinder box that resulted in revolutionary change in the Alabama city.

In 1961 and 1962, the movement toward equality continued in Albany, Georgia, where attempts were made to desegregate city facilities.

In 1963, Birmingham, Alabama, sheriff Bull Connor presided over an insurrection of protest for months that culminated with the bombing of a black church in a seminal moment of the civil rights movement. Four young black girls in attendance were killed.

That was the year, as well, that Nobel Prize winner Dr. Martin Luther King, Jr., led a March on Washington of some 250,000 people and delivered his seventeen-minute "I Have a Dream" speech.

Dr. King did not dream about basketball. What he did imagine is a day when all Americans would be free and equal and enjoy the same opportunities. That included playing basketball.

Les Hunter, the burly center who was often at odds with Ireland's strict methods, gave him credit for what he did—regardless of motive. "The thing that I can say about him is he was a guy who chose to play and recruit blacks when others wouldn't," said Hunter, who was one of those African Americans. "That's got to be a plus any way you look at it. I think he did it more for selfish reasons than for any type of humanitarian efforts, and maybe I'm totally wrong."[21]

But Ireland did what few other college basketball coaches were doing in the early 1960s.

The City

The black population of Chicago and other Northern cities was expanded by the Great Migration of the first part of the twentieth century. African Americans learned there were jobs to be had in factories and moved their families from Deep South states by the thousands and thousands. The grandchildren of slaves, still discriminated against in every aspect of life in Alabama, Louisiana, Mississippi, and other Southern enclaves hoped for better life opportunities in every way.

No city of the North was more ethnically divided than Chicago. Neighborhoods might as well have had Berlin walls dividing them, not invisible markers. Bridgeport, where Mayor Richard J. Daley came from, was Irish and stayed that way. Polish families lived in the Back of the Yards. Italians resided on the South Side, but north of Thirty-fifth Street where the White Sox home of Comiskey Park was located, and African Americans lived on the South Side, but south of Thirty-fifth Street.

Blacks in Chicago generally found life to be improved over life in the rural South, but at the same time no panacea, either. In 1919, a five-day race riot broke out in protest over the drowning death of a black man at a local beach when a white man was blamed for allowing him to die.

In 1955, in one of the most highly publicized cases of the civil rights era—still widely known today—Emmett Till, a Chicago teenager, went to Mississippi on vacation and never returned. Kidnapped and murdered, Till's alleged crime against white sensibilities was that he whistled at a white woman. The nationally known incident happened in Mississippi, but was always remembered in Chicago.

Beginning in the 1940s, Chicago was in the forefront of constructing high-rise, segregated housing projects such as the infamous Cabrini-Green project. Families could find no alternatives for living in the city and fair housing was an issue that was at the forefront of African American grievances for decades. Later, in the mid-1960s, Dr. Martin Luther King, Jr., led marches protesting the conditions—and he was hit with a brick for his trouble.

As segregated as Chicago was, it was still a major African American destination. If Harlem, in New York, was the unofficial capital of black America, Chicago was at least the focal point of African American life in the Midwest. It was not as cosmopolitan as New York, but it was a big, energetic city with much to offer.

College scholarships were at a premium for African American athletes. Most were happy to grab one if offered, even at a school like Clarence Gaines's Winston-Salem in a Southern town. To be offered a scholarship from a George Ireland, to attend a predominantly white university like Loyola in a Northern town, was much rarer.

In the early 1960s, a pervading belief in the United States was that the South was still fighting the Civil War, if not in full armed conflict then in diehard attitude. For decades, African Americans had been demonized and demoralized by institutionalized policies determined to keep them second-class citizens.

The families of what were probably the two most famous American black men of the first half of the twentieth century followed the Great Migration route. Joe Louis's people uprooted from Alabama and relocated to Detroit, where work was found in Henry Ford's automotive plant. Indeed, even the future heavyweight champion was first employed in the manufacture of automobiles before his fists became the fundamental tools of his career. Similarly, Olympic sprint star Jesse Owens's family left Alabama behind for Ohio long before his feats with his feet made him famous.

Louis and Owens excelled in what were essentially individual sports. It was even more difficult for athletes to create their own opportunities in team sports. Many times, doors were still bolted shut and blacks were not welcome on a team—or even in a housing development, or at a private club. The greatest taboo of all was interaction between the sexes. A black man was supposed to know his place when it came to white women. Interracial dating was forbidden. Sometimes conversation even in the "liberal" North was frowned on.

In Chicago, Ireland recruited young black men to play for his Loyola University basketball team, but that didn't mean everyone on campus agreed they should be there. That didn't mean the citizens of Chicago welcomed them as saviors. And it was far from Ireland's nature to be a den mother, to watch over his guys' social lives and personal habits. He cared mainly that they developed their basketball skills and did well enough in their course work to stay eligible. He told their mothers they would graduate, but he mostly left it up to them—white and black players alike—to demonstrate responsibility in the classroom.

By the end of the 1950s, the end of Dwight Eisenhower's presidency and the dawning of John F. Kennedy's promised age of Camelot, Ireland had been at Loyola for a decade. He had had a few good teams, a few average teams, and a few subpar teams. By the time Ireland made his Walter November connection in New York it might be said that he was stuck in mediocrity.

Clarence Red was Ireland's first great black player. Red was from New Orleans, with aspirations to become a dentist when he enrolled in the fall of 1957. Between that season and 1961 he averaged in double figures three times, with a high of 20.3 points per game during the 1958–59 season. He also averaged 16.8 rebounds a game as a sophomore and twice more averaged in double figures in rebounding despite standing just six foot five.

Red, who became an orthodontist, was not only a first-rate player; he was also the type of man who could help ease the transition to Chicago and to Loyola for other black players. Red was a huge get for Ireland. A stubborn man with a hunger to win, Ireland realized that if Red could perform at such a high level then there were many other Reds out there being overlooked in the basketball world. Red led to Jerry Harkness who led to Les Hunter, Vic Rouse, and Ron Miller, who led to Pablo Robertson, Billy Smith, and others. All of that group came from New York through Walter November.

"When Harkness arrived here he was taken under the wing of Clarence Red, the first of our great Negro stars," Ireland said in a syndicated Associated Press interview of 1963. "If, during his stay with us, Harkness had not been treated right, or had not been satisfied, the whole recruiting complex would have broken down. He and all the rest of our boys are a credit not only to their race, but to their school. They are well-disciplined players and their fair treatment by us is reflected by the way they put out in a game."[22]

In talking about their undergraduate days, Harkness, Hunter, and Miller often used a variation of a phrase applied to many aspects of daily life, of basketball life, and of travel. Essentially, with only a word or two of difference, they said, "You've got to remember the times."

They say it with matter-of-fact inflection. They say it in a manner that suggests, "What do you expect?" "The times" they refer to were ones of overt racism, of ugliness in daily American life. The times meant a black man just walking down the street could be hassled by a police officer because he was in a white neighborhood, or someone in a passing car might shout out a searing insult delivered casually.

And still it was better than being in Alabama, where a sneering sheriff might order you bashed over the head, or in Mississippi, where someone standing up for his rights might be hijacked off the street, driven to a remote location, and killed.

Loyola's black players were safer than that in Chicago. A white man who ran a college basketball team had plucked them from the wide pool of talent and revamped their lives by invitation-only.

As someone who grew up there, Emmette Bryant, the future professional who attended nearby DePaul, also understood Chicago's DNA and the implications of being in the wrong neighborhood at the wrong time.

"We grew up knowing not to go to Cicero or Back of the Yards," Bryant said. "We went all over the city to play games, but after the games you had to leave."[23]

Ron Miller said he was barely seventeen when he enrolled at Loyola and was not of a mind to roam the city, so he never had a firsthand "bad" experience because of his skin color. He did hear stories about other blacks having insults yelled at them, but not around Loyola.

"I tended to stay in my comfort zone," Miller said. "I stayed at Loyola or at the North Shore. Everyone in that vicinity knew who you were. I was very shocked Chicago was like that, though. It was almost an unwritten code how cliquish they were."[24]

Harkness said the Ramblers didn't ramble too far from Loyola to other parts of Chicago. For the most part, there was no compelling need to drift to different neighborhoods in a spread-out city, but occasionally racism did rear up.

The barbershop located about a block from the dormitory where the black athletes lived would not cut their hair. "We couldn't go to the barbershop," Harkness said.[25] To get their trims in a style they felt was acceptable, the players journeyed the short distance to Evanston. There a friend of player Rich Rochelle's family cut their hair—as well as that of Northwestern's black athletes—in his home.

Otherwise, "we stayed within the area," Harkness said. "It was not until later in life that I discovered if I went five or ten blocks from Loyola, I couldn't live there."

Having graduated and joined the workforce, Harkness put a deposit down on an apartment on the near-north side, but when he returned, "The guy looked me in my face and told me it had already been rented."[26]

Many years later Harkness was sought out by a stranger, a doctor, who told him he wanted to apologize for that incident. The doctor turned out to be the racist man's son, and he invited Harkness and his wife to attend an American Medical Association meeting. After that reach-out they stayed in touch.

"I accepted his apology," Harkness said.[27]

The African American Loyola basketball players never for a moment forgot that they were black. It just wasn't until many years later that they thought of themselves as perhaps being foot soldiers in the same war that Martin Luther King was leading.

No, under no circumstances were the black Loyola basketball players ever going to forget they were black simply because they were attending an urban-based university in one of the major Northern cities of the United States. A half a century later, the players who joined Harkness a year after his own college career began vividly remembered an incident that kicked off their Loyola experience.

They were attending a dance, a dance at which the black players learned just how few members of their race—especially women—were enrolled at their new school. They began dancing with the white girls, other freshmen, other students, just like them. Only their skin colors made them not just like them.

It didn't take long for the chaperones, men of the cloth, priests, to inform them that that sort of thing—race mingling—was not done on the dance floor at Loyola. Welcome to Chicago, guys. This was one incident that seared itself in the minds of the black players—perhaps because it was on their own campus. The campus should have been a safe haven and this showed they could not count on that.

Coach Ireland tried to act as a buffer to a certain extent, but he was not a human shield. He did not hover, did not micromanage his players' lives. He wanted them to have good experiences in Chicago, but he couldn't protect them every waking minute, either.

Judy Van Dyck, Ireland's daughter, who graduated from Loyola two years before the 1962–63 season but knew all of the players, said her father "would protect his ballplayers the way he would protect his kids."[28]

Players referred to the ultraorganized Ireland, who carried a planner in his pocket, as "The Man" in conversation because of the way he meted out discipline, and that didn't bother Ireland at all. But The Man did not have the kind of power that could overrule the religious leaders at Loyola who wanted to prevent African American basketball players from dancing with white girls.

The one thing that Ireland could do was buck accepted convention and bring in as many African American players as he could to make a difference on his team, even if he was going to take abuse for it, even if it was going to set him apart from other coaches, and that's what he did.

"There was an unwritten rule if you had black players, 'Hey, one or two is OK,'" Harkness said. "Maybe that happens that there are two on a team at a time. We didn't see too many teams with more than one or two black players in our era. Most of them were white."[29]

Not at Loyola. Ireland refused to be restricted by unwritten, unfair rules, whether in the coaching ranks or in the city of Chicago.

Jerry Harkness of New York City came to Chicago to play for Loyola. Coach George Ireland recruited him with the promise that the Ramblers would have a special team that could become a big-time winner. Courtesy of the Loyola Sports Information Office.

Jerry Harkness was the captain and leading scorer of the 1962–63 Loyola NCAA champions, averaging more than twenty points per game. He was the clutch scorer when his team faced its biggest challenges. Courtesy of the Loyola Sports Information Office.

CHAPTER 3

THE ALL-AMERICAN

It was a mini-miracle that Jerry Harkness ever wore a basketball jersey for the Loyola Ramblers given where he came from and the unlikely path he followed to Chicago.

Harkness was the glue for the Ramblers. He was the star player, a two-time All-American, who was not especially tall for a forward at six feet two and a half inches (often rounded up to a basketball height of six three). But he could score on just about anybody.

Harkness, born on May 7, 1940, was also older than most of his teammates by the time his senior year arrived, and he was also ahead of them by a year at Loyola University. The 1962–63 team was his team as captain, his team as the leader, and his team by virtue of seniority, with all of the other regular contributors being underclassmen. The key player on that squad had not even heard of Loyola and George Ireland by the time he graduated from high school.

A child of poverty in Harlem, Harkness was raised by a mother who was on welfare. His father was rarely in the picture. During World War II Harkness believes his father, Lindsey, was in the army. He has a distant, childhood memory of leaping into his arms for a hug when he was about five years old when his father returned from the service.

Mostly, though, it was Harkness and mom Lucille together, she trying to fend for them in any financial way she could in a community that at that time was essentially the African American capital of America. In Harlem in the 1940s, black Americans were predominant and black entertainment thrived in nightclubs. The Cotton Club was king. Duke Ellington and Count Basie ruled. But the underbelly of the community couldn't afford to spend its money on the finest musical entertainment. For people like Harkness and his mom the focus was on survival, staying one step ahead of the bill collector.

"I remember the stress my mother was under," said Harkness decades later when he resided in a well-off, single-family-home neighborhood of Indianapolis. "I remember trying to turn on the gas after we couldn't pay the bill and they came and put a lock on the gas meter."[1]

At the time no gas meant no heat, and while New York winters do not rival Alaska's, the heart of the season carries a serious chill and brings regular snowfall. It also meant no gas to cook with for the stove. So as soon as the gas company left, the Harknesses pried the lock off. "We had to eat," Harkness said. "Other times I remember having just bread and honey."[2]

Harkness was one of three children. His mother had her first baby out of wedlock and was disowned by her parents for doing so. Jerry was born next, and his sister arrived one year later. The pressure of trying to provide for her family became too much for Lucille and she suffered a nervous breakdown when Jerry was seven or eight. An aunt helped raise the children and for a time they moved in with grandparents.

Father Lindsey was less helpful, at least on a consistent basis. Jerry recalls him being more interested in running on the streets and being involved in night life than showing an interest in his family. "I forgave him later on in life," Harkness said.[3]

He was not in such a forgiving mood when he was a youngster, though, when hot meals were a rarity and his mother was in Bellevue Hospital trying to hold things together. Just about every day of his childhood was a struggle, and although that was a long time ago Harkness has not forgotten where he came from or what challenges he faced to get somewhere in life.

The road to success, as it does for so many growing up in poor communities, began in the sports world. For Harkness, his first athletic involvement was not basketball, but in track and field. At Frederick Douglas Junior High Harkness went out for the team and discovered he had the lungs and staying power of an endurance runner. While other competitors faltered, Harkness could keep going.

This innate ability, which he built upon, later became an essential component of his basketball game as well. Loyola's reliance on the fast break put a premium on players with superior stamina. It is a cliché to say that an athlete can run all day without tiring, but that's how Harkness's Ramblers teammates viewed him. His track-and-field training helped him. If anyone was suited to playing all forty minutes of a game it was Harkness because of his running background.

While most of the world was familiar with 125th Street and with Harlem being a magnet for big-time entertainment figures and those who wanted to see and be seen the way Hollywood figures gather in Los Angeles today, it was also easy for young people to run afoul of the law.

Crime follows desperation and Harkness knows it would have been easy for him, without a father around, without an older brother to keep him in check, and being raised in circumstances where every dime spent mattered, to make bad choices. It would have been so easy to drift into a habit of stealing, or even robbery.

Crossroads life choices come early in the types of neighborhoods where Harkness lived, and as a youth he leaned toward sports rather than crime. The first organized structure he had in his life was the Police Athletic League. Playing sports served as a good influence, but so did his mother. Lucille may have had her issues, but her philosophy was clear and succinct in raising her boy. "I don't know if my mom instilled in me to do the right thing," Harkness said, "but I wasn't a crowd follower. I could have gotten into some trouble as I moved up the line, but I mostly focused on doing good stuff."[4]

One of those good things was hooking up with a local amateur basketball coach named Holcombe Rucker. Rucker became famous later for starting the New York summer basketball league called the Rucker League, a circuit that was the highlight of playground play in the off-season for local legends, college and pro players looking for a game, and competition for anyone trying to make himself a name.

Rucker became the Harlem playground director for the New York City Parks Department in 1948, a job he held until 1964, and was the head of a touring basketball team. Harkness made the squad, and for a boy who had pretty much never been beyond the border of New York's boroughs, getting to travel a bit was a thrill. Rucker was later credited with helping about seven hundred young people obtain college scholarships through basketball.

The beginning of the push toward more integration in the school system in New York City was taking root when Harkness completed junior high school, and he ended up attending predominantly Jewish DeWitt Clinton High School starting with tenth grade. He rode the subway to school in the Bronx.

Always an easygoing person, Harkness was usually a quiet guy in high school. He did not rate himself highly as an accomplished student, but he got by, and he loved running on the track team and playing basketball. He said he fit in well enough at the school despite being a black-skinned minority because he was clean-cut and did not get into trouble.

Harkness was a pretty good basketball player, but he excelled at track. Running well and winning races is what gave him his self-confidence at that age. Actually, when it came to track Harkness was more than self-confident. His performances in junior high made him cocky and did not immediately endear him to his Clinton coach.

"I thought I was just gonna knock everything on its head and I didn't have to practice," Harkness said.[5]

His first high school race taught him differently. Employed as the anchor man on a relay team, he received the baton in fourth place. There was a big collision in the passing zone and three other racers fell. Suddenly, Harkness had the lead. The other runners scrambled to their feet to give chase, but Harkness was well positioned to breast the finish-line tape. Just as he was about to claim victory for his school the entire herd of anchor men from the other schools burst past him. He had blown it and was so deflated he refused to climb back up to the stands to get his clothes. All of the girls who had come to the meet were watching him.

"I sent a guy up to get my clothes," Harkness said. "I wasn't going back. I was oh, so embarrassed. They all caught me and I lost. The coach said, 'Well, you haven't been to practice. You haven't done anything.' So after that I said, 'Man, I'm not this good.'" There was a lesson in defeat about working hard and it stuck with Harkness for the remainder of his sports career. "I worked out really, really hard in the sprints."[6]

Harkness remembers the humiliation of the loss, but another strange thing happened. Even when he began working extra hard all of the old junior high sprinters he beat regularly began beating him. He didn't realize that by growing his body had changed and he had lost some of his speed. The short, powerful guys outperformed the lanky, long-legged guy. Harkness was quite depressed. "I was not worth anything," he said.[7]

Harkness wanted to quit the team. He told the coach how he felt, but the coach thought quickly and did not let him go, merely redirected him. Harkness was a little confused when the coach pointed to a different group of runners, who all happened to be white, and told him to try working out with them. Harkness was being tried as a distance runner. The one-hundred-yard dash was no longer in his future, but cross-country running was.

From the moment he shifted, Harkness fit in well with the distance runners. He stayed up with those teammates in workouts, and by the time the cross-country season began in the fall he was the top harrier on the squad. He won the race that made him the best runner in the Bronx and finished near the front of the pack in the all-city championships at New York's famed Van Cortlandt Park course.

His newfound stature allowed Harkness to compete in the prestigious Penn Relays in the spring at the University of Pennsylvania, too. Harkness usually won his races, but he did not win at Penn. He nearly tripped and fell and couldn't get his legs straightened out smoothly enough to unleash his usual kick. Harkness was running in second place, but he could not catch the leader. More than fifty years later, demonstrating how strange it is what people remember, he could recall the last two hundred yards of the race with clarity.

"I should have beaten the other guy," Harkness said. "I came up on him and he moved right in front of me going down the straightaway. I had to break my stride to go back out and to go around him. I never could get the speed up again. It was the first time I got outsmarted and I should have won the race."[8]

Those occasions were rare. Harkness adapted and became a star anew in half-mile and mile races. At that time he steered clear of basketball for a couple of years. He felt he was a better track man and that his future lay in that sport, so his sophomore and junior years he did not go out for the high school basketball team. Instead, he dabbled in intramurals. One game he scored twenty-four of his team's twenty-eight points and his friends got on his case, lobbying him to go out for the school team his senior year.

Fearing failure, Harkness resisted. He was admired and appreciated for his track success and he did not wish to risk his status at school by being cut from the basketball squad. He finally gave in and prepared for an assault on the roster. If the basketball coach knew Harkness at all, it was because of his running exploits, so he would have to start fresh in the sport. Over the summer between his junior and senior years of high school, Harkness spent hours and hours working on his shot at the local YMCA.

A minor incident at the Y boosted Harkness's confidence. A stranger watching him shoot told him he looked as if he was not that bad a player. Harkness's eyes opened very wide. That little compliment made more of an impact on Harkness than the flood of comments from his friends, and it was the clinching motivator to try out for the team.

Harkness remembers what would seem to be a casual remark so many years later because of the man who delivered it. Just sticking his head in the gym, the observer thought to encourage the lone player. It was Jackie Robinson, the former Brooklyn Dodgers Hall of Famer.

Robinson had played basketball as a kid and he occasionally dropped by the YMCA because he knew the director. Sometimes Robinson spoke to the young black athletes briefly. "That's all he said," Harkness repeated. "'You're not that bad.'"[9]

Robinson was right. Harkness wasn't bad at all. He tried out for the Clinton DeWitt team and made the roster. Then he worked his way into the starting lineup. The team kept getting better and at the end of the season it faced powerhouse Boys High School for the city championship. Boys High was so good that future star pro Connie Hawkins was a bench-warmer. Although he was two years younger than Harkness and may not have come into his own yet, it is difficult to believe Connie Hawkins sitting on anyone's bench. But he had a good seat to watch Harkness play tremendous ball and help carry his team to the upset.

Hawkins was later the subject of a book called *Foul*, about his career. Harkness read it and remembered a passage that referred to the Boys High loss to Clinton. "He was really upset because he was on the bench as a freshman and he was in tears because his team lost," Harkness said.[10]

Basketball aside, Harkness had shown the goods that made him an attractive catch for a college team in track. St. John's offered a scholarship and he felt that's where his life path was taking him. Outside of the thick walls of his own school, and perhaps in the minds of many hoops observers, Harkness was still an unknown in basketball. That was until he showed up for Rucker League play after he graduated from high school in June of 1958. It was a chance to be seen playing against the best and with an opportunity to shine against the best. Harkness's first coach was Howard Garfinkel, who became a legendary figure in high school basketball for starting and developing the Five-Star Camp that showcased high school stars for coaches in later decades. After a bit Harkness switched to another team, this one coached by Walter November.

One thing that made the Rucker League an aberration was its simple existence. The late 1950s was still a time when the best athletes in a high school played more than one sport. Most competed in football, basketball, and baseball. Almost no one played any sport year-round.

New York City was a hoops town above all else, though, and two thousand people a night might cram into cramped bleacher seats or find spots to stand to watch the premium talent on display in one of Mr. Rucker's games. Hawkins played. So did Roger Brown, later a star with the Indiana Pacers. So did Doug Moe, Larry Brown, and Billy Cunningham. Wilt Chamberlain became a regular.

Just being on the same court as players of that caliber was a boon to the still-raw Harkness. Despite the offer of a track scholarship, he had not thought very much about college. His grades were not very good, certainly not eye-catching enough to entice one of the finest academic institutions. In fact, after St. John's checked over his transcript the New York school realized Harkness had not been taking the proper college prep courses. That offer vanished.

November, who had played basketball at Scranton College and called coaching his amateur team "a hobby," believed in Harkness. "I thought Jerry was tremendous," November said, "my shining light. But he had no place to go. His grades weren't so bad. This was no basketball tramp. But there was one gimmick. The colleges around New York thought he was too small to play forward and that's the place Jerry had to play. They told him to pay his own way through school."[11]

Harkness couldn't afford to do that. Still, November told Harkness, "I'm gonna try to get you into college."[12] Harkness believes November was the only one saying that to players like him. It so happened that Harkness had a very timely great game against some big-name players, and a coach from New York University took an interest. First thing the coach did was promise Harkness a summer job.

The next step was for Harkness to take an NYU entrance exam. Then he would be good to go. Harkness was ready to move into a dormitory in a new part of New York and had his suitcase packed when the coach called and said, "Jerry, you didn't get in." "I said, 'What?'" Harkness recalled. "He said, 'You didn't do well. You didn't make it.'"[13]

Harkness had finished high school. His family was still poor. He didn't want to go back to living in Harlem. But his interest in college had come too late to rescue his earlier indifference about studying. He was very down. He really didn't know what he was going to do, not only with his long-term future but with his immediate future as well. Harkness's thinking at the time was, "Oh, my gosh, I'm in trouble."[14]

During this life lull, Harkness, the goody-goody kid who never got on the wrong side of the law, came close to getting involved in much bigger trouble than he had ever faced. An individual that Harkness knew (but not well) and recognized as being on the periphery of the New York basketball community approached him with a proposition. The guy asked if he knew two players from DeWitt Clinton who had been first-rate basketball players. One was then playing for the University of Connecticut and one for the University of Toledo. Harkness knew the players, but not well, either, because they were a year ahead of him in school and he had never been their teammate.

The man asked Harkness, "You want to make a couple of grand?" A couple of grand! Harkness was stunned. As poor as he was it was like someone asking if he wanted to suddenly come into twenty-five thousand dollars. He said he did. The man asked if the players knew him and Harkness said yes, although he was not really sure unless they knew about his track stardom. The man said they were playing in games at Madison Square Garden the next day.

Harkness had walked right into the middle of what would later emerge as a college basketball point-shaving scandal. The man said he should go to Madison Square Garden, seek out the players, and tell them to win the game, but "just kind of take it easy." Harkness asked what he meant. He said, "Well, they don't have to get their fifteen points or twenty points. They're key players on the teams. They can still win the game, but they can maybe hold the score down."[15]

Harkness's role was the messenger and he asked, "Two grand just to do that?" The man said, "Yeah, we'll take care of you."

Harkness drove to midtown Manhattan. All of his time in the car he kept turning over the assignment in his mind and kept running up against a roadblock. He just didn't know the players that well and kept wondering how in the world he could approach them about something as sensitive as this. "I could not do it," Harkness said. "I turned around and came back."[16]

Out of nowhere (not that uncommon at the time), Harkness heard from coaches interested in him playing at Texas Southern. It was Harkness's only college option at the time and he was prepared to move to Texas. Just before he hit the road, however, a major fire swept through the campus. Among the Texas Southern buildings ruined or damaged was the dormitory he was scheduled to move into. "Everything burns down," Harkness said.[17]

The St. John's track scholarship offer had been rescinded. New York University didn't work out. Texas Southern didn't happen. Harkness had a brief flirtation with a college in Bridgeport, Connecticut, following a tryout arranged by November and nothing came of that. Harkness's chance at easy money went by the boards—fortunately for him—something that could have embroiled him in the sport's cheating scandal when it was exposed, and wrecked his career. Harkness was looking at a future that was a void.

It turned out that Loyola's Ireland had seen him play once, but he played poorly that day and so he was bypassed for a scholarship offer. As the leaves began falling from the trees signaling the end of autumn, Harkness had absolutely nothing going for him except Walter November.

November had seen enough of Harkness's good days on the court and knew his talents well enough to become a believer. He felt Harkness was a diamond in the rough in basketball, someone who would shine with more experience, and although his grades were mediocre November also felt the youth was a good person who could make it academically.

November dialed up Ireland and bent his ear a little bit more about this Jerry Harkness guy. He told Ireland that Harkness was a good player and no one knew about him and that while his high school grades were not good, he was basically a solid young man who wouldn't get into trouble.

New York was loaded with basketball talent and it was easy for a very good player to be overlooked. Those who won honors like All-City had their names out front and were the first ones grabbed by colleges. But players like Harkness could also be of significant value. When November talked him up, Ireland remembered seeing Harkness on that off day, but added, "He's not a bad player." It was something very much like what Jackie Robinson had uttered in Harkness's ear.

One day the phone rang in Harlem and George Ireland and Jerry Harkness had a conversation. Ireland was very anxious for a talent upgrade for his Loyola team. Harkness was very much in need of a landing place to further his basketball and school education. With November as the man who brokered the connection, Harkness was offered a college scholarship.

An entire school year had passed, filled with hopes and overflowing with dashed dreams, between the time Harkness graduated high school and the time he traveled to Chicago to enroll at Loyola. Even then his odyssey was not over. Although Ireland had offered that scholarship, Harkness's grades were such that an academic official had to approve his entrance to the school.

"Ireland took a chance," Harkness said. "He took me to the dean of students and we all sat down." Then Ireland began his selling job. It was not unlike his stopovers in those family living rooms or kitchens when he convinced mothers to turn sons loose into his care. Once again Ireland was lobbying.[18]

The first thing the coach said was, "We're going to have a great team and Jerry is going to start it." Harkness heard that and blinked. "I'm sure he didn't believe that. But he thought it might be the beginning of something. I don't really know what he thought at the time." The next thing Ireland said was, "But he needs a little work."[19]

The dean bought the sales pitch, as so many mothers had. He agreed to accept Harkness, saying, "OK. But if he doesn't perform, he's out of here."

Harkness knew that Loyola was doing him a favor by accepting him with his weak grades, that if he had sent a blind application it would have landed in the reject pile. One incentive to make it stared him in the face the moment he walked into his dorm room. In a way he felt he had entered a higher-class world as an outsider. The dorm room struck him as exceptionally clean and neat and nice, nicer than where he lived in Harlem. Harkness had worn what he considered to be his good clothes, but he soon felt, "I wasn't dressed well."[20]

Loyola, the private school run by Jesuits, was opening its doors to him, and it seemed something akin to a four-star hotel with classrooms. He may have been a year older than the typical freshman, but Harkness was as wide-eyed as any of them. He was in a new environment and it would take some adjusting, but someone was giving him the chance of a lifetime. To hang onto it he would have to work harder in school than he ever wanted to and harder on the basketball court than he ever had.

Harkness never overlooked the pivotal role that November played in his life. He stayed in sporadic touch and many years after graduating from Loyola, he had the chance to introduce November to members of his family.

"They didn't know he was white," Harkness said. "They were shocked."[21]

It didn't compute with them because family members didn't figure any white man would act as a conduit for black teenagers needing a break in life without any kind of compensation.

"He didn't want anything," Harkness said. "He was a real good man."[22]

CHAPTER 4

RACIST AMERICA

You had to live through it, really, to believe it, to understand what the history books tell you now. How the hatred contorted the white faces of well-dressed women screaming at little girls as they shook in their black patent-leather dress shoes trying to negotiate a gauntlet of illogical resentment instead of skipping up a path to the school door. But the photographs don't lie.

You had to see it, the stupidity of it written in block letters on signs above the two water fountains at a public park, side by side, one spout for the white folk, one for the colored, to read the reality of America in the late 1950s and the early 1960s.

You had to witness it, the burly, uniformed man with a billy club in his right hand, smacking it—slap, slap, slap—into his bare left hand, the message clear in his eyes that if you gave him any reason, any excuse at all, he would love it, relish the chance to break that stick over your black head, or over your white head, you nigger lover, for being with them in the streets, when you should have been home in New York, or somewhere far away, minding your own business.

There was evil in the land.

They never understood the simplicity of the movement, the backwards thinkers, those who wanted to stop the march of progress in their yards, those who fought to keep America from discovering the equality as it was written about in all the documents that made America great and different. In the Constitution. In the Bill of Rights. Yes, they were rights, this equality that black people sought in the streets of their home states.

The big cause was fairness. It was the right to go to school together, whites and blacks both, where the best teachers were, and the subjects were the same, and the dreams were the same. The big cause was fairness in the

Team picture of the 1962–63 NCAA Champion Loyola Ramblers. Coach George Ireland is kneeling, holding a basketball. Also kneeling is assistant coach Jerry Lyne. Courtesy of the Loyola Sports Information Office.

ability to vote for whomever you wanted. It was about candidates being on the ballot who had black skin. All of the fundamentals.

All of it had been written. All of it had been espoused. All of it was guaranteed. And yet there had been a war between the states to free the slaves. Slaves! American slaves! Lord, there had been so much blood shed and the country had come such a long way. Yet still men suffered to drag equality forward where it belonged. That was the big stuff. Curing blindness took so long, so much sweat equity, in so many places. Patience was counseled, but that was absurd. It was all long overdue.

Yet so many hearts were so twisted, so frightened of the big stuff, that in 1962 and 1963, when Loyola University played basketball with a team heavily featuring African Americans, young men with black skin, society as a whole seemed at best ready for timid progress. If that, in some places. Not even that, in other places.

Oh, George Ireland knew what he was in the middle of, what he was part of, whether he acknowledged it aloud or not (and he didn't do so to newspaper reporters or other basketball figures very often). He didn't expect to be anointed with the Nobel Prize for Peace. His goal was to put the best Loyola Ramblers team on the court. He understood the era he lived in, the limits, and how he was testing them.

Most of the time during the 1961–62 season, when most of the main players were sophomores, Ireland started three black players. That was a huge number for the time. The players on the team felt he should have been starting four along with white point guard Johnny Egan.

Ireland knew he was pushing limits with the top officials at Loyola, with the alumni that had watched the team for years, and with the public in Chicago. Always, he had to wonder what the reaction would be when he took the next step. In the early 1960s few major college basketball teams had three black players on the roster. No one started five African Americans and many still started five white players. A large number of schools, especially those located south of the Mason-Dixon Line, had no African American basketball players on their teams.

Ireland did not stand on soapboxes and make speeches about equal rights. Chicago was segregated enough, even if it was light-years ahead of the Deep South in race relations. The marches in the streets, the bloody confrontations between unarmed civilians and militaristic police units, took place in Mississippi, Alabama, Arkansas.

In his heart of hearts, in his best basketball judgment, Ireland knew that four of his best five players during the 1961–62 season were black. The odd man out as a starter was Ron Miller. He played plenty, but he was not in the starting lineup.

"One time he told us, 'I can't do it. I can only play three [blacks] at a time,'" Miller recalled Ireland saying. Then the next year, the championship season, he took things one step bolder by regularly starting four black players. During that season, Miller said, Ireland told him, "'I don't care what they say, you're starting.' There was a lot of pressure."[1]

Still, there were exceptions. On a road trip to a southern state Ireland might start only three African Americans instead of four, though that was inflammatory enough in some of the places the Ramblers visited. "Oh, Coach Ireland always kept track," Miller said. "He told us which games he could only start three black players and which games he could start four."[2]

In this more primitive time of communication, before e-mails, never mind Twitter, most of the time Ireland could tell which way the wind was blowing because of his postal mail delivery. The letters came in from the local community and from afar if people heard about or read about Loyola having so many African Americans on the basketball team. College basketball was hardly ever on television at that time, so a large portion of the country was in the dark about Loyola's reliance on so many black players. All many fans might see was the score of games with the Ramblers rolling over the competition.

Word spread, anyway, and Ireland received mean and nasty letters. Sometimes those vicious pen pals called Ireland "a nigger lover." Sometimes there were death threats. He put the letters in a file rather than tear them up, perhaps saving them for fuel one day, as motivation for himself, for posterity, or even to get himself angry when he needed the spark. He grieved briefly for the world he lived in and then set out to cope with it.

The modern world is so dramatically different from the 1950s and 1960s that those growing up later find the history books where horror stories are recorded to be almost like reading fiction. Even for someone who grew up and through the time period and is now growing older in the 2000s, that bygone era is something difficult to reflect on. The reality of hatred and discrimination was harsh and so very hard to fathom.

"It's very hard when you think of those things," Miller said from the vantage point of 2012. "How could it have been like that? It almost doesn't seem real. How could it have been that bad? The country is great. I struggle sometimes with the Founding Fathers. They supported slavery. It always crosses my mind that there is a whole group of people out there who never got chances because they were black."[3]

It has frequently been observed that sports were ahead of most of American society on the topic of integration, yet for all of their leadership in that realm, sports have little right to boast, either.

Major League Baseball, the national pastime, was the bellwether sport of the United States throughout the first sixty years of the twentieth century, at least. Moses Fleetwood Walker is credited with being the first African American major league player in 1884. A few others joined him in the lineups of the old American Association, then a major league, and the National League. But Walker played his last game in 1887 after an outcry rose against black players. It was not until 1947, when Jackie Robinson joined the Dodgers, that the majors again featured an African American player.

There were a handful of black professional football players in the 1920s, such as Fritz Pollard, but then not again until after World War II. The National Basketball Association, which was not formed until the late 1940s, saw three black pioneers enter the league simultaneously in Earl Lloyd, Chuck Cooper, and Nat "Sweetwater" Clifton for the 1950 season.

By the early 1960s, sports were at the forefront of integration, at least on the professional scene.

The rosters of the American League and National League baseball all-star squads of 1963 included numerous African Americans, including Willie Mays, Hank Aaron, Willie McCovey, Bill White, Maury Wills, Leon Wagner, Earl Battey, Jim "Mudcat" Grant, and Elston Howard, as well as Latinos such as Juan Marichal, Roberto Clemente, Orlando Cepeda, Julian Javier, Luis Aparicio, Juan Pizarro, and Zoilo Versalles.

In pro football, the Green Bay Packers of 1962 and the Chicago Bears of 1963, consecutive champions, had barely a half-dozen African Americans on the rosters. Big change had yet to arrive.

In pro basketball, the Boston Celtics had ruled almost without interruption since 1957. Center Bill Russell, soon to be labeled the greatest winner in team sports, would also soon become the first African American head coach of a major American professional sports team. Russell was complemented by numerous top black players throughout his career, including such standouts as Sam and K. C. Jones and Tom Sanders on the 1962–63 team. During the 1964–65 season Celtics coach Red Auerbach fielded the first-ever NBA all-black starting lineup.

When it came to American society getting used to the rise of the black athlete, however, nothing compared to the impending burst onto the sporting scene of a new heavyweight champion. He had won the Olympic light-heavyweight gold medal in 1960 as Cassius Clay, but soon after winning the heavyweight crown in February 1965 he announced a conversion to Islam and a name change to Muhammad Ali.

Not only did Ali, who won the title at twenty-two, stand up for racial pride, but in perhaps his single most controversial stand, he spoke out against the Vietnam War and refused to accept induction into the army when drafted. The so-called police action with American "advisors" was escalating into a real shooting war.

The times were turbulent. President John F. Kennedy faced down the Soviets in the Cuban missile crisis. Before the end of 1963 Kennedy would be assassinated. That year Dr. Martin Luther King, Jr., would send his letter from a Birmingham jail, defending his activism as president of the Southern

Christian Leadership Conference and with the pronouncement "injustice is here." It was difficult to believe otherwise if you were black. On January 14, 1963, George Wallace had taken office as governor of Alabama with his own declaration of "segregation now, segregation tomorrow, segregation forever." In so many ways America seemed to be coming apart at the seams, but in other ways incremental progress was being made in civil rights, the Wallaces of the world notwithstanding.

College basketball was different from the pros. There were schools all over the country. In the Deep South, African Americans had zero opportunity to compete for a major state or private university. The Southeastern Conference did not integrate until the 1966–1967 season when Perry Wallace enrolled at Vanderbilt. Homegrown black ballplayers who wanted to play college ball and obtain degrees in the region could play for Tennessee State, Winston-Salem, Grambling, Norfolk State, or any of the many primarily black schools spread among various states.

In terms of geography, Indiana is usually viewed as a Northern state. North to South it is more or less a rectangle with the northern tier where the city of Gary is located, where Notre Dame is located, essentially in the orbit of Chicago. South of Indianapolis, the capital that is in the center of the Hoosier state, the area has a much closer relationship with the South. The southern tip of Indiana borders Kentucky. Indiana University, in Bloomington, is south of Indianapolis.

Also, Indiana, as much as if not more than most places, had been under the sway of the Ku Klux Klan from the 1920s into the 1940s, to the point that the Klan influenced every major election and state government policy. It was against this backdrop that a group of black civic leaders lobbied university president Herman Wells to work harder to integrate the school that was supposed to be the state university for all Indiana residents.

In Wells they found a like-minded advocate. Wells was a fair man who saw the wrongs at his school and was determined to open up previously closed doors at as brisk a speed as he could without antagonizing his board of trustees so much that they fired him.

It so happened that in 1947, a talented young black player named Billy Garrett was the finest high school player in the state. He led his Shelbyville High School team to the state championship and was selected Mr. Basketball, emblematic of the best senior player in Indiana. Indiana's entrenched and legendary coach Branch McCracken had already passed on other top-notch black Indiana basketball players (and he would later notably whiff on Oscar Robertson). Wells put pressure on McCracken to give Garrett a chance. Garrett was committed to Tennessee A&I when local leaders convinced him he had to take his shot at Indiana for the greater good.

To that point there had been exactly one African American player to suit up in the Big Ten, a backup at Iowa who rarely played. Garrett became a starter and star, and he is the one praised as the pioneer who opened opportunities in the league for future black players.

Remarkably, it took the combined forces of black community leaders, an open-minded university president, and an all-star player to gain just one African American entrée to a prominent university roster. The war was not won in a day, either.

Throughout that time and all through the 1950s and into the 1960s, Clarence "Big House" Gaines was coaching the team at historically black Winston-Salem. He was a keen observer of the recruiting scene and watched from afar as year after year white universities snubbed black players who could have been starters or stars for them. He also operated in a region where in several states it was illegal for black and white basketball players to take the court to play against one another, never mind with each other.

When Gaines's teams took their Southern road trips, always by bus because of a limited budget, they stayed in hotels operated for black clientele, and if they had to stop for food along the way they were forced to go around to the back of restaurants to obtain meals.

"I guess it may be hard for people of any color under the age of 50 to understand how black people were treated in those days," Gaines said. "In my youthful days, black people simply deferred in all ways to white people. We rode in the back in public transportation. We had separate water fountains and bathrooms. We did not question their authority and we put up with their irrational laws, such as the one making it illegal for black women to try on hats in white-owned stores in downtown Baltimore or Washington, DC."[4]

Gaines, who was born in 1923 and saw the world change during his forty-seven-year coaching career at the same school between 1946 and 1993, said that when white colleges began recruiting black players in the 1950s and into the 1960s, the pace was still slow and measured. "You could recruit an excellent black player," Gaines said, "and you could recruit a second good black player to be his roommate in the dorm and on the road. But if you started to recruit any more than two, you ran some risks. The biggest risk was angering the alumni because most of them were white. The administration and coaches believed the alumni would not identify with black athletes on the floor. If you angered the alumni, you ran the risk of losing their financial support. If you lost your financial support, you lost your coaching job. This was true of all white colleges, not just those in the South."[5]

George Ireland was well aware of the thinking, but he took that risk. Clarence Red had been a star for him. Jerry Harkness could be. But Ireland was not involved in tokenism. He really did hope to build something special. So he went back to Walter November and he listened when his friend called on the telephone from New York.

After Harkness shaped up as a premier player, Ireland was always open to suggestions from November, and November steered good players his way. Ron Miller, Billy Smith, Earl Johnson, and Pablo Robertson all came from New York. In time, Ireland began describing his bounty from New York as "Sturdy players hath November."[6]

Ireland also recruited Les Hunter and Vic Rouse from Nashville, Tennessee, and he signed Rich Rochelle from suburban Chicago. All of them were black.

Smith was one of the New York players in the November-Ireland pipeline. He said November was a good man and "I still love him today." Smith followed Harkness and Miller. Smith knew Miller, and November used that as a selling point to ship Smith to the Midwest.

"Walter said it would be a nice thing," Smith said of going to Loyola. "He was a salesman that just had your interest at heart instead of his."[7]

By stocking up on African American players, Ireland knew that he was bucking the conventions of the time. There were no white schools bringing in five, six, seven black players. This may sound amazing to the modern-day college basketball fan since many schools routinely now start five black players, and some NCAA Division I teams may have only a couple of white players on the roster. Such boldness by Ireland was virtually unheard of then. The only schools in the country that had more African American players on their squads, counting the freshman team, too, were the schools that were in Gaines's league. The notion that a predominantly white university would play three black players at a time was an extreme rarity. The notable exception was two-time defending national champion Cincinnati, which had won titles in 1961 and 1962.

"The unspoken rule then," Ireland once said, "was [playing] two blacks at home, if you had to play them, and one on the road. I played four and rarely substituted."[8]

By the 1962–63 season, that was definitely true. Some of the African American players Ireland brought in as freshmen either didn't cut it in school or weren't good enough for the varsity, facing the same winnowing process as some of the white players did in those days when entire freshmen-only rosters were filled.

Ireland's right-hand man was assistant coach Jerry Lyne, who eventually succeeded him. "No matter where we went, people didn't like us," Lyne said years ago of the early 1960s.[9]

The Ramblers were more than disliked in some places and either saw it vividly or sensed it. The late Vic Rouse, one of the Tennessee migrants, who starred at forward said of that time period, "We were, in fact, pariahs."[10]

After he made his determination that the only way to make Loyola basketball matter and to build the Ramblers into a contender capable of crashing the national scene, Ireland had to implement his strategy without funding. He did not have a large recruiting budget. In fact, he had little cash to spend on such an endeavor at all.

"Money was scarce," Ireland said once, thinking back to those times. "I didn't even have an office. My recruiting budget was practically nothing and we were playing in a gym that was already forty years old."[11]

Taking the occasional trip to New York to see many players in one place at one time amounted to maximizing his resources. Having Walter November as an ally was another way to keep tabs on players a thousand miles east.

Nobody mistook Ireland for a supersensitive guy. In his mind he recruited players who could play basketball at a high level and who would take advantage of the educational opportunities afforded by Loyola. He was not big on heart-to-heart talks with the players, who for many reasons had difficulties adjusting to the campus.

On the surface, a transition from the big city of New York to the big city of Chicago shouldn't have been traumatic. But the adjustment was huge for many of the players. Typical of freshmen, many initially had trouble keeping up their grades. The Loyola campus was small and the black population of the student body was even smaller. There were very few black women on campus. For Les Hunter and Vic Rouse, who had grown up with segregation in Tennessee, mingling with white people on a regular basis was an enormous difference from daily life in the South.

"Coming to Loyola was a tremendous adjustment for me," Hunter said.

"I'd lived in a segregated environment all my life. I didn't understand whites and they didn't understand me. And Loyola, on the far north side of town, was geographically wrong for us then. The girls we could date were on the South Side. It was hard even getting a haircut where we were."[12]

At one time or another most of the black players considered transferring. Some of them were on the verge of flunking out because of a slow adaptation to the demanding curriculum. Some of them did flunk out.

Almost everyone lives in the moment. Few people have the patience, self-awareness, insightfulness, and introspection to realize at a given time that what they are doing will be one of the most important things they will ever do in their lives. Even living at a time of revolution when everything could matter, when something you do that seems routine is meaningful or significant, is not always readily recognizable.

The Loyola Ramblers were in a scramble to write basketball history, chasing a national championship during the 1962–63 season. Each player was after the most playing time he could get, hoping to contribute to every win the Ramblers could get. Back then the players did not feel that they were part of the history of the civil rights movement. Not until much later, as they aged and looked back and examined the turmoil of the times when they came of age, and of all that followed in their country over the following decades, did they feel as if they had been part of something much bigger.

CHAPTER 5

TENNESSEE TWO-STEP

J ust looking over the Loyola roster and scanning the list of players' home-towns, one might pause next to two names in particular and wonder how the heck they ended up in Chicago. Les Hunter and Vic Rouse, high school teammates in Nashville, Tennessee, rode the rails north to the Windy City and into George Ireland's lair.

Anyone inclined to say that Ireland got lucky in corralling two major components of his starting frontcourt from the same part of the country that had no connection to the Ramblers would face a retort that he had made his own luck by being a savvy recruiter.

What was once a major basketball tournament, especially in the black community during the 1940s and 1950s, played a part in Ireland obtaining two of the most important players he ever recruited. Hunter and Rouse were unlikely targets since they were Southern to the core and used to an environment where African Americans didn't get perks like scholarships. Then, all of a sudden a big-city Northern, white, religious university knocked on their doors.

In 1929, the National Interscholastic Basketball Tournament for Black High Schools was founded at Hampton Institute in Virginia in response to the racism that prevented schools with African American student bodies from participating in championship events. It lasted until 1942. In 1935, a second national black tournament was founded at Tuskegee Institute in Alabama and then moved to Tennessee State in Nashville, where it remained in operation through 1967.

It was said that Tennessee State coach John McLendon never had to leave his own gym to recruit the kind of talent that enabled him to win three straight NAIA national titles because all of the best black players in the country came to his doorstep to compete in the National Interscholastic.

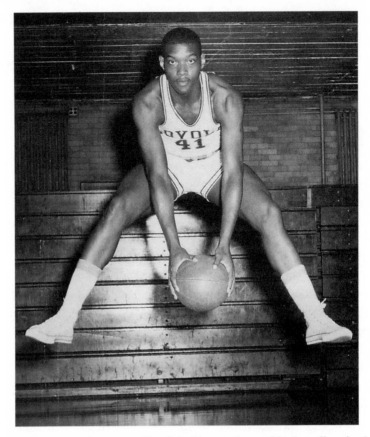

Center Les Hunter's nickname was "Big Game" because he saved his best efforts for the toughest games on Loyola's schedule. Hunter also had a solid professional basketball career with the NBA and ABA. Courtesy of the Loyola Sports Information Office.

For much of the time that the Interscholastic existed, it served as a fabulous recruiting tool for coaches at black institutions and as a showcase for players seeking scholarships.

Once in a while a handful of white coaches showed up in the stands, too, if their school was one of the brave ones willing to recruit African American players. Ireland was one of that handful. Actually, he said the year that he recruited Les Hunter and Vic Rouse for Loyola he was the *only* white coach in the stands. His appearance over the years led to his making the acquaintance of a curious Bill Gupton, coach of Nashville's Pearl High School, and the two became friendly.

During the 1962–63 season when Loyola was one of the best college teams in the United States, Ireland was asked how he got Hunter and Rouse to come to Chicago.

"Bill [Gupton] learned that I was a sincere and honest man and our friendship sprung from that," Ireland said. "A few years ago when I was scouting the tournament Bill had a player I was anxious to get. But he had his mind set on UCLA.

"Gupton saw I felt badly, but said not to worry. He said to come back next year and he would have two good ones for me."

Those players were Hunter and Rouse, and Gupton had accurately gauged their capabilities. "Gupton keeps an eye out for me in Nashville," Ireland said. "All he asks is that the boys be treated fairly. He knows this will be done."[1]

Rouse at first resisted entreaties to come to Loyola, Ireland said. "I had to use diplomacy to get Rouse. Ours is a Jesuit university. Rouse's father was a Baptist minister in East St. Louis, Illinois."[2]

Hunter and Rouse were longtime friends, and that made it easier to recruit them together. Hunter, who stood six foot seven and weighed 210 pounds before bulking up, played center at a time when many college centers were shorter than they are today. He was a magnificent rebounder and all-around star who later played professionally in the National Basketball Association and the American Basketball Association for several years.

Rouse was a tenacious player who also stood six seven and played as if he believed every rebound was his. More so than any of the other Loyola players he was intensely serious about his education and continued to earn additional degrees after his undergraduate playing days.

Hunter said that he and Rouse, who died in 1999 at age fifty-six, grew up in a strictly segregated white-black environment. The two black players felt the sting of discrimination in their daily life for their entire youth and growing-up years.

For a time when he was a youngster Rouse was forced to wear braces on his legs to recover from illness, a mild case of polio, but, teammates said, that did not impede his drive to become a college-level athlete later. "Rouse was just a dogged competitor," Hunter said. "He was a tiger on the boards. He would fight anybody."[3]

Hunter, who was blessed with strength and quickness, was originally more of a baseball fan. His father, Andrew, was a submarine-style pitcher, and although Hunter had easy access to Tennessee State's basketball facilities he loved baseball and wanted to play that sport. There was just one problem. Hunter said there was no opportunity for a black kid in his neighborhood to play organized baseball.

"They didn't have Little League for black kids when I was growing up," said Hunter, who was born in Nashville in 1942. "I played pickup games. I played a lot in the backyard. Everybody in the neighborhood played baseball. Everybody loved baseball. I ended up being better suited for basketball, but baseball was my first love."[4]

Hunter describes himself as "a chubby little kid," who grew gradually, and then suddenly. He was six four in high school and then had a three-inch growth spurt the summer after he graduated and before he enrolled at Loyola in the fall of 1960.

Soon enough Hunter's passion for basketball exceeded his love of baseball, although it took some time for his skill level to catch up to his enthusiasm.

"I played and I loved it," Hunter said. "Unless you've really got a passion for the game your athleticism may get you by, but you'll never really excel unless you're really, really saturated with it and infatuated with it. I can remember having a ball and playing imaginary games in my head, lying on the couch, just shooting up in the air in my den."[5]

When Hunter shot in his head the ball always went in and his team always won the game in the last seconds. "I think eventually my skill set caught up with my love and desire," he said.

Some of that kicked in when he was twelve or thirteen, but not enough. Hunter was cut when he tried out for his junior high team in the seventh grade. When he went back to try out again the next year, he was cut again. In ninth grade, the last year of junior high, Hunter showed up for tryouts again, only to be cut by the same coach for a third time. The coach told him, "You don't have time to develop here." Hunter was crushed. "You know when I did get some success down the line he claimed that I was one of his products. He cut me three times. I was not his product."[6]

Hunter might easily have given up on playing organized basketball, but instead he persevered with an "I'll-show-him" attitude. Others were willing to help a young man with a strong work ethic. Hunter came under the wing of Josh Grider, a former Tennessee State player who also played for the Harlem Globetrotters. Hunter and his family knew some administrators at Tennessee State and that gave him entrée to the gym.

So while Hunter's junior high team went on without him, he showed up for pickup games at Tennessee State. Many times guys off the street like him played scrimmages against the Tigers' varsity. Hunter's size helped open the door for him in the pickup games when he was just fifteen or sixteen.

"They would play three-on-three full-court," Hunter said. "They never had the air-conditioning on and the gym was always closed. There was the winners' court and the losers' court, but you were always fast-breaking."[7]

Hunter invested sweat equity and built stamina. He searched for other pickup games in West Nashville, an area Hunter's parents really did not want him visiting. "I was playing at community centers," Hunter said. "Anywhere there was a game, a lot of them outdoors in the projects. There were a lot of outdoor games in the projects."[8]

The outdoor courts had metal rims and chain nets. Park services in poorer neighborhoods always supplied equipment like that for durability. Hunter said sometimes the players pooled their change to buy nylon nets at a sporting goods store and hung them by themselves. At the least, for the big guys on the court, that meant when they jumped they would not tear open fingers on the chains.

During this period when Hunter crammed his schedule with every game he could find, he made an intriguing acquaintance who would not forget him. Before he became much better known as a National League All-Star outfielder for the Chicago Cubs, George Altman was a Tennessee State basketball player. He was also working toward a degree in education and teaching at Washington Junior High.

"I remember Les when I was doing my graduate work," Altman said, "and I remembered him later when they won . . . at Loyola."[9]

It was more of a small-world overlap than an important connection for Hunter. Hunter's intense commitment to improvement paid off at his new high school when he went out for the team in the tenth grade. Initially, Hunter made the team more because he was big than because he was outstanding. The polish was still coming. But he was in the door as opposed to being that kid who had been locked out of the junior high team and now had his face pressed against the glass.

Any youngster that gets cut from a team can be scarred by the disappointment. Any youngster who reads his name on the "keep 'em" list can describe the joy years later. "It was a good moment," Hunter said of making the high school's roster. "They had a junior varsity team and I also played on that. We had a really, really good team. We won a national tournament and we won the National Interscholastic at Tennessee State all three years."[10]

Hunter and his team both kept improving. His total playground immersion with hustle and hunger carried over to Pearl High School. Hunter blossomed into a very good basketball player, and by senior year he began to think he could become a college player.

"In my sophomore year I didn't really have much to do with us winning those championships," Hunter said. "But in my junior year I got to play a little bit more and we won the championships again. So in my senior year I knew the team was going to be depending on me and Vic. At the very least I knew I could go to Tennessee State and play."[11]

Hunter was a natural for Tennessee State. He grew up in the neighborhood. He used the school's facilities to make himself into a first-rate player. And people at the school already knew him. But Hunter says that Tennessee State didn't really bother much with recruiting him.

"I think if they had known that I was going to end up being six seven, they would have been more interested in me, but I was six four," Hunter said. "I developed more my last year after really growing over the summer, and that meant I could go into the pivot and play decently inside."[12]

No longer was Hunter just a middling-sized player who might have to play guard or be a small forward in college. He had become a rare commodity—a center with all the moves.

By coincidence, Hunter and his best friend Vic Rouse were the same size. Although both spent their childhood in Nashville, Hunter and Rouse did not really know one another until they ended up at Pearl High School. They quickly became close friends, blended neatly as teammates, and were inseparable off the court. Hunter was a year older than Rouse, but they were in the same year in school because the highly intelligent Rouse had skipped a grade early on.

Whether it was playing basketball for Pearl, visiting each other's homes, or hanging together at Hadley Park, a local community gathering place, Hunter and Rouse were usually found together.

Rouse was born in Nashville, but his family moved to East St. Louis, Illinois, when he was a kid because his father was named the minister of a Baptist church. (Ireland wasn't kidding about the religious side of Rouse's recruitment.) During Rouse's youth, and still today, East St. Louis was a poverty-stricken city that had a nasty, negative national image as a crime-ridden community unsafe for its young people. Rouse's father saw the problems up close and personal and sent his sons, Vic and John, back to Nashville for their high school years. They lived with their grandmother.

Hunter and Rouse, along with another player, Richard Bennett, were best friends. Bennett, who lived on Hunter's street was known for his deadly outside shot. He could fill up the hoop and played college ball at a predominantly black school, Bethune Cookman in Florida.

"He was better than Vic and myself during high school," Hunter said.[13] Although Bennett chose to matriculate at the Daytona Beach institution, Hunter and Rouse talked about the prospects of staying together to play college ball. They did not envision being courted by Loyola, however.

While Hunter respected Ireland as a living-room closer with recruits ("He had some skills there") he found his recruitment weird. Hunter came from a two-parent family, but his mother and father worked full-time and were not home when Ireland showed up at the house to make his Ramblers pitch. So Ireland delivered his spiel to Hunter's grandmother. From then on Ireland seemed to be under the impression Hunter was raised by the grandmother, even telling others that. Hunter could never figure it out. It was one thing that turned him off to Ireland and Loyola. The coach probably never quite fathomed how close he came to losing Hunter because of this faux pas.

College basketball recruiting in the twenty-first century is about as comparable to recruiting in the 1960s as a crop duster is to the space shuttle. Now every high school player knows a huge amount about every college team's prospects, history, successes, and defeats. They have mountains of material to pore over. Coaches see high school games, text players, call them, write them, whatever form of communication is available and legal under NCAA rules during a given "contact" period.

When Ireland recruited the high-caliber players that put Loyola on the map, college basketball teams were invisible on television and did not get much ink in local newspapers, particularly for road games. Furthermore, most coaches could not afford to travel great distances, did not see players in summer all-star camps, and didn't receive video highlight films.

Instead, coaches relied on the word of trusted friends, accidental sightings, and the voices of former players making recommendations. Ireland knew Gupton at Pearl, and Gupton put him on to Hunter and Rouse.

Similarly, when Hunter and Rouse chatted about playing college basketball together, they couldn't simply open a catalogue, point to a specific school, and assume they could go there.

"It was very closed," Hunter said of the number of non-African-Ameri-

can-oriented schools that would accept black players. "Now I would probably have been up at Vanderbilt because I could walk to Vanderbilt from my
house. But it was closed to us. Any Southern school, you couldn't go there."[14]

Ireland had been to the National Interscholastic and remembered seeing
Hunter play the year before. He had been trying to recruit Ronnie Lawson
at the time. Hunter and Lawson had played basketball together since Hunter
was in fifth grade. His mother was the dean of women at Tennessee State,
and that earned them the opportunity to play in the Tennessee State gym.
Lawson chose UCLA instead of Loyola, but Ireland was back for the National Interscholastic a year later.

Hunter and Rouse were leaders on their senior-year Pearl team that finished 32–0. The results made them a bit cocky about their abilities. They
talked about joining Lawson at UCLA. Hunter, who had relatives who had
attended Notre Dame, became enamored of that school. Hunter and Rouse
felt they had a great deal to offer, but neither Notre Dame nor UCLA was
interested in a package deal. So Plan A and Plan B didn't work out. There
was always Tennessee State, but the duo wanted to get out of town. At the
National Interscholastic, Ireland button-holed Hunter and talked up Loyola
and Chicago for both he and Rouse. At last someone spoke their language.

To that point in his life, his first eighteen years on earth, Hunter had seen
little that would lead him to trust white people. For that reason alone, he
didn't completely trust Ireland. He seemed a little slick to him, but Ireland
said all of the things Hunter and Rouse wanted to hear.

"I thought he presented himself well," was Hunter's first impression.
"I was always a little suspicious of him, but he was willing to take us on
and made a few promises. I guess everybody that's won a championship in
high school, who has been an integral part of that championship, thinks,
hey, they're going to be right there in the starting lineup in college. He kind
of told us what to expect and the tandem of us joining Loyola would help
make it a good team. Loyola didn't have a reputation, so we thought we
could be the guys who could go in and win right away."[15]

Coaches representing a program without an impressive track record have
a challenging selling job and that was Ireland's situation. He had a vision for
the future, sure, but he couldn't haul out the record book and show recruits
that Loyola had been a perpetual twenty-game winner because the Ramblers
had not been. The new guys had to take it on faith that what Ireland said
about building a program was going to become reality.

Ireland sold Loyola to Harkness with the same story: Great things are going to happen! Be part of something special! At the end of Harkness's freshman year—he was a year ahead of Hunter, Rouse, and several of the others—Ireland stopped him in school one day and said, "I've got some surprises for you." It was as if he wanted to prove to Harkness that what he had been saying all along was truthful, that Harkness really was going to be the cornerstone of a rising program. A surprise for him, Ireland said, like it was his birthday or something. "I'll never forget that," Harkness said.[16]

"Come on over here," Ireland instructed Harkness. "I want to introduce you to someone." The someone was some*ones*, Hunter and Rouse, his new six-foot-seven teammates. "I said, 'Oh, my gosh.' It was the height. I didn't know much about them until later on. They had won all of those tournaments in black competition. They were awesome. They were really good."[17]

Harkness was looking up at both of them. He also recognized the prestige of winning the National Interscholastic. "The competition there was absolutely awesome," Harkness recalled, "because all of these guys were there who couldn't play elsewhere. Absolutely awesome. So these two guys, six seven and six seven, come in and I just knew."

Harkness formed the impression Rouse was the player Ireland really wanted and that Hunter was part of the deal. From their statistics and size it seemed both were good catches, and in the long run Hunter had a much longer and better basketball career than Rouse, going on to the pros. But Harkness believes he heard the story of their recruitment this way: That Ireland approached Rouse with a scholarship offer and he said, "I'm not coming unless you pick my buddy, Les Hunter." Again, hearing secondhand, Harkness added, "Hunter was not as impressive as Rouse. And Ireland said, 'Man, I really need this Rouse and Hunter's not bad.' So he said, 'OK,' and he brought those two guys in."[18]

Whether that was an accurate depiction or not, Harkness did have Ireland's ear on recruiting issues. Maybe the timing of Hunter's three-inch growth spurt figured into it.

Ireland felt obligated to keep Harkness in the loop because he had made big promises to him when he imported him from New York. In fact, Harkness sometimes rode with Ireland to local schools to scout players. He did not accompany Ireland on longer road trips, but if a player was competing in a high school game in the Chicago area, Harkness might be in attendance. That's how he first saw point guard Johnny Egan play. Ireland took

Harkness to a St. Rita's game. Two of Egan's teammates were extra-large, six-foot-seven or six-foot-eight forwards, and Harkness spent most of the game studying them. He did not yet know that Hunter and Rouse were on the way.

"St. Rita had some big guys and I was thinking about two big guys to help us," Harkness said. "Ireland says, 'What do you think of him?' I'm thinking of the big guys and he said, 'No, well, the guard.' I said, 'He's OK.'"[19]

Egan, who came from a Catholic school background consistent with Loyola's outlook, and who is white, intended to become a lawyer. He had his heart set on attending the University of Iowa. At the last minute Iowa turned him down. Ireland said, "Jack [as Egan was also often called], I'll get you into law school here. We'll take care of you." Egan accepted, adding another piece to the future starting lineup.[20]

Despite his early difficulties in adapting to life in Chicago, one thing Hunter never contested about Ireland's pledges is that he did work his butt off to bring in good players to improve the team.

"Actually, when we got there," Hunter said of Loyola, "we found out it really was true. He had some guys there. He had just determined that he was going to have a pretty good team. Unfortunately, the faculty didn't agree with him as far as being on the same page as building a program because if you didn't make your grades, I mean by just a smidgeon, you were gone. They didn't give second chances."[21]

Of the two big men Ireland recruited from Tennessee, Rouse made the stronger first impression. Part of it was his demeanor. He was a scrappy player who had a fierce pride. He gave Loyola a toughness level with his play under the boards, even when going up against bigger and stronger players, and that was an intangible that spread through the team. "Vic was never intimidated," said guard Ron Miller.[22]

Rouse may never have been intimidated by any challenge he undertook. If it took some time for Hunter to grow into his body and gain the full benefit of his athleticism, Rouse was a smooth-as-silk guy. Although he worked very hard at everything in life he went after, on the court Rouse looked like a natural. His close friend Hunter not only shared daily life experiences with him when they were teenagers and in college, but he had the perspective to stand back and admire Rouse's positive character traits.

"Vic was more focused than anyone I ever met," Hunter said. "He had drive and determination. He absolutely refused to lose, whether in athletics or in the business world. But nothing was more important to him than his family."[23]

Miller said that Rouse was always like that, from the beginning, a guy who knew he was enrolled in college to set up the rest of his life. "He was more serious than the rest of us," Miller said. "He had goals. He had purpose."[24]

Of all the African American players that Ireland recruited for his teams during the time period when blacks could hardly find a predominantly white school to accept them, no one made more of his Loyola education than Rouse. For him it was just a starting point and he later earned three master's degrees and a PhD. Rouse collected college degrees like some people collect baseball cards.

Rouse may have come with his pal Hunter to play basketball for Loyola, but he had no intention of leaving Chicago without learning skills to prepare him for the postgraduate world. Yet, much like the other black players who came to town from elsewhere, Rouse had his moments of regret about choosing Loyola and times when he definitely felt alienated as a minority. Years later, when he reflected on his four years at the school, Rouse said he felt it had been worth it educationally, but not as much fun as it could have been.

"Retrospectively," Rouse said, "coming to Loyola was one of the best decisions I ever made. Academically, Loyola was very good. I had professors there who didn't even know I played basketball. I liked that. Still, I don't think back on my college years as a happy period of my life. As a black, and as a black athlete, I felt myself narrowly isolated in a white world. It was a physically and emotionally stressful time for me."[25]

The African American players that Ireland recruited to play, whether from Nashville or New York, were new to Chicago. Even those who brushed shoulders with white people on the subways of New York never had many direct dealings with white people. At Loyola the teachers were white and most of the student body was white. That took some adjusting.

In the South, in places like Nashville, the rules were rigid. A young black man like Hunter knew what to expect. In the North, in Chicago, on a mostly white campus where he had been asked to come, Hunter found the rules governing daily life to be fuzzier, more complicated. The priests made it clear that dancing with white girls was out. Dating white girls was a no-

no. There were rules about where you could live, too, and some restaurants might not make you feel welcome. It was hard to get a handle on just what people expected and what a guy could do without taking heat.

"I had not experienced any type of social awakening in Nashville," Hunter said of being an eighteen-year-old on his way to college. "I had always hung out within the black neighborhoods. I'd always interacted with blacks. I had always attended school with blacks. When I went to Chicago, it was a totally different feel. I was always minding my p's and q's. I was always quick to take offense at something I felt was a slight. It was hard to explain. I wasn't very happy. It wasn't a real integrated place in the community."[26]

The neighborhood just north of Loyola and just south of Northwestern University, the Big Ten school located in Evanston, is called Rogers Park. Rogers Park is pretty much a melting pot in the twenty-first century, but in the 1960s it was basically an all-white community. At that time, not all of the local citizenry received the black basketball players warmly. The ignorant few hurled insults at the African Americans and made them feel like aliens.

"You'd be walking across the street and people would yell out stuff," Hunter recalled. "On Sheridan Road. Strangers." Loyola is a block or two from Lake Michigan and the shore offers inviting sandy beaches. "If you went to the beach they'd tell you, 'Why don't you go down to your beaches?'"[27] The reference was to the South Side of town, that portion of sand along Lake Michigan near the mostly black neighborhoods. Some of the players reacted in disbelief. This was in one of the largest cities in America, and in the North.

"You know, I spent most of my freshman year trying out to figure out how to transfer [to another school]," Hunter said.[28]

One reason that Hunter did not leave Loyola was his own lack of awareness of where he could go and be welcome. If it was difficult to obtain a scholarship offer directly out of high school, it seemed more daunting and confusing how to go about getting one from another school in order to transfer. In the end, staying at Loyola was right for Hunter and he did reap rewards.

CHAPTER 6

FRESHMAN YEARS

At various times during its reign as the governing body of college sports, the NCAA has decreed that freshmen will not be eligible for participation in varsity sports. It may seem a quaint rule now, with college basketball players showing up on campus for a single year, uplifting the fortunes of a team, and then disappearing into the NBA draft. Yet off and on over the decades, before the cost of fielding separate freshman teams grew prohibitive and clashed with the notion of Title IX providing equal opportunities for women, the rule was in effect and shortened the normal college varsity athletic career from four years to three.

That rule prevailed when Jerry Harkness arrived at Loyola in the fall of 1959 and when Johnny Egan, Vic Rouse, Les Hunter, and Ron Miller arrived at Loyola one year later. They, along with the other recruits, some of whom would make it onto the varsity and some of whom would never play beyond the freshman level, were not eligible for George Ireland's varsity squad during their first year on campus.

One of the main reasons freshman eligibility rules were passed was to give athletes time to adjust to the college atmosphere after moving on from high school and the chance to adapt to supposedly more rigorous academic challenges. Since Ireland knew what he had waiting on deck, it must have been excruciating for him to supervise his 1960–61 team with so much grounded talent in-house.

The 1960–61 Ramblers played pretty well and finished 15–8. Harkness was a member of that team and responsible for a good bit of its success. He was sterling as a sophomore, averaging 22.6 points and 8.6 rebounds per game. The rebounding was particularly notable for someone who was usually one of the smaller forwards on the floor.

That year Harkness established his game and his role as a leader in the

When coach George Ireland risked the wrath of racists by starting four African American players, feisty point guard and Chicago native John Egan was the only white starter. Egan later became a defense attorney. Courtesy of the Loyola Sports Information Office.

program. But if the freshmen recruited a year later had known just how close he came to being exiled, they would have been shocked. Jerry Harkness almost never made it to the varsity.

Harkness had been admitted to Loyola despite his low academic standing due to Ireland's intervention and the pledge that he was capable of handling the demanding academic curriculum at Loyola. But he basically dribbled the ball off his own foot and was almost dismissed after his first semester. Harkness's report card was ugly, with four Ds and two Fs. "I'm on my way out," he said, analyzing his situation.

Harkness was already a budding star on the freshman team, so Ireland didn't want to lose him. Ireland said, "You've got to get your grades up." Harkness knew that and although he thought he had been working hard, he realized "I had to work my butt off." He telephoned professors at home asking for extra work to earn extra credit. He made sure he attended classes. He wrote bonus papers. Someone familiar with his surroundings in New York reminded him this was his big chance to escape the slums.

His best subject was English, and in the second semester, after all of that work, Harkness got his grades up to four Cs and two Ds. He was glad he was playing freshman ball instead of varsity because he needed every available minute to study and adapt to college. The coaches lobbied on his behalf with the dean of students, saying he was not only trying hard but had shown improvement after the horrible first semester.

"They won the argument," Harkness said, "and then we started getting into my major of sociology. One class was called Street Corner Society and I looked at the book and said, 'I know all of this stuff. I lived this.' So I got As and Bs in my major. I could have told them things because I had lived that street corner society."[1]

That street corner society came calling again a thousand miles west in the Loyola gym one day. Harkness looked up from a workout and saw a visitor he wanted nothing to do with.

"They came back," Harkness said of the men who had offered him two thousand dollars to deliver the point-shaving message at Madison Square Garden. "They tried to get me to shave points at Loyola."[2]

Harkness had become a go-to guy on Loyola, the key scorer, and the gamblers sniffed him out for a fix. Just maybe, they thought, Jerry Harkness, in his new role, could be helpful and win them a profit. The man advancing the proposition said, "Jerry, people are making money. You're talented. You can make money. I'm not asking you to lose a game. I want you to cut back in a game." Harkness responded with, "No, I can't do that." The man left and Harkness never saw him again.[3]

Within weeks, the 1960s college basketball point-shaving scandal burst into the headlines. Caught up in the fallout were many prominent players, including New Yorkers Roger Brown and Connie Hawkins, and their careers suffered because of accusations; they were never even convicted of a crime. When the news broke, Harkness went to see Ireland and told him that one of the fixers had come to him. Ireland was distraught.

"I told him, 'I didn't want it,'" Harkness said, referring to the money. "I was all happy I hadn't done anything bad." Ireland was upset. He said, "You didn't tell me." Ireland raced in to the telephone and reported the incident to the NCAA and "saved me. They checked me out, but there was no connection. None."[4]

Harkness was admittedly immature his first year at college and away from home. He did not drink or smoke, but he kept late hours and didn't always conform to dorm rules, which didn't always sit well with Ireland.

"He [Ireland] was a disciplinarian," Harkness said. "We got into an argument and I was ready to leave school. I said, 'I'm gone.' He would never go after anybody. I said to myself, 'He's coming after me.' I'm stupid, big-headed, and I go to the dorm. Well, he didn't come, so I got my bag ready. I felt I had to follow through on what I said."[5]

Harkness was angry and hurt. He was ready to say, "Forget it" and split for New York. Before he could leave, someone in the dorm stopped him and informed him that Ireland wanted to see him. So Harkness returned to the coach's office. Ireland talked him into staying but informed him he had to move out of the dormitory because he had broken the rules.

"I never had a drink, never had a cigarette, never even cursed in public," Harkness said. Now he needed to find new housing. "I stayed in Evanston [a few miles away] and I matured because I had to get on the bus and come in to school in the cold. I started to come around."[6]

As a coach, Ireland had the tendency to yell at players, but he did adapt when he learned his screaming could unduly upset some of them. He focused his ire on those who could take the criticism and serve as symbols for the team. Harkness was too sensitive for that. If Ireland yelled at him it only distracted him.

"If he was yelling at me like he yelled at other people, I'd lose it," Harkness said. "He learned to leave me alone because I could never have a Bobby Knight as a coach. Just because I'm emotional. I was always highly emotional. He realized at that point that I knew when I messed up and pointed to myself. We developed a connection."[7]

During that sophomore year Harkness emerged as the varsity's leader. The freshmen were around, practicing, showing off their talent, but on game day at old Alumni Gym they sat in the stands. By today's way of doing business, for Ireland it was like having an entire squad of redshirts, or injured players. The new guys were good, though, and everyone around the program knew it, including them.

The freshman team played a full game against the varsity team during the season of 1960–61. They were confident. They bonded quickly and brought an attitude to the court. "Our freshmen beat the varsity," Miller said. "Then he [Ireland] would not let us play them again."[8]

Miller may or may not recall that correctly, since others say they shoved it to the varsity all of the time. Either way, there was no doubt the freshmen were too good for the varsity. "We beat their brains out," Les Hunter said.[9]

By midseason Ireland was unable to restrain himself from boasting about his freshmen, telling sportswriters what kind of talent was hidden away in his on-campus gym. "In a regulation game they might beat my varsity by 30 points—maybe worse," Ireland told the *Chicago American* in January of 1961. "This is by far the greatest freshman team Loyola has had in my eleven years here."[10]

Ireland indicated the freshmen and varsity were facing off regularly. "We scrimmage them every night and they're just too tough," he said. "They always out-rebound us and most of the time they out-shoot us." He felt several of the freshmen could start immediately for the varsity.[11]

Although he did not want the varsity to get demoralized and become incapable of beating its regular-season foes, Ireland had to be quite pleased knowing that the players he had recruited were more talented than those he already had. It was a vindication of his judgment.

As Ireland spoke, the frosh, coached by Frank Hogan, were 8–0 and averaging just shy of one hundred points per game in their limited schedule. "The closest anybody's come to them is 40 points," Ireland said. "They beat five teams so badly that the return games were cancelled by mutual agreement."[12]

All evidence supported Ireland's recruiting coups. Les Hunter and Vic Rouse came from Nashville. Ron Miller came from New York. Jack Egan came from Chicago. Chuck Wood came from Racine, not far from Milwaukee. They and other recruits had different backgrounds, but shared the common ground of the game. They had to mesh as a unit and they did so, laying the foundation for future seasons. As different as their upbringings may have been, with the differences of skin color factored in, from the beginning the freshmen respected one another, seemed to enjoy playing together, and bonded in a special way. Their mix of talents blended, too.

"We were all good ballplayers," Miller said. "I think the freshmen were very competitive. Les was very talented. Jack had the heart of a lion who would not back off. Vic was the same way. I was only six two, but I could basically guard anyone. There was a mental toughness about everyone. We were all tough. Jack and Vic probably gave us the toughness. They had the attitude of 'take no prisoners.' I think the stars were aligned for us. We had no friction as teammates. We never had any arguments or disagreements. There was no jealousy."[13]

The country was imploding over racial matters. The South was a tinder box. The civil rights movement was the biggest domestic political issue. But that's not how it was at Loyola basketball practices. There were no blacks and whites on the team, only basketball players. "I have a lot of respect for them now," Miller said a half century since the group played its last game together.[14]

Other links were formed in the gym that freshman year. Some members of the varsity were still going to be around when the group became sophomores. Harkness knew he was seeing his future teammates every day. But John Crnokrak, a couple of years ahead of the freshmen, was the wrong age. He was a large six four, a former football player, and he identified with many of the newcomers as a big brother type who had been through many of the same experiences.

Crnokrak was from Gary, Indiana, the steel-mill town in the northeastern section of the state not far from Chicago. It was a basketball hotbed and a place where African Americans thrived in the game. Crnokrak was of Serbian heritage, so although he was white, he was also somewhat of a minority. When he played basketball in high school he sought out the best competition so he could improve. Gary Roosevelt High School, the black high school in town, had the best games, so Crnokrak either ran the five miles to the school or hitchhiked so he could play. He had been around black players most of his life, and when he teamed with Loyola's African American players he was appalled at what they sometimes heard from fans on the road. "It just broke my heart," Crnokrak said of some of the insults years later. "That's still so vivid in my mind."[15]

He felt a kinship with the black players because of his interaction with the guys back home in Gary. He felt connected to them in another way, too, because Crnokrak almost never made it to Loyola. When he was coming out of Gary's Edison High School, he was wooed by numerous schools. Wyoming was represented by the famous Milo Komenich, the onetime Gary star who had been a notable forward for the Cowboys and was also of Serbian heritage. Still, he wasn't on Crnokrak's radar. "I didn't know where Wyoming was," Crnokrak said.[16]

Komenich spoke Serbian and there was no way George Ireland or any other school's recruiter was going to top that living-room performance. That was enough for Crnokrak's father.

In the fall of 1957, Crnokrak dressed in a shirt and tie and headed for Laramie, Wyoming, riding a train to the Rocky Mountains. "The train made a few million stops," he said. When he alighted on the station platform Crnokrak felt he was slightly overdressed. Everyone was wearing cowboy hats, and if the locals were dressed up, they were wearing string ties.[17]

Crnokrak was seventeen years old and feeling so out of place and bored in Laramie that he saw the movie *Pajama Game* five weeks in a row. But not even gazing at Doris Day could keep him interested. He was homesick despite famed coach Everett Shelton telling him he was doing very well in hoops and that he demonstrated significant potential. Crnokrak quit school at the semester break and his unhappy father forced him to work in the steel mills and think about the chance he had blown by walking away from college.

Word of Crnokrak's defection from Wyoming spread to such interested parties as Branch McCracken at Indiana University, Ray Meyer at DePaul, and Ireland. The recruiting process began all over again for Crnokrak. Ireland made a home visit to the nearby city of Gary and focused on Crnokrak's mother. In English he told her, "I'll take care of your son."

"Like he's my father," Crnokrak said. If anything, Ireland laid it on a bit thick, especially by modern standards, when he raised his shirt and showed the family his scar from an ulcer operation. "I got that from caring for the kids," Ireland said. No one can accuse Ireland of stealing the ploy from President Lyndon Johnson because it wasn't until 1965 when Johnson made news by showing off his twelve-inch scar on his bare stomach following gall bladder surgery. The trend may just have been a sign of the times. Nonetheless, Ireland was convincing and Crnokrak was off to Loyola. He said he chose nearby Loyola "so my parents could see me play."[18]

What all this meant was that when players such as Hunter complained about being homesick and wanting to transfer, Crnokrak could understand their feelings. "In Chicago, they were homesick," he said. "They were me in Wyoming." Several times Crnokrak thought Hunter was going to transfer. "Four to six times would be my guess," he said. "I thought he was going to pack up and leave."[19]

The get-used-to-college plan for freshmen made for a dull basketball season for the new guys. Egan believes that thirteen guys were on the team at one time or another that year, several of whom would not stick with the varsity. Most of the attention the players got, he said, was from assistant coaches Frank Hogan and Jerry Lyne. Ireland was too busy supervising the day-to-day life of the varsity.

Fellow freshman Chuck Wood remembered things the same way. "I did not have a lot of interaction with him [Ireland]," Wood said. "I had ten times the conversations with them [Hogan and Lyne]."[20]

Practice, working together, beating the varsity, all combined to give the freshmen a feeling they had good things to look forward to once they were playing together on the varsity. But there wasn't much of a freshman schedule. Nobody spent much money on a freshman schedule, that's for sure. They played anyone handy a short bus trip away.

"We played nobody really," Egan said. "The only reason we got some recognition was that a few teams played us. I certainly had the sense that we would be good, but I didn't have enough information to compare us to other teams because I hadn't played other college teams. I wasn't a real basketball fan. I didn't know that much about other teams."[21]

The gathering of talent under one roof was a tiny bit awkward at first. Egan felt like all of the new guys from different cities were trying to impress everyone else. But when they played every day, everyone's strengths (and weaknesses) became apparent, and it became clear who deserved to start and who fit best with whom on the court.

It also became clear not everybody was varsity material and that Ireland had overrecruited in a sense. There were too many guys to ever line up on one roster and hope to get playing time. The weak links weeded themselves out, but unlike in the present day where coaches often run off players promised scholarships, Egan said Ireland did the honorable thing.

"Ireland really attempted to help kids that he asked to come to the school and that weren't going to make the varsity," Egan said. "The guy may have been a wonderful person and a great scorer in high school, but he wasn't going to play. Instead, he got a job in the trainer's room with a four-year scholarship. He [Ireland] was good to a lot of people that a lot of other people don't know about. He did not like the fact that he had to let a guy go. He had the outlook of, 'What am I supposed to do now as a coach?' Maybe a guy quit on his own. Maybe he [Ireland] wasn't going to make him quit, but guys made choices. A lot of guys don't want to sit when they're never going to play. I don't blame them. But I think Ireland was pretty good to most guys that he brought to that program."[22]

The stayers, the keepers, the ones who were at Loyola and were going to remain at Loyola, became friends that first year together. Egan, Miller, Rouse, Hunter, Wood, Rochelle—they formed friendships and maintained them, not only as they matured in college but also later in life.

That year, as freshmen, they started learning how to count on one another on the court, in the locker room, and as a team. The beginning of the journey to NCAA glory had begun.

Forward John Crnokrak played for Loyola, though his eligibility ran out the year before the title run. He was a protector of teammates when they needed his help. Courtesy of the Loyola Sports Information Office.

CHAPTER 7

GETTING TO KNOW YOU: THE 1961–62 SEASON

They were good. It was not just in their minds. Fueled by the group of sophomores and led by junior Jerry Harkness, the Loyola Ramblers began making noise on the national college basketball scene during the winter of 1961–62.

The Ramblers' rise was foreseen by at least one Chicago sportswriter, Jim Enright, in the *Chicago American*, who in his season preview started the story by saying, "This is Loyola's forty-ninth basketball season and could possibly prove its greatest in history." It was looking like the sophomore class was going to be a pretty special one, he noted.[1]

Coach George Ireland's game plan was simple, though not an easy one to execute. He demanded that his team play all out, all of the time. He believed in the gospel of the fast break on offense and the harassment of full-court pressure on defense. To carry out these commands, the Ramblers had to be in superb condition, for it meant running all of the time. The goal was to swarm, intimidate, overpower, and outlast opponents.

Although much of the basketball played in the early 1960s stemmed from a fairly stagnant, patterned offense, by this time the running style of basketball had been used effectively to win championships in some notable forums. The Boston Celtics of the NBA were winning world titles just about every year, and their preferred method of assassination was the fast break. In the late 1950s, one of the major practitioners of playing up-tempo basketball in college was Coach John McClendon at Tennessee State when his teams won three straight NAIA championships.

Not every team had either the personnel or the mind-set and will to make the high-speed attack and relentless defensive pressure work. It was an exhausting method of play, and the first issue was whether or not a team had the right players. Loyola did, and the dual offensive-defensive speed game became a trademark for the Ramblers. Soon enough, starting in 1964, UCLA would engage fans with the same methods and embark on a run of ten NCAA championships in twelve years.

But Ireland was ahead of UCLA on this. There was a certain kind of ruthlessness necessary to play this type of demanding game. It tended to allow a superior team to score points quickly and to dominate. Generally, it helped to have a fair amount of depth on the bench because scores could get out of hand against inferior teams and because even the finest players could tire more readily when there were no breaks taken to catch a breath during the action.

Ireland was a smart enough coach to recognize that he had the tools to run and run and run, but one thing about the coach that his players never quite grasped was why he had to annihilate foes. It was all well and good to have a killer instinct, but Ireland didn't seem to have an off button. Players said he acted nervous in the locker room at halftime with twenty-five-point leads and wouldn't clear the bench all of the time with fifty-point leads.

Leaving starters in the game with massive leads is regarded as piling on and poor sportsmanship. The Ramblers could never understand why Ireland didn't let the early-decided slaughter games play out more graciously. Many teams walked out of the gym after a game against Loyola not only licking wounds from a thorough defeat but seemingly so demoralized, whipped, and battered that they needed care from a MASH unit.

Games with wipeout scores have been around in sports forever, but rarely does a team perpetuate an execution on purpose and step all over the vanquished. As to why Ireland kept up that type of approach, only speculation is possible. The likely number one reason for massacring the opposition was to get more attention. That is the top theory espoused by Loyola players.

The Ramblers were a small-potatoes school on the national college basketball scene, and the swiftest way to get noticed was to win every game and win big. People would begin talking about you, and word of mouth was important because this was an era that long predated ESPN and nightly highlight shows on television. Also, this was an era before college games could be viewed nightly. That later played a role in a viewer making his or her own judgment about how good a team was. So for Ireland to succeed in his grand ambition of seeing Loyola nationally ranked and nationally noted, he first had to get the Ramblers on the sport's radar screen.

While that was a good explanation in the beginning, Ireland never showed the inclination to hold back once that purpose was accomplished. Maybe he felt his team would drop in the rankings. Maybe, as several players indicated, he didn't trust his bench players to hold leads. Maybe, as some also suggested, he believed no lead was safe and his team could still somehow blow a humongous margin. Whatever the reason that motivated Ireland to keep his starters in games longer than was seemly, opposing coaches could expect no mercy from the Loyola leader.

The first varsity game that featured Harkness leading the younger players resulted in a 95–44 victory over Assumption College. The second game was a 104–63 defeat of South Dakota. Wayne State fell next, 93–43, and then North Dakota, 96–73. Loyola had played small schools like that over the years, and when those teams scheduled the Ramblers there was little reason to think they were going to be sliced and diced so thoroughly.

"Their coaches were furious at George Ireland," Les Hunter said. "Just absolutely furious at him and I can understand it. Before, Loyola and those teams would have close games, and now we went to their places with all these black guys and beat them by forty or fifty points on their floors. You've been playing close, and all of a sudden you bring these black guys in here and embarrass their team. That's maybe why Ireland didn't get the respect that he deserved. A lot of those coaches would just shake their fists at him at the end of the games. I also think sometimes that he was just a mean guy and if he didn't like a coach he would run up the score. He didn't like Ed Hickey up there at Marquette. He used to talk about coaches. I think Coach Ireland was an incredibly jealous guy. He would never be gracious about the opposing coach, except John Wooden at UCLA. He was friendly with him. I think he [Ireland] was paranoid."[2]

Actually, Ireland was right to think that many people were out to get him. Certainly on the court every opponent wanted to beat his best teams. Off the court, irritation that he had recruited so many black players evidently (judging by that Africa joke) produced some jealousy among opposing coaches. It also created ill will among the narrow-minded on campus. To be hung in effigy is public ridicule and it was not something Ireland would easily forget. He was in the middle of building something different at Loyola and his best response to the symbolic distaste for his policies was to win. The more he won the more ammunition he had to shut up critics, and the bigger he won the more the rest of the country would take notice of what he was doing.

Although the freshmen had done little of official note besides fine-tune their game the season before, they had watched the varsity win fifteen games and they had seen some first-class teams invade Alumni Gym. They were building their own confidence without yet having recorded any accomplishments worthy of the attitude, but they did believe in themselves. Some of the graduating Loyola players tried to temper the outlook of the freshmen, saying they should wait until they play varsity and see just how good some of those teams on the schedule really are. Guard Johnny Egan refused to be intimidated by such talk.

"Are you telling me that these guys are so much better than our team is going to be?" he said. "You know what? I can't buy it. I don't believe it. Maybe it's going to happen to us that we can't keep up with the best teams, but I didn't see it. The guys [freshmen] were playing like guys I haven't seen before. I watched the varsity lose games and I didn't think the other teams were that good."[3]

One thing Egan knew about the Ramblers was that their speed could be devastating. He was fast. Les Hunter and Vic Rouse were fast. And from watching Harkness play every day as a sophomore, he knew he was underrated. Egan was right about it all and the Ramblers displayed their talents from the first game of the season.

Some trademarks of the team emerged quickly. Everything stemmed from defense. If Loyola made the other team rush a shot and miss, then the playbook-designed fast break kicked in. Hunter grabbed the rebound, turned, and looked up court, never dribbling. Ron Miller escaped the crowd around the basket and dashed toward half-court. The outlet pass went to Miller. Filling a lane on the opposite side of the court, streaking past back-pedaling defenders, was Harkness. Miller threw the ball to him as he cut in from an angle for a layup. Zip, zip, zip, it was all over in seconds, with Loyola scoring.

In a full-court press, teams rush to double-team the ball and trap a player, ideally near midcourt or against the sideline where the ball handler has less room to maneuver. However, this is a risky defense because it involves leaving one man open under the premise that with four arms waving in his face the man with the ball won't be able to find him.

Equally important, though, for Loyola, was what occurred defensively when the guards took chances. Sharp passing and poise could beat the press, and if the press was shredded by an accomplished playmaker Loyola could be in trouble. In those cases Hunter and Rouse, each standing six seven and with long arms, retreated to the basket area to catch the open offensive man, acting as insurance policies. This form of help defense stifled any advantage gained by other teams making a smart pass.

"Rouse and Hunter were saviors in a lot of respects," Egan said, "because when you're double-teaming, someone gets loose. But then you're afraid to go in for a layup with Hunter back there. So everybody helped out with each other's defense. Everybody hustled. We knew we could count on each other to do that."[4]

Five pieces make up a starting lineup in basketball, and what is expected from those roles is almost universally understood. Typically, there is a center, who is the tallest player; a power forward, who is usually a bruising rebounder; and another forward, who is usually a scorer. In the backcourt, there is a shooting guard and a playmaking guard, the one who carries out the game plan for the coach on the court and calls out any number of practiced plays. For Loyola, although there were sometimes changes, eventually those who filled the starting positions were Les Hunter, Vic Rouse, Jerry Harkness, Ron Miller, and John Egan.

Hunter, Rouse, Harkness, and Miller are black and Egan is white. There was no friction over color, no belief that Egan was a token starter and that some other black player could have filled his role if society had been more liberal. There was none of that. What developed, first for four of them as freshmen, and then with the mixing in of the older Harkness by their sophomore years, was a smooth-running machine. Everyone knew his role.

While basketball talents may be complementary and a coach succeeds when he knows how to best blend them together and squeeze the most out of his players, teams are not always cohesive emotionally. Players may be very different men in private life, but it is the chemistry on display during games that makes them a team.

Sometimes assumed from their coach, sometimes derived from a star player, sometimes a goulash of everyone's contributions, teams do take on personalities. Loyola became viewed as a team that would kill you with its speed, trample you with its fast break, annoy you to death with its pressure defense, and scrap with you for every loose ball.

At five foot ten, Egan was the shortest player on the team. But he may have been the feistiest. Like a choirboy at church, Egan could display the most innocent of looks on his face. Yet at the same time he could push the rules to their limits and drive an opponent crazy to the point that he wanted to punch him out. Egan delighted in distracting the other guy and breaking his concentration. He didn't talk trash, but he had as wide an array of facial expressions as Marcel Marceau.

Egan was tenacious, forced things to happen with his defense, set up teammates with passes on offense. He played with a swagger and his mere being seemed to be a lightning rod for opposing crowds. They could just smell his smug belief in Loyola being the best and it rubbed them the wrong way.

At times Egan even drove Ireland nuts. In one game that first varsity season Egan was getting open to take several shots, but none were falling. On several occasions he felt he had been fouled, but he wasn't getting the calls. Ireland, who could be heard a county or two away when he got wound up, began screaming at Egan. Normally, Egan would either ignore or not even hear things hurled his way because he was in such a zone when he played. But this time he was irked.

"I was throwing up horseshit shots, but I expected to get two free throws out of it," Egan said. "And it's not happening. It was hard for me to believe. There's a lot of contact and I'm not getting the call." The circumstances made Egan look bad, as if his shot selection was lousy, and Ireland screamed at him from the bench.[5]

Egan was irritated and that same weekend, at a practice, he confronted his coach. Egan said, "'Look, I know you want to win. I want to win. I know you could tell me to stop shooting. You can tell me anything. But talk to me. Don't scream because if you scream it won't do you any good. If you want this thing to be successful, don't scream at me.' And after that, for the most part, he didn't. He was good with that."[6]

His Ramblers teammates might be surprised to hear anything on the court disturbed Egan because he always seemed unflappable. Nothing enemy fans shouted seemed to faze him. John Crnokrak, who was a senior when Egan was a sophomore, sometimes played the role of Loyola enforcer. He may have been only six foot four, but he seemed bigger and he assumed the role of protector for the smaller guys.

One road game during the 1961–62 season a fan was dumping verbal abuse on Egan. Crnokrak decided to shut him up, so he climbed into the stands, looked down on the guy, and said, "One more word out of you and I don't care if I ever play again." Basically he threatened to so thoroughly beat the crap out of the tormentor that Crnokrak would be banned for life.[7]

Egan's response? "I owe you," he said to Crnokrak, "but you shouldn't have listened to him in the first place." Juxtaposing Egan's rabbit ears when Ireland yelled and when a stranger did so, he was apparently only sensitive to friendly fire.[8]

Crnokrak also admitted that when it came to fighting his own battles, Egan, size notwithstanding, might well be the guy a foe feared most. "He had the devil in him," Crnokrak said. "I would take him at my back in any brawl."[9]

Although college and professional basketball are as physical as ever with jostling for position under the basket, elbows being dug into midsections, and subtle body-banging in the paint, there is no fighting in the modern game. If a punch is thrown, a suspension is levied and a fine meted out. Actual fights were more common, especially in NBA games, a half century ago, and once in a while Crnokrak was in the middle of a fracas that in the present day, due to video repeats all of the country, might receive one hundred times the attention it did then.

With the addition of the talented sophomores, Crnokrak, who played three seasons for Loyola after his transfer from Wyoming, saw his playing time shrink. As a junior he averaged 5.0 points and 8.5 rebounds a game. As a senior he only got into sixteen games. One of those games was a midseason matchup with St. John's. After their scorched-earth start to the 1961–62 season, the Ramblers record read 11–2. The two losses were to Ohio State and Marquette.

For the St. John's game, Ireland assigned Crnokrak to cover a rugged forward named Willie Hall because of his dangerous offensive capabilities. "I want you to stay in his jock," Ireland ordered Crnokrak. Crnokrak was supposed to bother Hall into mistakes, take him out of his regular game, and cover him so closely teammates wouldn't even pass to him.[10]

The attention got on Hall's nerves and, according to Crnokrak, "he didn't like it and he hit me with an elbow so hard I got fourteen stitches." When Crnokrak saw his own blood he became infuriated and retaliated, punching Hall in the face. "You're dead, motherfucker," Hall replied. Hall rushed at Crnokrak. Crnokrak grabbed him and held him until the refs broke up the fight. Crnokrak said he found out later that Hall had been a New York boxing champion.[11]

During the early part of the season the Ramblers scored a 95–90 victory over Indiana. That was essentially a statement game, an indicator that Loyola could be a national player. This was pre–Bobby Knight, but Indiana had won national titles under Branch McCracken and was always regarded as a tough team. One of the Indiana stars of the time was Jimmy Rayl, a former Hoosiers schoolboy sensation and a future pro.

Rayl was a terrific shooter and you didn't have to be a genius to know that. But Ireland scouted more often than his contemporaries and provided a scouting report when Loyola was scheduled to go up against IU.

"He did all of that," Harkness said. "He didn't have film, but we knew what they were going to do." Up to a point. Harkness said at one point the scouting report became so detailed and complicated "we'd scratch our heads." When Ireland saw the confusion, Harkness said, he ripped up the papers and said, "They'll never get into any of that stuff. We're going to press them when they get out of the locker room." And that turned out to be the accurate assessment.[12]

One way players became closer friends was through the hospitality of six-foot-ten backup center Rich Rochelle. Rochelle was a local, from Evanston, only a few miles from the Loyola campus. Rochelle said he was lucky he even went to college and that the step was taken through no assistance offered to him at his high school. Although Ireland recruited him fairly heavily, Rochelle said coaches at Tennessee State, some schools in California, and Arkansas State also wanted him.

"I had a few offers," Rochelle said, "and I was the first in my family to go to college."[13]

Becoming the first member of his family to pursue higher education meant something to Rochelle, who graduated with a degree in sociology. But one way blacks were discriminated against at the time, he said, was being told by high school counselors they weren't "college material." "That was pushed at me. That was typical of that time. 'Go into woodworking.' All we were told is that we would be able to do things with our hands. I knew better for myself, thank goodness, than to let them hold me back. I didn't have the counseling you need. I did not understand what I could have done. You remember the times."[14]

As someone whose family home was only an L ride away on the subway, Rochelle many times brought teammates home to sample his mother Beatrice's cooking. Rochelle's mother always liked Ireland, more than he did, in fact, but she probably liked the boys coming over and eating well even more. Sometimes the menu featured red beans and rice, pork chops, or chicken. This open-door policy was especially helpful over holiday periods when the school shut down and going home to a distant place wasn't practical for all of the players. Instead, they joined Rochelle in Evanston.

"The guys came out to eat on a regular basis," Rochelle said. "Christmas dinner. They loved her turkey and dressing."[15]

After Loyola lost to Marquette, another Catholic school rival and a staple on the schedule, in the eleventh game the Ramblers ran off twelve straight wins. But they beat Marquette in a return game, 98–84, and topped Bowling Green, 81–68. Bowling Green was a national power featuring center Nate Thurmond, a future seven-time professional all-star and Hall of Famer, and guard Howie Komives, who led the nation in scoring with a 36.7 points per game average two seasons later.

Another notable triumph came over the University of Detroit and its star forward Dave DeBusschere, who became the youngest coach in NBA history and helped the New York Knicks win an NBA title. Loyola won the game DeBusschere's senior year, 90–76. Harkness believes that was one time when the still-growing Ramblers really showed what they could do by playing together. Although Harkness averaged twenty-one points a game that season, he insisted he wasn't really a scorer so much as playing the role of a scorer for a team that needed him to do so.

"I fit that piece," Harkness said. "I could run all day. I ran all game with the press. I guarded DeBusschere and he was six foot six or so, and he got his points, but at the end of the game when we made the run, he was gone. I mean, he was a great athlete, but I ran him to death. I just ran him all over. In the end we got layups. I got layups and short jumpers. I got on the foul line a lot, too, because I was a lefty and that was an advantage."[16]

The Ramblers' last regular-season game was a loss to Xavier, but the big wins earned Loyola some notoriety.

"It was a good team," Hunter said.[17]

And as Ireland had hoped, it was also a team that was starting to get a national reputation as one of the best in the land. In the early 1960s, the National Invitational Tournament at Madison Square Garden, or the NIT, was still nearly as prestigious as the NCAA championship. The NCAAs were about half the size that they are now, and it was very difficult for an independent team like Loyola, with no league affiliation, to obtain an invitation to the postseason event. Instead, sitting with a 21–3 record, Loyola accepted an offer to play in the NIT.

This in itself was a goal fulfilled for Ireland. Before the 1961–62 season the Ramblers had been invited to participate in exactly two postseason tournaments. They had never been to the NCAA tournament, and only twice were they courted by the NIT, first at the end of the 1938–39 season and again at the end of the 1948–49 season. That was it.

For all of the big victories, for all of the acclaim coming their way, for all of the potential demonstrated when they were at their best, the Ramblers were still a young team and one that had not yet challenged on the national stage.

As always, too, with this group, there was the backdrop of race. By the middle of the season, at the latest, it was clear to the team that four African American players should be starting. The best lineup was Egan, Harkness, Hunter, Rouse, and Miller. It was Miller who became more of a sixth man specialist because Ireland was feeling heat over how many black players he used at any one time.

"The sentiment we had was that Ronnie Miller should have been starting," Hunter said. "I didn't know why, but naturally I assumed it was racial. I know Ireland said he couldn't start more than three black players because of the community. There absolutely was pressure. I didn't know about his pressures, but I thought it was racial. I didn't know if it was pressure from outside or whether he just didn't feel that he wanted to start more blacks. I do know that when he hadn't been playing blacks he hadn't won. He'd be 12–15 or 15–12, or something like that, and they were playing nobody schools athletically, a bunch of little schools."[18]

Miller was one of the New York players Walter November had steered to Ireland. He had known Harkness when they were both in school in the Bronx. Miller played basketball, football, and baseball as a youngster and might even have been a better baseball player than basketball player. He said St. John's talked to him about a baseball scholarship.

Like Rochelle, Miller felt himself being pigeon-holed by a racist attitude that could determine his future. He was attending a high school that was for the trades and being directed to become an electrician.

"I hated the school," Miller said.

A friend attended Christopher Columbus High School, which was out of his district and a forty-five-minute subway ride away, but he convinced his single mother, Edith, a thirty-seven-year career telephone company worker, that he would be better off at that school, even if it was mostly white, Jewish, and far away. It didn't hurt any that Miller's friend lobbied the basketball coach and informed him he could get a good player out of this scheme. Miller stood about six foot two, weighed around 170 pounds at the time, and was very quick.

He was fortunate that he coincidentally lucked into a relationship with a basketball coach who really did know talent. Roy Rubin, who was such a savvy defensive coach that he wrote a book on it, later was a hugely successful coach at Long Island University and coached the Philadelphia 76ers.

Rubin became a large influence in Miller's life, not only taking him and friends to Madison Square Garden to watch big-time college basketball, but also inspiring him in philosophy.

"He dominated my life completely," Miller said. "He made sure I took the right classes. There was no hanging out and goofing off. He used to say, 'If you hang out with bums, you'll be a bum.'"[19]

Miller was never a bum or a troublemaker. He was quieter than his Loyola teammates and didn't always hang out with them either. He laughed when describing his circle of friends in Chicago as being "non-basketball guys, nerds."

While Miller believed he should have been starting his sophomore year he heeded Ireland's comments about being unable to start four African Americans. Harkness, Hunter, and Rouse started alongside Egan. A white senior named Mike Gavin usually got the nod for the fifth slot. The way Ireland worked his rotation for some time, Miller would come in for Hunter, Rouse, or Harkness, meaning there were still only three black players on the court at once.

Later in the season, given the undeniable truth that Miller needed to play more, he would still not start but would come into the game as a substitute and stay on the court, making four African Americans running the floor for Loyola at the same time. "It was so obvious to everyone that I should have been starting," Miller said.[20]

Miller appeared in all twenty-seven games and averaged 10.2 points and 4.4 rebounds, while shooting 44.5 percent from the field and 75.3 percent from the free-throw line. There was no doubt that his numbers supported the starter argument.

Miller sometimes saw indications that Ireland felt badly that he was the one losing out as a result of the racism of the times. He took the time to tell Miller that he just didn't feel he could start four African Americans and that he received hate mail that put the focus on Loyola and ramped up pressures preventing him from doing so.

"He was not a buddy to anybody," Miller said of Ireland's relationship with the players. "He was not a guy you would ever be close to. When I look back on it I thought he had a lot of insecurities. He had feuds with people like Ray Meyer. But he was not a negative or vindictive person. He was out of sync a little bit with what was going on with the civil rights movement. Things were changing."[21]

Just not fast enough for most African Americans.

CHAPTER 8

BAD NEWS IN NEW ORLEANS

The Ramblers saw the hate in person in New Orleans.

The most memorable road trip the Loyola men's basketball team made during the 1961–62 season was the most unusual, and the journey demonstrated up close what the six o'clock news and the front pages of big-city newspapers were discussing.

What was ostensibly a simple trip to Louisiana to play a game against what was presumed to be a kindred-spirit Jesuit university also named Loyola, proved to be evidence of conflicting worlds as the civil rights movement unfolded and attempted to drag, kicking, screaming, and protesting, the Southern states back into the Union, an effort thought accomplished a century before.

One Loyola University, based in Chicago, featured several African Americans on its basketball roster. The other Loyola University, based in New Orleans, would not allow white people and people with darker skin to sit together in the same bleachers. New Orleans, supposedly one of the most sophisticated of American cities, with its polyglot population of whites, blacks, and Cajuns and its reputation as a world-class tourist destination, proved to be as backward as rural Alabama when it came to race relations.

It might be argued that Loyola of Chicago had no reason to schedule a game in the Deep South at all. Still, since they were two Loyolas, of the same faith and outlook in theory, the opponent did make sense.

Just what would occur when the Ramblers showed up to prepare for and play a college basketball game with its band of black brothers in a city that had zero tolerance for interaction between the races was difficult to imagine. Did coach George Ireland really believe the arrival of his team in the city by the Gulf of Mexico would go unnoticed? Not according to his players. They said they were forewarned by Ireland that things might get uncomfortable when they reached the Big Easy.

John Crnokrak was deeply moved and disturbed by the racial discrimination that his black teammates suffered on trips to the South. Courtesy of the Loyola Sports Information Office.

Before boarding a plane to New Orleans, Ireland conducted a team meeting. At first he seemed to be calling for the team to vote on whether or not to travel to Louisiana and play the game. Then it morphed into a sort of pep talk about how the Ramblers were strong young men and how they could put up with and conquer all obstacles.

"It's going to be rough down there," Harkness remembered Ireland saying. "Things are segregated down there in the South and it's going to be rough." The speech continued: "We're going to have to do this. We're going to have to do that. But I want to give you guys the chance because you're dedicated. You're strong men. But I want to get your OK to go down there."[1]

Harkness said the players looked at one another and after absorbing Ireland's warnings about how bad things might be when they got to Louisiana, they said they weren't going to go.

"He was shocked," Harkness said. "He thought his young guys would face all this. It was 'Uh-uh, we don't want to go down there.' Oh, my goodness. Then he changed his tune. We didn't want to go down there if they were going to treat us like that. I forget what he said, but he changed our minds."[2]

One issue not discussed was where the team would stay. There seemed to be at best a vague understanding of what the accommodations would be like when the Ramblers got to the segregated town where whites did not rent hotel rooms to blacks. Then, when the team arrived, the players heard there was an offer on the table for all of them to bunk at Xavier of New Orleans, whites and blacks.

"The problems seemed exaggerated," Harkness said. "Xavier of New Orleans, a black school, said they'd let us stay in the dorms. We would have no problems. They'd take the whole team. They called and said, 'You can all stay here and we'll take care of you.'"[3]

But Ireland declined the offer. It was because of that decision, declining accommodations that would have provided a relatively peaceful solution to the problem even if the Ramblers would not have stayed in luxury, that Harkness and other players became suspicious of their coach's motives. They began to wonder just what he was thinking.

"He didn't accept that [opportunity to stay at Xavier]," Harkness said. "That's a good offer. But Ireland wanted controversy."[4]

By controversy, Harkness and other players meant that they thought getting attention for being shunned because the team had black players would help the school's national reputation. In any case, new arrangements were made. The white players were going to sleep in one place and the black players were going to sleep in another place. This was the only time the team split up all season.

Rich Rochelle assessed Ireland's motive similarly. "He wanted attention," Rochelle said. "He wanted the limelight. We could have stayed together."[5]

Why would Ireland not have accepted the easy solution?

"Just national recognition," Rochelle said. "I can't get into the gentleman's mind. Making a spectacle."[6]

The team was divided by skin color and loaded into taxicabs. Harkness, Miller, Rochelle, Vic Rouse, and Les Hunter went one way, to the suburb of Algiers, and John Egan, Chuck Wood, and the other white players went another way, to a local hotel.

Ron Miller was always skeptical about Ireland acting as if this whole business about where the team could stay sneaked up on him.

"He said, 'I didn't know this when we booked the trip,'" Miller said. "There's no way in hell he didn't know. He acted hurt that he actually had to go through with it [splitting up the team]. Jerry was the one most upset."[7]

"We were looking at each other and laughing, acting silly, you know," Harkness said. "Ireland split us up right there. We go off to the black community and we don't see them again."[8]

Actually, there were indications that Ireland did not know all that his team might be in for in segregated New Orleans. He jumped into a cab with the black players intending to make sure they got properly settled. One of the players joked, "C'mon, Dad." Only the black cab driver didn't think anything was funny about this situation. The man said to Ireland, "I can't take you." Ireland said, "Don't worry about it, I'll pay." The man said, "They will take me to jail."[9]

That was a sobering message—taxicab service was not integrated. The black players did not really miss him in their private surroundings, however. They were treated like kings. "The black guys had a great time," Miller said. "That was the best trip. The best food. The best partying. The best."[10]

Nonetheless, the division of the unit was strange to all. "I'll never forget looking through the window and seeing the guys looking over at us and we're looking over at them," Hunter said. "I heard it was against the law for whites and blacks to ride in the same taxicab."[11]

For two years the players had acted like the Three Musketeers, with the one-for-all and all-for-one attitude, and they did not want to be split up. While the outside world may have looked on them as whites and blacks and naturally different, they had come together over the common ground of trying to form the best basketball team possible. Players did not speak of race being a problem between starters and backups, whites and blacks, stars and end-of-the-bench players.

"Color didn't matter," said white backup forward Chuck Wood. "There was no question of color. Everyone got along. The egos never got in the way. You never hoped this guy didn't do well. If they did well we all did well."[12]

Only New Orleans had such a disagreeable problem with whites and blacks sharing off-the-court abodes.

The day before the game, in a conference call with Chicago newspaper reporters (none traveled with the team to regular-season road games in those days), Ireland said he was under the impression that the team was going to stay together at Xavier, but although he did not explicitly explain the reason behind the change, the plan was altered.

"I've had nothing but trouble since we got here," Ireland said. "Our five Negro players can't eat with the rest of the team, can't ride in the same cabs, or live in the same building." He announced that he would no longer schedule games in the South as long as such discrimination continued.[13]

Although the Ramblers had not accomplished much on the court yet and were only just beginning to gain a reputation as a nationally ranked program, the African American players on the team were welcomed and fêted as celebrities by the black community in New Orleans.

The black players were parceled out as honored guests to individual homes, were wined and dined and visited the local entertainment establishments. And without Ireland around to supervise, impose curfew, or jump on rule-breakers, their bedtimes became flexible.

Ironically, Egan, who had been shepherded in the other direction because he was white, suspected as much might occur as soon as he heard the African Americans were going off to stay elsewhere.

"At the time I don't remember that the white guys were that offended," Egan said of his group of nineteen-year-olds. "I don't remember feeling that this was terrible. I thought they were just going to have too much fun."[14]

Maybe the racial overtones of the entire situation didn't seem that big to Egan then, or maybe he just knew his teammates well, but that feeling was correct.

"We knew that was going to happen," Egan said of being split up. "I don't think we were all that uptight about the fact that we were separated. We just accepted it. I am sure if I was black I wouldn't have accepted it so calmly. Even though I might have had a good time where I stayed, it would piss me off.

"It was at that time I think that Ireland really intended to make a point about segregation for a couple of different reasons," Egan continued. "Not only did it exist, and he personally was against it, no question about it, though I don't believe he was a crusader, but it was a great opportunity for him to make waves about it. He could show himself as a person who stood up against racism, which is a great recruiting tool because he was then recruiting New York."[15]

Although this adventure was a new thing for most of the Loyola players, the school had a longstanding home-and-home arrangement with the other Loyola. It was just that the Ramblers did not have many African Americans on the roster when they visited New Orleans two years earlier. John Crnokrak, with roots in northern Indiana, had been on that team. Nothing in his background prepared him for the sight of "white" and "colored" water fountains.

"I ran over to the faucet to take a drink of water and I was shocked," Crnokrak said.[16]

On that trip, when he was a teammate of Clarence Red, Crnokrak said, Loyola was at first assigned to stay at a segregated hotel, which would have sent Red elsewhere for accommodations. Red, Crnokrak recalled, reacted simply, saying, "Bullshit."

"We voted we weren't going to stay there," Crnokrak said. "That [the threat of being split up] tore me up. We were a team. That tainted me so bad."[17]

Crnokrak remembers Ireland commenting on the hate mail that came in because of his use of so many black athletes on the floor, and he later remembered hearing about those poisonous writings from Judy Van Dyck, Ireland's daughter, who still has them.

Was Ireland a pioneer in the vein of Alabama football coach Bear Bryant or simply an open-minded coach who could tell the world of college sports was changing and felt pragmatism was a wise course? It has been said that Coach Bryant, who was a far greater legend in his domain than Ireland was in Chicago, recognized that he had to start recruiting black players for his Crimson Tide football teams but couldn't because his superiors tied his hands.

During a 1970 football game, University of Southern California's black fullback Sam Cunningham led the Trojans to a three-touchdown trouncing of Alabama, and some say that was the galvanizing incident that opened up Alabama and the Southeastern Conference to the recruitment of black football players. Jerry Claiborne, who then was a Bryant assistant before embarking on his own head coaching career, said, "Sam Cunningham did more to integrate Alabama in sixty minutes than Martin Luther King did in twenty years." The strict accuracy of the statement may be questioned, but the point was sharply taken.

"I think George [Ireland] was like Bear Bryant and was far thinking," Crnokrak said. "George realized these young men had talent." And was he practical, too? "That's well said."[18]

At first, Harkness did not recognize how unusual it was that Ireland was recruiting black players. In New York sometimes the teams he played on competed against white teams and no hullabaloo was made about it. So for him to be recruited to play at a predominantly white university didn't make that big an impact on him at first. Neither did he realize that Ireland might be going out on any kind of limb to recruit African Americans.

The first clue for Harkness that race relations were not all hunky-dory in Chicago was that dance where a black player danced with a white girl, only to be told by a priest, "No mingling."[19] Then, on another occasion, some of the black players got wind of a dance in the nearby suburb of Mundelein. They showed up at an all girls school and one of the black guys was rebuffed by one of the white girls. The young man got angry, feeling the girl was acting as if he wasn't good enough for her.

"The next day Ireland called us all in because the nuns at that school had called him and told him his black players were acting unruly," Harkness said. "You could see the standoffishness with the girls in some of the dorms on campus. We weren't really involved in much of the social stuff. They didn't know how to react to all of us. Even at lunch, we'd all eat together. We automatically just clung to each other."[20]

Harkness said Ireland tried to be diplomatic about their visit to the girls' school, but he got his message across. It went something like this, Harkness said: "Maybe down the road this is going to change, but right now people are leery about that and the world's not ready for you guys to be hitting on white girls." One of the guys jumped up and said, "I don't care if they're purple, green, or yellow, if they're fine we will hit on them." Ireland said, "Now, wait a minute. You can't. This is not the way it's going to be."[21]

As a result, the black players went where the black girls lived, the South Side of Chicago. They held their own parties in the dorms, where they brought black girls in. That was OK.

Ireland was sensitive to what being a nineteen-, twenty-, or twenty-one-year-old guy was like. He also did not like that it was out of his control to say it didn't matter to anyone at Loyola if his players were involved in interracial dating.

From a recruiting standpoint, Harkness agreed, though, that Ireland was ahead of the national trend on the issue of recruiting black players virtually without limit. "He got out there. He jumped that gun," Harkness said, "and it truly did not matter to him how many black guys were on the team. He didn't care about a quota. No *ifs*, *ands*, or *buts*, by the time I was a junior and those other guys were sophomores, he started four black guys."[22]

Not every game and not everywhere, however, at least not until the end of the season. Ireland was hardly dumb, so he was aware that taking his team to Southern towns for games and playing his usual complement of African Americans could become a flashpoint.

The better the Ramblers played, the more excited Ireland got because he could see his long-term plan bearing fruit. He was getting beat up by sarcastic remarks from other coaches asking him if he only recruited Africa, but he had a blunt retort for them: "I'm winning." Only once did Harkness and some of the other black players doubt Ireland's color blindness.

During one practice, when Ireland had a tendency to blow a gasket periodically, anyway, Harkness said Ireland made an inappropriate remark to Ron Miller. All of the African American players grew angry when they heard about it, he said. They talked about the comment (Harkness remembers it being something on the order of "Chocolate Boy" or "Thunder Boy") and decided they had to confront Ireland.

"I'm sensitive to stuff like that," Harkness said. "Ronnie mentioned what he said, but Ronnie is not as sensitive as I am. Ronnie got along with whites and blacks. He was articulate. He was up on politics. He knew about a lot of things. He didn't go to parties with us. He was a good guy, just different. We expected him to say to Ireland, 'Yeah, I didn't like it.' Ireland goes, 'Ronnie, did I bother you? Hurt your feelings?' And Ronnie goes, 'No, you didn't hurt my feelings.' He said, 'No, Coach, it was all right with me.' I was so mad at Ronnie when I got up out of that meeting. Even though Ronnie brought it up, I should have known better than to take it to Ireland. But it was something I had to confront Ireland about for the future, anyway. You know, 'You can't do that. You've got to think twice.' That was the end of that. He did not do it again, so it was good. He had to understand us. He had to understand our situation."[23]

However, decades later, Miller says that he doesn't know what Harkness is talking about. He has no recollection of any incident. "I don't remember Ireland ever saying anything to me out of line," Miller said.[24]

If time has muddied memories of what did or did not happen that day in practice, it has not had the same effect on recalling the New Orleans trip. The situation in New Orleans was clear enough: Loyola was not particularly welcome as an opponent. The seating at the school for the game was segregated. Some blacks in the community had called for an attendance boycott because of that and that did affect the number of African Americans who came. Blacks who did attend were on one side of the gym and whites on another. Although it was a home game for Loyola of New Orleans, many of the black fans rooted for Loyola of Chicago. The white fans, not so much.

Harkness had not felt close to Egan at first, partially because of Egan's connection to St. Rita. The school Egan's family had attended for five generations had been embroiled in some fights with black schools. Harkness wondered how Egan really thought. To Harkness, one of the key moments of proof that he was on the black players' side came in New Orleans.

"He just played so hard that game," Harkness said, "because he knew the pressure we were under because of this racial thing. He played his heart out. I just thought it showed he was on our side. He didn't know that, but in my mind that's how I was thinking. I just remember him diving and playing hard, and although I saw that a lot from him it really hit me there. We walloped them. It was pitiful. At one point I think we had them by forty. I knew we had something to prove there."[25]

An atmosphere of hostility prevailed in the arena at Loyola, but more as a low current of electricity than as a churning, roiling mood of impending danger.

"It was us versus them," Rochelle said.[26]

Nasty cracks came from the gallery. Sometimes a fan would yell, "We're going to show you what some white boys can do." Rochelle used politer language than the spectators did to describe some words hurled at the Ramblers, calling them "catcalls."[27]

Loyola from Chicago was too good for Loyola from Louisiana, winning 95–73. After all the angst surrounding the trip and confronting racial issues, it was a game the Ramblers had to win.

An account of the game in the *Chicago American*, pieced together from wire service reports, was headlined, "Racial Peace Prevails; Loyola Wins." The story called the game "a rare integrated sports contest in this southern city. The game was played without incident, despite the threat of a boycott by Negro leaders in protest of segregated seating. There were about seventy-five Negroes on hand. New Orleans is in the middle of an election which has segregation as a bitter principal issue."[28]

It was noted that when Loyola forward Vic Rouse, who scored twenty-four points, came out of the game he was given an ovation by the approximately one thousand fans.

About that time, the Ramblers began to develop the attitude that they should win every game. Harkness said the younger players were more confident than the older players had been. They hadn't lost much, so they didn't believe they should lose. Harkness said he had conversations with upperclassmen that went this way: "We're gonna lose this one." "Oh, we're not going to beat so-and-so. We can't." And he replied, "We're not gonna lose this game."[29]

A road game at Marshall in Huntington, West Virginia, for the 1961–62 team was again an invasion of what seemed to be the active Confederacy. "They called us names," Harkness said.

Les Hunter remembers being called "a black bastard" by one of Marshall's players during the game and he was thinking of ways to retaliate. The player kept it up, chirping at Hunter, irritating him. Hunter was in danger of losing his temper, and in a huddle he told Ireland what was going on. "I'm going to punch this guy if he keeps calling me names," Hunter said.[30]

Forward John Crnokrak spoke up and said to leave the offender to him. He recognized if Hunter retaliated there might be a race riot. Crnokrak said, "I'll get that guy." As the game ended, Crnokrak went after the other player, chasing him into the tunnel that separated the locker rooms from the court. At the same time the crowd was coming out of the stands.

"We were in peril if they decided to attack, but the police kept everybody off of us," Hunter said. "Crnokrak was going after this guy because I couldn't go after him."[31]

Something that always stuck with Hunter was that Marshall had an African American player. What must it have been like for him playing with such a teammate? "It was rough enough for me in Chicago," Hunter said, "and it had to be real rough for him with a teammate like that."[32]

Chuck Wood said that he, Egan, Hunter, and Rouse went out to find something to eat in Huntington. They saw a hamburger joint and went in.

"We were told, 'The blacks will have to sit in that booth back there.' Egan said, 'No, that's not going to happen.'"[33]

Wood said they ordered hamburgers and malts to go from the counter, but they were disgruntled by the situation. "The person behind the counter says, 'You guys had better knock it off. If one of my customers calls the police these guys [Hunter and Rouse, the black guys] could be thrown in jail for disorderly conduct,'" Wood said. All he could think was, "What the heck is going on?"[34]

What was going on was the American South in 1962. What was also starting to go on with Loyola basketball, though, was winning everywhere. The Ramblers captured that game, 88–80, whether local fans liked them or not.

In those moments Loyola was very much a team, a group, a single-minded unit, and although the players never recall a minute of racial problems between the whites and blacks on the team, they were not all buddy-buddy all of the time away from the games, road trips, and practices, either.

"Still, a lot of the time the white players went their way and we went our way," Harkness said. "Sometimes we ate together in the dorm and it was good enough that we were really good on the court. There was never a spillover of any white and black problem, never. Never whatsoever."[35]

The glimpses of the United States on its worst behavior could have demoralized the players and interfered with Loyola's performance, but the players didn't let it. They kept winning, and as the regular season ended with a 21–3 record the Ramblers were invited to play in the NIT championships in New York.

At that time not only was the NIT a much bigger deal than it is now, when it is viewed as a consolation tournament compared to the NCAA, it was also elite enough that only twelve teams were invited to play. These days, if the NCAA is the Big Dance, then at best the NIT can be considered the Square Dance. Now, although many more teams are invited to participate, the majority of the games are held on campuses. In 1962 all of the teams traveled to New York for the tournament and fought it out at Madison Square Garden.

Harkness said he believes Loyola could have gone to the NCAA tournament that year but that Ireland chose to enter the NIT as a favor of sorts to Walter November, who, after all, was based in New York.

Loyola opened against Temple University from Philadelphia and won, 75–64. In the second round, the Ramblers faced Dayton, but they played one of their worst games of the year and lost to the eventual champion, 98–82. During that era the tournament held a consolation game and Loyola won that, 95–84, over Duquesne.

Unheralded at the beginning of the season, Loyola had finished third in a national tournament. Not all of the Ramblers felt so good about their 23–4 record and final placing, as might be expected. "We should have won the NIT," Hunter said.[36]

Hunter pins the defeat on Ireland for mixing up his starting lineup at an inopportune time. While it was felt that Miller should have been starting, which would have given Loyola four black starters, Ireland had resisted, being wary of a likely increase in criticism for using too many African Americans on the court simultaneously. But he changed plans abruptly and inserted Miller into the lineup at the NIT. The problem was, he made several switches, not just one. Hunter said he was making sure that all of the New York guys recruited by November got into the lineup so November could see them have starring roles. Hunter, the starting center from Tennessee, was taken out while the smaller New York guys started as a sort of doff of the cap to November.

"Ireland wanted to show him that if he steered guys to him they would play," Hunter said. "But he didn't want to start more blacks. We couldn't get any boards and they [Dayton] jumped out to a ten-point lead just like that. He put me in and I had a tremendous game, but it was too late. After that Ireland began starting Miller and that was the beginning of it, the first time four blacks started at Loyola."[37]

Ireland was on a hurry-up schedule and going 23–4 made a statement to other teams about how good his Ramblers were. Adding a national title would have been sweet, but all of the key players returned for the next season, and some other good ones, more blacks included, would join the varsity for the 1962–63 season.

Most important was that all of those sophomores were coming of age. They joined Harkness and they formed a potentially lethal outfit. The one thing those players lacked at the start of the 1961–62 season was experience. They had that now. They had never lacked for confidence, but now they had both of those key ingredients going for them to supplement their talent.

There is no question that the success of 1961–62 set up the success to come in 1962–63. The tremendous season that ended in disappointment was a tremendous element in the growing process. Most championship teams need a seasoning period. Loyola crushed the easiest opponents on its schedule, bested most of the good ones, competed in a national tournament and showed well, and off the court matured by sharing and dealing with emotional challenges. That 1961–62 campaign was essential to Loyola's development.

"We were together and we were learning from each other," Harkness said. "It truly, truly did develop us for the next year. Everybody was starting to talk about us."[38]

Jerry Lyne was the Ramblers' assistant coach during the 1962–63 championship season. When his mentor George Ireland retired, Lyne succeeded him and led the program for five seasons. Courtesy of the Loyola Sports Information Office.

CHAPTER 9

A GREAT START

Many coaches prefer to have their teams ease into the regular season, sort of like beachgoers who approach the ocean and dip only a few toes into the surf to test the temperature. George Ireland set up his Loyola schedule that way for 1962–63.

No ranked teams, no big-name programs, no major threats were lined up for his guys to confront as action began in December. In consecutive games the Ramblers blitzed Christian Brothers, North Dakota, Milwaukee, and South Dakota by a combined 126 points. C'mon in, everyone, the water's fine.

Loyola opened the season with Christian Brothers and thrashed that hapless bunch, 114–58. Next, the Ramblers smashed North Dakota, 110–56. The third team on the schedule has improved and prospered over the years, becoming a Loyola rival in the Horizon League, but a half century ago Milwaukee was far removed from any hint of being a powerhouse and the Ramblers won 107–47. After trouncing South Dakota, 105–58, the Ramblers were 4–0.

On those occasions, everyone in uniform got into the games. Even Ireland couldn't really worry about his bench not being able to sustain a fifty-point lead. The regulars did the job, but bench guys like Billy Smith and Pablo Robertson also scored in double figures against North Dakota, with fourteen points and ten points, respectively.

Backups like Jim Reardon, Chuck Wood, Rich Rochelle, and Dan Connaughton all collected season highs during that four-game opening sweep. It was merely a matter of flexing a few muscles in disposing of that quartet. Jerry Harkness, embarking on an All-American season, scored eighteen points in nineteen minutes against North Dakota.

In almost no time the Ramblers had established themselves as a fearsome offensive force. A correspondent in the *Chicago Sun-Times* claimed they "shoot with the precision of William Tell," and by the second game of the season the newspaper had raised (although cavalierly) the issue of whether or not this was a national title contender. Loyola, it was noted, "may ultimately be rewarded with a high national ranking. Even the championship—who knows?"[1]

After devastating demolitions of the first foes, the Chicago newspapers were writing that Loyola possessed a "high voltage basketball attack, which has left chaos and destruction in its wake." By mid-December the Ramblers were ranked number three nationally in the United Press International poll. Defending national champ Cincinnati was ranked first and Duke was ranked second.[2]

Western Michigan, in the fifth game, was a different type of opponent. The Broncos played the same kind of up-tempo game and dared to run with the Ramblers. The point differential was twenty-one, a 123–102 final in Loyola's favor, but it was as much of a horse race as the Belmont Stakes, fun to watch, exhilarating to be part of.

Jerry Harkness pumped in thirty-four points, Vic Rouse twenty-five, Les Hunter twenty, Ron Miller eighteen, and John Egan sixteen. What a display of firepower. And the defensive pressure set up the explosive running game.

"Jerry and Jack [Egan] could run the trap," Miller said. "I would rotate to the guy who thought he would be free and intercept the pass. We could pass and we could run."

Western Michigan ranked somewhere in the middle when it came to assessing Loyola opponents. The Broncos were incapable of a slowdown game. They came at the Ramblers strength against strength. There was no time to go buy popcorn at that game without missing something.

"That was a track meet," Miller said.[3]

Loyola was 5–0 when it faced Indiana. Playing against the Hoosiers was a whole 'nother deal compared to lining up against a team like Christian Brothers. Even a half century ago Indiana had a reputation as one of the finest programs in the land. The Hoosiers were Big Ten Conference contenders each year, and they had claimed two NCAA titles.

Indiana was one of the big names on the schedule. After brushing aside the early annoyances with massive point production, Loyola took on the Hoosiers in a game for respect. The traditional national power was close enough to Chicago geographically to cast a shadow. The Big Ten was the

league most Chicago sports fans followed—that and then-independent Notre Dame—and it meant something if the Ramblers could topple IU. Trim-
ming the Hoosiers would be far more significant than blasting Christian
Brothers.

The Ramblers put up 106 points on Indiana, a team that prided itself on
defense, beating the Hoosiers 106–74, in Bloomington.

"You know a lot of black fans came up to me and were cheering for us
at IU because they had never seen anything like it," Harkness said. "We beat
them and we started to think we were pretty good."[4]

By clubbing Indiana, Loyola made a statement that it belonged among
the best teams in the country. The Ramblers shredded IU's D. Scoring more
than one hundred points against Indiana was an exceptional achievement.

"We knew that we were pretty good," Harkness said. "We were third in
the nation and we knew we had to prove it."[5]

A pattern was developing. Unlike some teams that relied on one super-
scorer, Loyola featured diverse scoring capability. Harkness always got his,
but several other players complemented him on a given night. Against Indiana Hunter scored twenty-seven points, Harkness twenty-four, Miller seventeen, Smith fourteen off the bench, and Egan thirteen. That was a sweet
win and it was clear Loyola had too many weapons for most opponents.

The Ramblers had trailed Indiana at the half, but during the game's last
ten minutes they shed the shackles the Hoosiers had placed on the offense.

"Hunter was a giant for me at Indiana, and that Harkness is a real gar-
bageman," Ireland said. "You know, the kind that will stick right in there
and grab anything that doesn't go into the basket. Then he puts it in."[6]

The wins kept coming and so did the points. The Ramblers beat Seattle, Arkansas, and Memphis State. Loyola was scoring like a pro team, even
though the college game's length is forty minutes compared to the NBA's
forty-eight. Seattle also preferred a high-octane style of play. When Ireland
spoke to Chicago reporters before the contest he actually suggested the Ramblers might play a slowdown game, the antithesis of their usual style. No one
knew whether to believe him or not.

"I have a lot of confidence in this ball club," Ireland said of his team. "I'm
sure they can adapt themselves to any situation and if it is to our advantage
to slow this Seattle club down, we're going to do it. What makes this team
great is that I have five very good scorers and six boys averaging in double
figures."[7]

At the time Seattle, which has drifted back and forth between NCAA classifications over the intervening decades, was a powerhouse. Hall of Famer Elgin Baylor, a huge NBA star with the Los Angeles Lakers, is the school's most prominent basketball alum, and the Pacific Northwest squad was ranked nineteenth in the country when Loyola beat Seattle, 93–83.

After the first four games Ireland was not as free with his substitution minutes as he had been. Entire games came and went with Connaughton, Reardon, Rochelle, and Earl Johnson, (before he left school in February) sitting for the duration. Wood, too, but that was as much because he had contracted mononucleosis, which kept him out of uniform for eleven games.

As the Ramblers worked their way through the schedule, Harkness was almost always the high scorer, but the other starters always contributed their share. Against Seattle, six players scored in double figures, three in the twenties, but the showdown was one of Loyola's closest games during the first half of the season. Seattle was a formidable foe, although the Ramblers did not walk the ball up the court and try to slow the pace, as Ireland had threatened. Seattle, however, tried to make the Ramblers' own medicine work against them, employing the same kind of pressure defense to keep the game tight.

"We played a good first half," Ireland said. "Then we made some mistakes like bad passes and wild shots that let Seattle close in. It wasn't so much Seattle's press as it was our miscues, but we proved we could bounce back as we had a few nights earlier against Indiana."[8]

As the end of 1962 approached, Loyola headed for Oklahoma City for the All-College Classic that was a hallmark of the Christmas season in college basketball and the biggest such event at the time in the Great Plains area. The event is the oldest college basketball tournament, dating its founding to 1935, before even the NIT and NCAA championships began. By that time Duke had taken a tumble in the Associated Press poll, but Loyola stayed third behind Cincinnati and Ohio State. In-state foe Illinois was ranked fourth.

In Oklahoma, Arkansas loomed as the Ramblers' first opponent. Ireland was one of those coaches who thought one way and talked another. He knew how good his team really was, but he took the football aw-shucks approach, talking up opponents, generally indicating that every team Loyola faced was so good it should have been going head-to-head with the Boston Celtics.

"Arkansas is much bigger than we are," Ireland said. "We're going to press. If Arkansas stops our press, we'll drop back on defense and I think we proved against Seattle that we can play defense when it's necessary."[9]

Against Arkansas four players scored in double figures, with Harkness firing in twenty-two points and Hunter next in line with fifteen. Although Loyola did give up inches in the matchups, the Ramblers controlled the boards. The Ramblers started slowly, but when the fast break got going they took over and won, 81–62.

As usual, Loyola was spectacular to watch, filling the hole with break-aways, jump shots, and feeds down low, plus playing the suffocating defense that caused opposing point guards to panic in their attempts to find an open man.

The victory over Arkansas moved Loyola into the semifinals of the Oklahoma City tournament, facing Memphis State, and the Ramblers topped the Tigers, 94–82. That win pushed the midwestern bunch into the championship game against Wyoming, a game that turned out to be important for more than perpetuating Loyola's unbeaten streak.

"Miller and Egan are tremendous guards," Ireland said, "good drivers and sharp at drawing fouls from their opponents. You've got to score one hundred points with a gang like that going for you."[10]

Ireland said one of his new practice strategies that season seemed to be paying off, even if his players didn't like it at first. At home Alumni Gym, Ireland ordered the installation of smaller rims inside the regulation baskets. This required more pinpoint shooting.

"They complained about it for a while," Ireland said. "But as the practice season wore on they got used to it and once we took the inner rim out they were really pouring it through there."[11]

Ireland had no hesitation about working his guys hard in practice, and the players sometimes felt he was more on the ball in practice than on the sidelines. During games he wasn't as animated, and it sometimes seemed that assistant coach Jerry Lyne did more of the talking.

"I always thought Ireland was a better practice coach than game coach," Ron Miller said. "He drove us hard in practice. He didn't swear, but he yelled a lot."[12]

Within a team a dynamic always forms, often in response to a coach's personality. On some teams the coach can be like a father or big brother. On others he is the disciplinarian inspiring a little bit of fear. Ireland did not wish to play the head-of-family role for his players or act as a sibling. He was the boss.

For all the shouting that went on during practice, Miller believed Ireland knew what he was doing when he raised his voice. Some players responded to tongue lashings and others didn't. Miller was of the type that didn't handle being screamed at and Ireland recognized this. "I was the one he didn't yell at," Miller said. "He once told me that he thought my fundamentals were so sound and that I grasped what he wanted us to do, so he didn't need to."[13]

For Loyola to be a permanent fixture in the national poll's top five was intoxicating.

Still, compared to schools like Cincinnati and those in the Big Ten, Loyola remained a little-known program. Only gradually did the Ramblers become aware of just how good they could be, so it shouldn't have been a surprise that other teams and fans elsewhere weren't clued in yet, either.

"Jerry Harkness, he was the Michael Jordan of that day," said center Rich Rochelle. "You have the best basketball player in college at that time. You have a great leader on the floor in Egan. Ronnie Miller ended up being phenomenal. Les was just a phenomenal ballplayer—his ability to get off the floor. He could jump very fast and very high. He was able to control the paint. He wasn't a brute. He was just an outstanding all-around center for his height."[14]

Many took note of what the Ramblers accomplished the previous season at the start of the new season, but poll support seemed fragile when Loyola dropped to fourth, falling behind Ohio State despite remaining unbeaten. Although it was meaningless at the time, at the end of the season when the NCAAs were over, one might look back at this poll and recall that when Loyola was number four, Mississippi State was number five. In hindsight, it might seem as if the two schools had been on a collision course all along.

After beating back all early-season challenges, and coming on the heels of the 23–4 season of 1961–62, Loyola was in the national discussion.

Up close, familiarity was impressive but also confusing. Did Loyola players realize just how good they were? Frank Perez was on the freshman team and as such practiced against the varsity every day. "We were their punching bags," Perez said. "I don't think any of us really did understand how good they were, but it was, 'Wow, this team has won so many games in a row.'"[15]

The wins kept mounting.

"About one-third of the way through the season we realized what we had," Rochelle said. "We'd seen some of the best teams in the country and nobody had been able to run with us. The ball went down the floor very fast and it went up very fast." And it went into the hoop very often.[16]

At 8–0 the Ramblers advanced to the championship game of the Oklahoma All-College Classic, ready to meet Wyoming.

Many years after the achievement was recorded, Loyola men's basketball coach George Ireland stood outside of a campus building where a banner hangs commemorating the 1963 NCAA title team that he led. Ireland died in 2001 at age eighty-eight. Courtesy of Paul Smulson.

CHAPTER 10

BREAKING BARRIERS IN OKLAHOMA CITY

eorge Ireland and Loyola shattered a barrier at the All-College Classic late-December holiday tournament in Oklahoma City in 1962 by accident. At one point during a still-tight game against the University of Wyoming on December 29, 1962, Ramblers point guard John Egan got into a flap with a referee and was ejected from the game. He was replaced on the court by backup point guard Pablo Robertson. That personnel switch meant that Loyola had five African American players on the court.

Although the milestone passed uneventfully, many years later officials at NCAA headquarters determined that was the first time in major college basketball history that a school had fielded five black players simultaneously. Actually, during that game Ireland only used seven players, and six were black.

The noteworthy occurrence, which the NCAA official said was going to be entered into the college governing body's book of firsts, did not mean there had been no colleges competing in college basketball up until that time without full lineups of black players. Historically black universities such as Clarence Gaines's Winston-Salem team and John McClendon's Tennessee State club always had lineups consisting of all-black players. But they competed in the NAIA and later, when the class was created, the NCAA Division II.

From the time he began playing two or more black players regularly in Loyola games Ireland had been a boat rocker. However, he was not going to risk sinking the boat by starting four black players, never mind using five at once. Not at first, anyway.

Although Loyola met Wyoming well into the 1962–63 season, the Ramblers were still undefeated. The Cowboys were a tough team and the solid program owned one NCAA title, though it dated to 1943. Loyola maintained a reasonable lead through the game and won 93–82, but the contest was not a blowout.

Ireland, always nervous about playing from the front and fretting about how another team could catch the Ramblers, was not going to lessen his team's chances of winning a game merely for the sake of inserting a white player into the lineup whom he didn't think was the right fit. It's not known how much thought Ireland gave to his substitution when presented with a midgame situation where he had to act quickly. More than likely he was preoccupied by the threat to his team's winning streak.

After Ireland's skittishness about starting four black players during the 1961–62 season, he acceded to the reality of the strengths and weaknesses of his personnel for the 1962–63 season. There was no more juggling to make sure there weren't more than three blacks on the court at one time. That policy was gone. The starting lineup was locked in with Egan, the sole white player, at the point, Ron Miller as his backcourt partner, Les Hunter at center, and Jerry Harkness and Vic Rouse at the forwards.

The top two subs were also African American, Pablo Robertson, a guard, and Billy Smith, a forward. They were New Yorkers and had also been sent to Ireland by Walter November. The only white in the eight-man rotation besides Egan was Chuck Wood.

The always-eager Egan was at the root of the incident that led to the all-black five. Typical of his never-let-up playing style, Egan became embroiled in a jump-ball fight with a Wyoming player late in the second half. Egan grabbed his half of the ball while kneeling on top of the player, who was stretched out on the court. The contact produced conflict and Egan and the Cowboy exchanged elbows.

Egan was usually sly enough to gain on-court revenge in one manner or another without losing his temper, but he did not respond well when the referee started lecturing him about being too aggressive. Too aggressive! Heck, that was the hallmark of his game. If you were five foot ten in a game of giants, you had to be. Egan's return comment was a snappy one. He told the referee to just put the ball in play for the jump ball.

In this particular case, although he did not curse (an automatic cause for ejection), Egan did open his mouth. Usually, he was more subtle, but his reactions to theoretical bad calls made against his team could infuriate others. "He could not say a word—and he did not say a word—and still make you angry," teammate Rich Rochelle said of Egan, whom he believed could win an Academy Award for his acting. "He did it with body language. That night he had a thing going with the ref. He [Egan] could look at you in such a way that you wanted to grab something and beat him with it. He could get under your skin, but he was very much in control of himself. If I remember, that night they had to grab the referee."[1]

Hunter said it was very much out of the ordinary for Egan to say anything. As Rochelle noted, Egan had other ways of expressing displeasure to a referee. "He wasn't a guy who argued with refs," Hunter said. "If he said something he probably had something on his mind because he didn't yell at refs, or even talk to them. He was real quiet on the court."[2]

Tweet! The official blew the whistle on Egan and said, "You're out of the game!" The ref tossed him for insubordination. No doubt the confrontation had the three thousand or so fans in the arena chirping and booing. So Egan went to the bench and Ireland had about a minute to dwell on who to use to replace him on the court. It made sense to replace a point guard with a point guard, and in came Robertson, the regular backup. Nothing was made of this development at the time, even in the minds of most of the Loyola players.

Not even all of the players seemed to recall the occasion once it passed. It seemed like a blip on the radar, the minutes where five black players competed together, passing swiftly. Miller, for one, did take note. He might have been expected to watch such things more closely since he had been kept out of the starting lineup for months the year before simply because of his skin color. "We knew everything that was going on," Miller said of the black players' reaction to the uniqueness of the situation. "We knew about it."[3]

On the contrary, as best as he can recall, Hunter said he did not hear anything about Loyola's slice of history until ten or so years ago. "I said, 'Wait a minute, I never heard that.'"[4]

One reason the Wyoming team was so hard to shake was that the Cowboys featured sharpshooting guard Flynn Robinson, who later had a lengthy NBA career. Harkness recalled Robinson, who was born in Elgin, Illinois, right outside of Chicago, almost choosing Loyola for his college before deciding on Wyoming. (Maybe he investigated the gym.) Miller said there was definitely more focus on shedding Wyoming and remaining unbeaten than there was on the fact that five black guys had taken the court together. For Loyola, it was not so unlike some practice days. "I don't remember that anyone made a big deal about it [at the time]," Miller said.[5]

Harkness agreed that the fact five African American players had competed for Loyola simultaneously was more or less lost in the pleasure of the victory, but when he realized it, he said, "That was beautiful. I'm sure Ireland realized, 'Oh, my.'"[6]

When Miller thinks back on the team's visit to Oklahoma City that holiday week between Christmas and New Year's another memory shoots to the forefront. After the game ended late, the players who had won the famous tournament were on the prowl for something to eat. Most of the restaurants were closed.

"The one or two restaurants that were still open wouldn't serve us," Miller said. "We ate at the Greyhound bus station." That night, Loyola wrote history but had to fight for the right to eat dessert, in both cases because many of the players had black skin.[7]

By the time Loyola disposed of Wyoming, the Ramblers were 9–0. Unlike the previous season, Loyola was not catching teams unaware. The squad's 23–4 record in 1961–62, the third-place finish in the NIT, and having all of the key contributors back meant that the Ramblers did actually have a national reputation in the preseason.

There are many more magazines, wire service polls, Internet sites, blogs, and the like now that deal with preseason college prognostication each October, but the landscape was not completely barren fifty years ago. Wire service polls existed and so did some magazines. The general feeling amongst those who studied college basketball was that Loyola was going to be about the fifth-best team in the nation.

This was a huge leap in public consciousness for Ireland and Loyola, even if it was the kind of paper attention that rewarded gut feeling more than specific accomplishment. The number one team in the country was the University of Cincinnati. The Bearcats were the two-time defending NCAA champs and were loaded with talent. No one saw any team lurking on the horizon that might be capable of knocking them off when it counted.

Ireland was a great believer in getting off to a fast start and he was a pick-and-choose scheduler. Although he wanted to show off this team and pit it against the best in the country, he also wanted to make sure the Ramblers put together a great record. As was his habit, Ireland scheduled a few cupcakes to start the season to make sure Loyola was running on all cylinders before taking on any big boys.

The high-speed offense and the clamp-down defense combined to produce points at supersonic speed. Run, run, run was the theme, and the Ramblers stole the ball often enough to score points in bunches, baskets coming just a few seconds apart.

"It looked like we were wild, but it was organized chaos," Harkness said. "But after playing together for a year we knew each other. We even started to think things like, 'If I go here, Rouse has my back. Maybe I can double-team. I can get back in time and pick up his man. We had so much confidence in each other's offense that when a guy put up a shot I'd just leave, start to go back on defense."[8]

Miller said the perfect team fast break was Hunter clearing the glass, making the pass to him near half-court, and then Miller finding Harkness for an open shot before the other team's defense was set. Sometimes, Harkness said, it paid to run the half-court game just to keep everyone involved in the play.

"I'd think, 'Man, we're fast-breaking this team to death,'" Harkness said. "But I could see Hunter felt a little bit out of it and I thought, 'I've got to get the ball to Hunter. We're not using the play inside.'"[9]

Loyola beat up those smaller basketball schools, scoring around 110 points a game, to begin the season. They intimidated teams like that, but the Ramblers also knew that the Marquettes, the Indianas, teams with more tradition, were not just going to faint in their tracks because Loyola was supposed to be so great.

Although he is not sure exactly what early-season game it was (perhaps the Western Michigan game), Miller recalls Ireland's pursuit of perfection extending to his critiques of half-time leads that may have been less than twenty points. While just about any coach in the universe would be satisfied with an eighteen-point intermission lead, Ireland once amazed the Ramblers by ripping them in the locker room in that circumstance.

"He was saying we had played bad," Miller said. "We had to play better in the second half. He wasn't mad. He wasn't angry at anyone in particular. He kind of just raged for the heck of it."[10]

Maybe Ireland was just looking for something to do at halftime. When a team is playing so well and there is nothing to correct, the fear is that the players will become complacent, stop going hard, and let the other team back in the contest. That may have been Ireland's motivation.

The Ramblers, almost the same Ramblers squad that had injected itself into the national picture a year earlier, was sending out very strong, 50,000-watt messages to the world during the first half of the 1962–63 season. This was a team that could do it all, that played hard, that had overwhelming speed, and that might be the best team in the country. Rankings at Christmastime put Loyola as high as number three.

Loyola was collecting victories in a dominating fashion, its explosive game making it the highest-scoring team in the land. Its blend of superb athletes, deep bench (when Ireland bothered to use it), and clicking-in-all-ways lineup was just pouring it on against helpless teams, even on the road.

"We knew we were good," Miller said. "We knew we were absolutely loaded. With Billy Smith and Pablo Robertson we were great off the bench. All seven of us could have started. There was no drop-off when they came in."[11]

Egan was the sparkplug. From the coach's standpoint he was the most trustworthy player on the floor just because he carried out the game plan. Although he was usually the only white player in the game, Egan earned the black players' appreciation through his play and his attitude. Being heaved from a game, as had happened versus Wyoming, was not a usual occurrence. Normally he kept score for revenge in his head. That's where he measured payback. He was often the smallest player on the court, so he wasn't going to be an intimidator, but Egan made sure neither he nor any of his teammates were taken advantage of physically or in any other way.

Billy Smith remembers a game in the first half of the 1962–63 season when a player on the opposing team submarined Les Hunter, knocking him to the floor. On one of the next possessions, Egan dribbled that player right into Vic Rouse, and somewhere in that little crowd of bodies an elbow was delivered to the miscreant's head.

"I respected him for what he did," Smith said of Egan. "He was sly. That's what I liked about him. You have to have that mental attitude when you're small that you're not going anywhere no matter what they do—mental toughness."[12]

On another occasion Smith remembers Egan buzzing around a seven-foot, 280-pound center like a mosquito, driving him nuts. Egan couldn't bang with the guy or block his shot, but he was quick enough to slap at the ball.

Smith did not have the same patience as Egan did to bide his time for payback. During a game at Kent State in Ohio the crowd was shouting insults at him (it might have been under the guise of missed free throws, not racial issues), and Smith wasn't of the mind-set to just ignore it. So he flashed the finger, the universal fuck-you symbol at the fans.

"You're young, you get angry," Smith said. "You've got to curtail it [your temper]. You don't think that you have to remember that all choices have consequences."[13]

Smith flipping the bird at fans would have been much more highly publicized in the 2000s. He would have been a video star on the Internet and late-evening Sports Center on ESPN. He did not get into nearly as much trouble for the action as he would have today. However, his comment about choices and consequences became a haunting one given what happened soon afterward to Smith and Robertson.

The two New Yorkers arrived at Loyola together, but in the middle of their sophomore year, they exited together, too. It was not planned that way, and their lives took very divergent paths after that, but players good enough to start on many, many college basketball teams, good enough to play key roles on a nationally ranked team, abruptly became players without a home.

Billy Smith was forced to leave school during the middle of the team's title run because of poor grades, but he later returned and became a top scorer for the Ramblers. Courtesy of the Loyola Sports Information Office.

Frank Perez (33) in action during a Loyola game. A freshman during the 1962–63 season, Perez could not participate in varsity games but was a keen observer of the championship team. Courtesy of the Loyola Sports Information Office.

CHAPTER 11

BILLY AND PABLO

George Ireland's starting lineup was locked in for the 1962–63 season. The group that came together at the end of the 1961–62 season had grown together, learned together, and become a cohesive, overpowering unit.

Four African Americans were in the starting lineup now, and that wasn't going to change. As Ireland showed with his limited substitution plan, he had found his guys and he was going to ride them as long as he could with only periodic rests.

Also, as the season unfolded, it was obvious that the first subs, the sixth and seventh men in the rotation, were also black. Ireland felt there was a clear line between their talents and the others on the bench. Forward Billy Smith and guard Pablo Robertson were the guys Ireland was most likely to call upon when those running up and down the court at the frenetic pace Loyola set needed a blow.

There was one exception. Chuck Wood, one of the white players, who came from Racine, Wisconsin, was a six-foot-three swing man. Sometimes he came in for Vic Rouse or Ron Miller if either needed a brief rest or got into foul trouble, or once in a while for Jerry Harkness. However, Wood contracted mononucleosis and missed eleven games while recovering. The debilitating illness is very difficult for an athlete to overcome and regain full stamina.

Rich Rochelle, the six-ten backup center from Evanston, seemed to be in Ireland's doghouse. He said he concluded partway through the season that he and a few other Ramblers weren't going to see much action short of some kind of catastrophe where most of the starters fouled out or were leveled by a chickenpox epidemic. "We would only be on the floor if one of the first five died," Rochelle said years later.[1]

To a man, the starters and the backups felt that Ireland could have and should have given the bench players more PT, especially on occasions where the final score wasn't in doubt. But he was very stingy with minutes and most of the backups sat and sat. They had very nice views of the action as Loyola ran up victory after victory, but most of their contributions were in practice.

"He [Ireland] called it his Iron Man Team," Rochelle said. "It was a panic thing. He was afraid to play the bench."[2]

Afraid to lose big leads, in Rochelle's mind, even when it seemed virtually impossible. The margins were too large and the clock was ticking down too swiftly to allow for a comeback.

There was no doubt that Smith and Robertson, both from New York, both sent west by Walter November, were very skilled, athletic players. They did not have the seasoning of the starters, but their raw ability was impressive, and they did damage when they came into the game.

Robertson was a point guard who could spell Egan. The 1960s style of basketball was really just beginning to be played at higher speed and above the rim. Ball handlers, for the most part, were expected to be fundamentally sound, and fancy dribbling was supposed to be for members of the Harlem Globetrotters or guys like Marquis Haynes on the spinoff Harlem Magicians. The Boston Celtics' Bob Cousy, who essentially invented the modern point guard role, delivered behind-the-back passes and each one elicited an ooh or an ahh from the crowd. There was always meaning behind a fancy Cousy play, though.

Robertson was from a different mold. He could pass behind his back and, before such maneuvers became commonplace, could dribble between his legs. This was borderline heresy, but opposing teams had no defense for such a slick ball handler. Robertson pretty much had to play with such verve because he stood just five foot eight. But he liked to make his trick plays with no clear-cut plan, and his shooting was not as solid as Egan's was from outside.

It was not as if Robertson was impressive only because he was playing against slower college players, either. Later, he became a regular with the Harlem Globetrotters, the one team in the world that unequivocally and enthusiastically embraced trick passing and dribbling.

"Oh man, Pablo was a natural," said Frank Perez, another Loyola player who was aimed at Chicago from New York and roomed with Robertson as a freshman. "He was an excellent ball handler. That was his game. He tried to make passes no one else would. He had that Globetrotter game."³

As befitting someone who would become a Harlem Globetrotter, Robertson was the jokester on the team, too. If someone was going to crack a joke and keep the group laughing, there was a good chance it was Robertson. He was lighthearted, had a winning personality, and had always been that way, as far as Perez could determine.

"We played against each other in high school," Perez said. "He definitely had personality. He was an interesting guy. He was funny, oh man, yes."⁴

Smith and Robertson represented a tandem in that they joined Loyola at the same time as freshmen during the 1961–62 campaign. Robertson, said Smith, was born to run the fast-break game that Ireland loved and was sure to gain more playing time as his career went on, though he was not going to displace Egan as a starter any time soon.

"I think Pablo was shifty," Smith said. "When you were playing with Pablo, you were running. You kept moving. I could run and Pablo made sure I got the ball. I loved him. He was a monster on the fast break because he was so quick."⁵

Smith says he likes to think of Robertson as a minipackage of dynamite akin to the Hall of Famer Earl "the Pearl" Monroe. But Robertson never achieved anything like the fame of the big scorer Smith compared him to, nor success as a pro in the NBA. Smith says it was the way Robertson handled the basketball, the way he moved when he dribbled, that made him think of Robertson as a Monroe type.

"Shifty," Smith said again. He kept coming back to that word as he pictured Robertson in his mind's eye, a quicksilver player who could dart through little holes and fool defenders the way he leaned with his body at the same time he was bouncing the ball. "He was always rocking back and forth," Smith said.

Robertson was one of those guys who made friends wherever he went. He was so outgoing he seemed to think everyone would like him as long as they got a chance to know him. He would chat up anybody, seemed to be color blind after a lifetime in New York, and didn't seem to get the message that not everyone was.

Both Smith and Perez say that Robertson did not seem to acknowledge any roadblocks between making friends with white girls on the new campus. It was Robertson who, during freshman orientation, was singled out by a priest for dancing with a female white student.

Smith was of the mind of, what did you expect?

"You've got to remember the times," Smith said, making the frequently blunt statement that so many Loyola players uttered when harkening back to the racism rampant in the United States in the early 1960s. "I didn't have those expectations," Smith added. "There were no black women around. To put it mildly, to put it into perspective, I didn't speak to white girls. For a young black man on campus, there were no social attractions. There was something wrong with the way things were done, but I understood the times."[6]

Robertson and Smith climbed on a Pennsylvania Railroad car in Manhattan and rode the train to Chicago to enroll at Loyola. They traveled together and they came for a college education and the chance to play college basketball at a place where both Walter November and George Ireland told them a program was being built that would make them proud and that they could help lift to new heights.

They both excelled as freshmen during the 1961–62 season as they witnessed the varsity going 23–4 and making its first inroads into the national scene. They hoped to start the next year, but that was not in the cards. The Loyola starters were as set in concrete as the mid-highway barriers on the new Dan Ryan Expressway on the South Side.

Robertson had his admirers among his teammates, though, both for the way he made them chuckle and the way he passed the ball. Dan Connaughton still remembers how Robertson was like a stand-up comedian. "Oh, my God, he was funny," Connaughton said. And Connaughton took the risk of noting that this Robertson reminded him of another player with the same last name who is on the short list of the greatest players to ever take up the sport, Oscar Robertson. "Pablo was a magician," Connaughton said. "He was just a fabulous ball handler, just going behind his back and through his legs."[7]

At times, the way Connaughton recalled it, the ever-nervous Ireland was not completely tolerant of Robertson's gifts. "He got irritated sometimes," Connaughton said. "He would say, 'Cut out that fancy crap, that monkey business.'"[8]

Connaughton enjoyed Robertson's company more than Ireland did, he thinks, but at times even he was amazed by the occasional Robertson stunt. As freshmen, when the newcomer squad played teams all within driving distance, Connaughton said the transportation "was so high-tech back then. Students drove us."[9]

On one of those short trips, he believes to a game at Valparaiso in northern Indiana, Robertson pulled out a thermos or some kind of container that held liquid refreshment and made an announcement to his fellow passengers. This was not ice water or something akin to Gatorade, which hadn't yet been invented (that was two years away).

"He said, 'I've got a little special something,'" Connaughton said. "'This will get me right before the game.' He made himself some screwdrivers. Then, in the game, he put on a show, passing behind his back, dribbling. He was a character. He had unbelievable natural instincts."[10]

The feeling seemed to be unanimous among the other players that Robertson was the type of guy who could have excelled in appearances with David Letterman, even if pregame drinking was behavior that tilted to the outrageous side. "Pablo was a laugh a minute," forward John Crnokrak said.

Starting point guard John Egan was not going to relinquish his job to Robertson or anyone else, but he does believe that Ireland should have used Robertson, Smith, and all of the other bench players more.

"I don't remember ever saying, 'I'm tired,'" Egan said. "I don't ever remember saying that. I don't think anyone else ever said that or anyone else felt it, either. But once we were pressing full-court the whole time and we were up by twenty-five points and I said to Ireland, 'Why don't you put somebody else in for me?' He said, 'What? What are you talking about? Get in there and continue to press.' I went in there and fouled the next two guys that came across the half-court line and I fouled out. Somebody else had to come in."[11]

Egan never expressed any outward insecurity about Robertson encroaching on his territory. Egan was a better scorer, a player more in tune with Ireland's thinking of what a point guard should do, so in truth he was never going to be replaced by Robertson on a regular basis. Much later Jerry Harkness said he believed Egan felt a pang or two wondering about that, wondering if Robertson's brilliance at hitting the open man on the court might cause his displacement.

"I think Egan felt a little sensitive to the fact that Robertson was that good," Harkness said, "that so many people thought Robertson was tricky. He was flashy and good and Egan might have almost felt like, 'Am I being given this because I'm white?' That's the way life is. That's the way blacks have felt a lot of times during the civil rights era. 'Am I getting this because I'm black?' But the answer is no. Egan fit that group picture, the overall group. He was a piece in the overall picture. Now this guy might have been flashy, but I don't know if Pablo had the drive that Egan had. He was a good playmaker, probably better than Egan in getting it to the big guys on the break and all of that. But he didn't have the drive, the outside shooting, the leadership of Egan."[12]

Egan did think Robertson was an exceptional player, aided in his passing skills by having large hands. But they had one offbeat, off-court incident that could have driven a large wedge in their relationship.

Of all things, Egan said a stewardess had given him a phone card that was for calling long distance free and told him to vary a letter in the code periodically to keep it going. Egan was from Chicago and all of his relatives were from Chicago, so he didn't really have a need for the benefit. Instead, he gave the card to Robertson. Sure enough Robertson used the card often, but he didn't alter the code frequently enough and he got nailed.

"Pablo is using it all the time," Egan said. "Pablo gets collared and the police come to the university and Pablo says I gave him the card. That was nice of him, since I had no benefit from using it. He tells them I gave it to him, so I get called in. Ireland's there for this meeting. The police are there. Everyone indicates Pablo says I gave him the number. I said, 'He'll do anything to start.'"[13]

Egan shot them the snappy, clever comeback instead of a denial. Then he said, "Are you kidding?" Somehow serious punishment was evaded.[14]

Robertson's specialty was ballhandling, but Smith had the capacity to score big. Smith was a terrific scorer in high school, and he had the makings of a major-league scorer in college. He was born in Harlem in 1943 and was often in trouble as a youth, sometimes for black pride reasons. He said when he was twelve, starting junior high school, an assistant principal called him "nigger" and his response was to heave him to the ground, a distance of about four feet. Next thing he knew a police officer was pointing a gun at him and he thought he was going to be shot on the spot.

"He cursed at me," Smith said, referring to the police officer. His basketball coach appeared on the scene seeking to defuse the situation. Smith was asked to apologize, but he refused, saying, "He'll have to shoot me first."[15]

Smith attended Commerce High School in New York, near the Lincoln Center for the Performing Arts, and by age fifteen he was sneaking off to the Catskills to play in summer games for pay of a hundred dollars a game at resorts like Grossinger's in Liberty. If discovered, his eligibility would have been ruined. "I was playing in places I shouldn't have been playing," Smith said. "I went to play against the house team. We weren't supposed to accept money. I was under radar."[16]

One high school game put him on the radar for college recruiters. Smith had an eighty-eight-point game before graduating in 1961. "It got me a scholarship," he said.[17]

Besides Loyola, Vanderbilt, Western Michigan, Wichita State, and a few other schools came after him. They believed he was a six-foot-eight player for a 28–3 New York City team, but he was only six five.

Influenced by Walter November and the fact that Ron Miller, whom he knew, was already in Chicago, Smith chose Loyola. He wasn't quite sure what to make of Ireland when he became very demonstrative in practice. "He was excitable," Smith said. "He was very feisty. He knew what he wanted to do. He had a lot of moxie. I kind of remember him sort of hitting a guy in practice and the player shrugging it off with a what-are-you-going-to-do reaction. I'd probably be busy trying to kill him."[18]

Smith scored more than twenty points per game for the freshman team, and since he had always been a big gun, a go-to scorer, he believed he could step right in and do the same thing for the varsity. But that wasn't going to happen, not with the Loyola lineup clicking on all cylinders. Becoming a guy off the bench was a difficult adjustment for Smith. He subbed for Vic Rouse or Les Hunter most of the time.

"When you have started all of your life and you are told you are coming off the bench it plays with your head," Smith said. "If you score only seven points in a game it can be deflating to your ego. We had a hell of a team so I couldn't squabble with the way they were playing. It wasn't that I wasn't playing at all."[19]

Still, Smith could do things no one else on the team seemed capable of with his smooth athleticism and, once, Ireland was tempted to juggle the lineup. He experimented briefly with moving Harkness to guard alongside Egan, inserting Smith in the frontcourt, and again resorting to cutting Miller's minutes. It didn't last, though.

"He was so good that they moved me to guard some plays," Harkness recalled. "But he shot too much. He was real good, but he shot so much that it seemed as if he didn't know how the team worked. He got everything out of whack taking so many shots. I was hardly getting any. The other guys weren't, either. Smith was not a great passer. We were playing fast, but something was missing. We blended much better the other way even though Bill had more talent than I've got. He could jump better than me for sure. But we didn't need that because Rouse and Hunter were so good. He [Smith] didn't have the endurance that I had, that I gave them. Little things like that fit that team and were key. We just blended like you wouldn't believe, and Ireland recognized that."[20]

Frank Perez said Smith was a "tough player underneath." Unlike Robertson he wasn't outgoing. "He was one of those guys who kept to himself most of the time. We were friendly. I would go by his room, but I was friendlier with Les and Vic. On the court Billy was all business. Most of his baskets were in the paint. He had to be tough because in practice he guarded Les. He and Les used to go at it every day in practice."[21]

Rich Rochelle also said Smith kept to himself a lot, even calling him introverted. "He was a very strong individual," Rochelle said. "A very intelligent young man." Rochelle also remembered Smith as an outstanding chess player, though it would be proven that he did not make all the right moves when he was attending Loyola.[22]

Although no one ever suggested there was any racial conflict on the team, John Egan and Billy Smith were definitely not buds. They just didn't get along. Egan said that on one overnight trip to Milwaukee to play Marquette Ireland made room assignments that put a black player and a white player together and of all people Egan drew Smith as his roommate for the one night.

"It was not good," Egan said. "We didn't get along. There was no specific incident. Billy Smith was the center on the freshman team and we would scrimmage against them all of the time. He was a very aggressive player and a real strong rebounder. But he would just follow me around the court and hit me hard. I would tend to hit him hard when I drove to the basket. Nobody ever said anything about it, you just did it. I thought he was a racist."[23]

That night in their shared room Egan and Smith had a frank conversation before they went to sleep. It was not a good airing out of the issues, either. Smith told Egan he was just using the white university to get whatever he could out of it and had no special feeling for Loyola. Egan told Smith that the only reason white students hung around him was because he was a basketball player.

"It was not a nice conversation," Egan said. Then, and Egan couldn't remember which one of them uttered the harsh sentence, it was said in the late-night darkness that "if I ever saw you on the street after all of this is over, I would never acknowledge your existence."[24]

For the time being that's where things lay between them, an agreed-upon dislike, but with a mature unwillingness to disrupt the team's overall chemistry. They played together and when they shared the court during the 1962–63 season, they were on the same side.

Indeed, Smith characterized the team's overall relations as "fantastic." He said of Egan, "I would fight to the death for him and I didn't particularly like the guy."[25]

There was not a shred of doubt that having Smith and Robertson as the sixth and seventh men in addition to the other bench players made Loyola a better team than the 23–4 squad of the year before. The duo's addition meant the club had great depth and that the Ramblers had no weakness.

And then, not long after the historic game against the University of Wyoming in Oklahoma City, things nearly came unraveled. Loyola—and Ireland—demanded that the basketball players, especially ones the coach had to argue for with the dean of students, go to class and make good grades. There was very little give in the rules. Much was expected and players had to deliver to stay eligible.

Unlike today, in 1963 there was very little organized support for students on athletic teams who were lagging behind. In an era when coaches barely had room in their budgets for an assistant coach, there were no full-time academic advisors. The responsibility to keep up was placed almost completely on the shoulders of the student. And basketball players at Loyola were not going to be taking any Basket Weaving 101 courses.

As the first semester ended along with the first half of the season, Loyola decreed that Pablo Robertson and Billy Smith were ineligible and had to leave school. No probation, exile. It was a stunning ruling that surprised everyone connected with the team. Les Hunter, for one, from the vantage point of years in the future when teams go to great lengths to keep their players in school and playing, believes that Loyola could have done more to help Robertson and Smith.

"You know, I think their grade point average was only off by about one-tenth of a point," Hunter said. "This was a team that was undefeated, on the verge of doing something great for the first time in school history, there was money pouring in at the gym and we were packing them in, and they would kick two guys out. Instead of putting them on the sideline, or sending them to extra classes, or to a school nearby to make up the credits to take a course or something, they were just told good-bye."[26]

Not every team could have withstood a double blow like that. Smith and Robertson were important players—not starters, but regulars in the rotation. They helped make the Ramblers go. The loss of two players for the season in the middle of a run like that, whether to injury or for any other cause, can be extremely disruptive. Sometimes even if a team rights itself it takes time and it takes a few humbling defeats to get past the upheaval.

"I was concerned," Hunter said. "I was really concerned about that. We only had nine players, not even two fives to practice with."[27]

The practice thing may sound like a minimal disruption, but it was an issue. Bill Jauss, a longtime Chicago sportswriter who covered that Loyola team during the 1962–63 season, said having only nine players on the roster made for some joking. "I tell the story, only half-kiddingly," Jauss said, "that if you were walking down Sheridan Road and you were under the age of thirty, there was a chance you might be dragged in to scrimmage."[28]

Nobody was looking for a shakeup and this one was not welcome. The core of the team was intact, but it was as if someone had cut off a couple of fingers. Something irretrievable was lost and it was unclear how the Ramblers would make up for those missing pieces. "They were absolutely good players," Egan said. "I don't remember a feeling of devastation, but I knew it was a loss."[29]

Wood said everyone knew that they had to go to class and that if they messed up, "you were just gone."

That was the situation for Robertson and Smith. One minute they were teammates, important teammates, and the next minute they were on the outside looking in, the same as other students who had never set foot in Alumni Gym as a member of the Ramblers. It seemed like harsh justice because everything occurred so abruptly.

Frank Perez said that by his junior year, which would have been after Smith's and Robertson's departures, the team had a tutorial program to help players with their study habits and he took advantage of it. That opportunity might have been created as a result of Smith's and Robertson's jettisoning and Ireland seeking to be careful never to have a repeat. "I don't know what their grades were," Perez said. "Maybe four Ds? They're not going to do that at Loyola and be kept."[30]

Perez said he sometimes felt some members of the team had a kind of resentment toward Smith, not a strong one, but a feeling that by flunking out he could have cost them all something very special.

John Crnokrak, who had already graduated but had developed friendships with the starters the year before during the 23–4 season, did not sugarcoat his analysis of what transpired. "They didn't go to school and the college sent them packing," Crnokrak said. "Ireland made sure we went to class."[31]

If there is simmering resentment about being let down, it seems pretty mild. Ron Miller said he doesn't recall the players ever having a major discussion about how the departure of Robertson and Smith would affect them, and he never thought about it. By then the Ramblers had such a strong belief in their talents they figured they could beat anyone and it didn't seem to Miller that not suiting up Robertson and Smith was going to be a fatal blow.

Given how Ireland operated, he figured, the coach would just squeeze more minutes out of the starters instead of going to the bench. And Miller was right about that. Ireland just relied more and more on his starting five, and gradually they did turn into an iron man quintet. Certainly that was a risky strategy, but Loyola kept rolling.

One thing changed, for sure, though. When an opposing team scouted the Ramblers, invariably a comment would be made suggesting they had a terrific starting five, but no depth. It was the only conclusion to draw since Ireland hardly gave any of those guys on the bench much chance to prove themselves.

Smith was not easy on himself when he looked back at the young man he was at the time. When he was kicked out of school, Smith said, "The grades were horrible, Cs and Ds. There was a standard you had to meet. It's damaging to your psyche when you think you're pretty smart."[32]

High school work didn't adequately prepare him for the rigors of a Loyola education, Smith said, and he was also guilty of staying out late and partying a lot. "Your inner-city education did not come anywhere close to what it should have been," he said. Smith said he knew he was in trouble when he was summoned into a meeting with assistant coach Jerry Lyne. "I was the fourth child out of ten and the first of my generation to go to college. It was very sad for me to leave. I had to go back home."[33]

Loyola told him that if he got his grades back up he could re-enroll, but there was no way to make up for his mistakes quickly enough to rejoin the 1962–63 season. That was a lost opportunity.

"I dismissed myself," Smith said. "It was a disappointment. No doubt about it. I let my teammates down. I let myself down. Sometimes you must accept the consequences for what you did."[34]

Smith had traveled from New York to Chicago with high hopes and big dreams, accompanied by Pablo Robertson. Instead of living up to what they imagined they could have done, they left Loyola after a year and a half, at the worst possible time, missing out on being part of a very special team.

"We came together," Smith said of him and Robertson a half century later, "and we left together."[35]

CHAPTER 12

HOUSTON NIGHTMARE

The Loyola of New Orleans game was a year old when Loyola of Chicago embarked for a road game at the University of Houston during the 1962–63 season, and there is little doubt the Ramblers were blindsided by the intensity of hatred they felt from fans in the stands during that game in February of 1963. The vitriol Loyola faced was worse in Texas than it was in Louisiana and maybe it rattled the Ramblers a little bit more because it was unexpected.

Coach George Ireland had been careful about warning the Loyola players that the reception for them in New Orleans might be harsh. Although the team was splintered and players assigned segregated quarters, everyone got through the trip, through the experience, and thought, "Well, that wasn't so bad."

Not so the trip to Houston.

Maybe because Texas was in the Southwest, not the Deep South, maybe because Houston was part of a state that was more identified with ranching and cowboys than lynching and racism, maybe because Houston was a big city, but Loyola players did not expect the road trip to Houston to be fraught with as much tension as it produced.

The Ramblers were 22–1 by the time they journeyed to the Lone Star State. They had lost Billy Smith and Pablo Robertson, a development that could have been traumatic, but that challenge had been eased through with little impact on the win-loss record. The Cougars, for their part, were not a significant power at the time, although some of their greatest college basketball success loomed just a few years ahead.

Season records aside, for all of the advance notice they received about New Orleans, Loyola's players remember Houston as a nasty, racist visit that took the prize for the worst place they traveled to during their college basketball careers. "The Houston trip, that was brutal," said guard Ron Miller.[1]

Ron Miller was one of several
Ramblers who came to Chicago
to play for Loyola out of New
York City. He became one of
the title team's starting guards.
Courtesy of the Loyola Sports
Information Office.

Name-calling was louder and more vigorous in Houston than it had been anywhere else they played. Fans in the stands threw small objects at the players. Chuck Wood was sitting on the bench and was hit hard by a small pellet. "He thought he'd been shot," Miller said.[2] The situation did not get that far out of control. It was a piece of ice that hit Wood.

Being a team that started four African American players in 1963 was essentially a beacon inviting harassment from juiced-up racist fans wherever Loyola traveled. Most of the schedule played out in the Midwest, and there were not notable racist receptions, but during the periodic trips to Southern communities the host school's fans could not believe their eyes. Even if they did not know about Loyola's composition, they reacted strongly when they saw that the team's contributors were mostly black and that others on the bench were also black.

Any team Loyola faced in the South was all white. The idea of integration at any level, in any way, was touchy at best and despised at worst. The extremes taken to prevent racial mingling, from insane laws up to the threat of physical violence, meant that Loyola had to be on guard. By the season's midpoint the Ramblers were used to hearing a certain amount of heckling and harassment from the stands. But the contest against Houston raised the verbal lashing to an unprecedented height. Once, Miller was lunging for a ball near the sidelines and a woman seated in the front row simply snarled "You nigger" at him.

"We always heard some stuff," Miller said. "This was so different. It was so obscene and so ridiculous." Fifty years later Miller remembers the intensity and absurdity of the scene, the verbal abuse, but it is not as if he has been haunted by it. Whether Loyola's strong unity or the resilience of youth played a role, he said they actually got over it somewhat quickly. "Maybe we were so young and we just wanted to play basketball," Miller said.[3]

Yes, they did, but playing basketball and putting up with harassment were two different things. Forward Dan Connaughton, who is white, called the journey to Houston "an intense trip. The racism was palpable and it was real."[4]

As one of the bench guys he never got to unzip his warm-up jacket in that contest, but that just meant he had nothing to preoccupy him like dribbling, shooting, and playing defense for most of the night. It meant he could hear the flung insults more clearly.

"The guys sitting behind me were wearing ten-gallon hats and these shit-kicking boots," Connaughton said. "They were yelling all the time, things like, 'Why don't they take these guys back to Chicago?' It was very ugly."[5]

Houston would later field some of the finest teams—integrated teams, too—in college basketball, but in 1963 the Cougars were really just getting going under Coach Guy Lewis, who had yet to construct his legend at the school. Lewis took the reins of the program in 1956 and it took until his sixth season to produce a winning record, and that was only 13–12. Lewis's first top-notch team was the 1960–61 club that finished 17–11 and made the NCAA round of sixteen. The next year the Cougars finished 21–6.

Under Lewis, Houston bounced between leagues a couple of times during his first half-dozen years, but by the early 1960s the Cougars were an independent. That is what made them ripe for Ireland to schedule. Neither Loyola nor Houston was a member of a conference, something that presented a challenge to scheduling, so it made sense to face other independents that had the same dilemma.

Of course one easy team for Loyola to schedule, even for a home-and-home series, would have been nearby DePaul, situated just a few miles away. But although they were neighbors, Loyola and DePaul were not neighborly. There was a longstanding feud between Ireland and Blue Demons coach Ray Meyer. During his three-year varsity career at DePaul, guard Emmette Bryant said he made friends with some Loyola players, but he never faced them on the court.

"We were never allowed to play each other," Bryant said recently. "They [Ireland and Meyer] wouldn't play each other. It didn't stop us from going to each other's games. I didn't have any misgivings. We managed to go to tournaments. I never envied those guys [Loyola players]."[6]

So instead of the easy road trip to DePaul, one could say the horrible trip to Houston served as a substitute.

Lewis, who coached Houston for thirty years and recorded twenty-seven straight winning seasons, had lost numerous key players from the 21–6 team, and the bunch that met Loyola finished 15–11. But Lewis was building something in Houston. He eventually led the Cougars to the Final Four five times and to the NCAA title game twice. Among his greatest players were Elvin Hayes, Don Chaney, Hakeem Olajuwon, Clyde Drexler, and Otis Birdsong. During one stretch in the early 1980s Lewis's team consisted of so many spectacular athletes who could dunk that it acquired the nickname Phi Slama Jama.

Lewis also held dear to one of the quirkier idiosyncrasies of any big-time college coach. While Jerry Tarkanian was known for chewing on a towel during his days leading the UNLV program, Lewis acted more like the Linus character in the comic strip *Peanuts* who always dragged around a blanket as a security prop. Lewis was famed for holding tight to a bright red-and-white polka dot towel on the bench during games.

There was never any suggestion that Lewis was a prejudiced man, but it was obvious in his first years of coaching that his all-white teams appealed to the school's audience. The hostility was so aggravated toward the Loyola visitors it is likely Lewis would have also been hung in effigy if he attempted to recruit and play a number of African Americans during his first seasons with the Cougars.

Eventually, the hunger for victory trumped the desire for the separation of the races in Houston. The best way to ensure championship-caliber teams was to sign up superior talent. Each one of Lewis's biggest stars, Hayes, Chaney, Olajuwon, Drexler, et al., was a black man. Lewis's first African American recruit was Chaney, a six-foot-five guard who later played on Boston Celtics championship teams in the NBA. Chaney came to Houston in 1964, a year after Lewis's Cougars were bested by Loyola, 62–58, in one of the fiercest games the Ramblers played that season.

More significant was Lewis's pursuit and signing of the six-foot-nine Hayes in 1965. Hayes turned into one of the greatest college players of all time. He was from Louisiana and grew up with segregation, but with an excellent supporting cast at Houston he put the Cougars on the college basketball map in the late 1960s. Houston, with Hayes, became the most dangerous rival to UCLA and Coach John Wooden's title teams featuring Lew Alcinder, the player who later changed his name to Kareem Abdul-Jabbar.

In January of 1968, Hayes and Houston faced UCLA in a regular-season game that attracted more than fifty-two thousand fans to the Astrodome and was the first nationally televised nonchampionship game. Hayes and his cohorts under Lewis upset UCLA in the contest that earned the appellation "the Game of the Century." Houston entered the game 14–0 and UCLA came in 13–0, but also riding an overall forty-seven-game winning streak. UCLA was ranked number one in the polls and Houston was ranked number two. Houston pulled off the upset, 71–69.

Lewis pretty much followed George Ireland's pattern, though in a more volatile climate. UCLA was the best team in the country, overwhelming opposition with racially mixed teams and a regular stream of African American All-Americans. Lewis was not content with his Houston teams as semi-powers in their region. He wanted more. For Houston, Hayes was the most important recruit of all time, a game changer, a perception changer, a social history changer.

"I liked the idea of going to Houston, of helping desegregate athletics here," said Hayes, who also had an outstanding professional career and became a member of the Naismith Basketball Hall of Fame. "I knew Coach Lewis wanted to do just that, so I went." When Hayes was on the court at home in Houston his fans screamed support, yelling, "EEEE!"[7]

Houston became the first school in its region to rely so heavily on black players. Chaney arrived two years before Texas-Western bested Kentucky in a game that included five black starters for the Miners and five white players for the Wildcats. Integration did not come to the Southeastern Conference in basketball until 1967, two years after Hayes enrolled at Houston.

Hayes campaigned for Lewis to be enshrined in the Naismith Basketball Hall of Fame. Lewis won 592 games in his career and was already a member of the College Basketball Hall of Fame. His coaching win total, plus being on the right side in pioneering integration in the Southwest, were arguments in favor of Lewis, Hayes believed. In September of 2013 Lewis was inducted into the Naismith Hall.

"There were no schools in the South, basically, recruiting black athletes," Hayes said. "He paved the way in basketball. You watch LSU, Kentucky, Alabama now, they have all these great black athletes. These schools weren't even looking at them back then."[8]

Lewis's imagination might have been powerful enough to picture such a scene for his team only a few short years in the future, but that was not something easy for Loyola players to envision given the level of harassment they faced during their close-game victory in Houston.

The treatment was so sour Miller said that after the game an old friend of his from high school who was living in Houston came out of the stands to talk to him. "He was in tears," Miller said. "He was so upset about how they had treated us."[9]

It was hard to ignore.

"I wasn't expecting that in Houston," said John Egan. "There was a lot of screaming at us. I thought it was directed at all of us, not just racial. It could have been because Houston was an all-white team at that time."[10]

Egan said he had actually been recruited out of high school by Guy Lewis to come to Houston, so it was interesting for him to see Lewis on the opposing bench, but as he typically did, Egan tried to block out anything in the environment that wasn't happening on the court.

"I assumed the screaming was primarily racial, but I didn't really hear it," he said. "They threw coins at us. We were in a huddle talking and there came the coins. I don't know that anyone got hit or hurt. Maybe I was just surprised it was that bad."[11]

By "that bad" Egan meant the crowd as a whole. It was a surly, seemingly potentially violent gathering and that was unsettling. The noise level was decibel-high enough to shake the players out of their Chuck Taylor rubber-soled shoes. Egan was so successful in focusing on playing basketball—every bit of concentration was needed in the close game, anyway—that he did not hear about many of the offensive comments hurled at Loyola players until later when his teammates were talking about the night.

Having coins thrown at the players stuck with Egan as much as anything because they could hurt. The scene rankled him even more than some of the black players because he had given serious consideration to attending Houston. What would that have been like?

"It was a shock," Egan said of the game-day behavior. "I wasn't thinking about race when I considered going to Houston. They played in the Missouri Valley Conference and that was an integrated conference with Cincinnati." Houston had left the Missouri Valley after it recruited Egan.[12]

Perhaps it was being naïve, but the Loyola players just didn't think of Houston, which was a big city, as a place that might be as mean as the Deep South. Usually, they were unflappable, and they had been through all types of experiences together. But this time Jerry Harkness said he almost lost his poise. He was fearful he was going to cost Loyola the game.

Winning was always a pretty solid antidote to heckling. Walking off the court with a victory was very satisfying after the fans harangued you. The reality was you had the *W* in your pocket and there was nothing else they could say. You proved you were the best and all of the rest was just talk that washed away. It was like writing in chalk on a sidewalk before the rains came. It would have hurt much more to lose to a team while being viciously jeered.

From the start of the game the Houston experience bothered Harkness. Loyola players came through the tunnel into the arena and before they even reached the court fans were throwing things at the players and screaming racial comments. "They were hissing and calling us names," he said.[13]

This was before the opening tip. It was as if the fans had their minds made up to hate this group of strangers on sight, and it was all about skin color, not basketball.

"I was jittery," Harkness said. "They scared me. I had a pretty good first half, and we were up big, about fourteen or sixteen points. I don't know what it was, but I began to hurt the team. I missed shots. I was nervous. They were screaming. They were yelling. A priest had come with us on the trip and they had been on him."[14]

Harkness was Loyola's team leader. He never lost his cool. He tended to rise above the pressure and played his best when the Ramblers needed him the most. This time his teammates, the other main men like Les Hunter and Vic Rouse, were impervious to the heat, but not Harkness. "I was the only one," he said. "I was taken aback. My shots were in and out. They were rallying on us. They were coming back. Because of our talent we should have blitzed them. They were making a comeback, but I knew we were better. I hurt the team. It was awful."[15]

Still, Loyola prevailed by four points. Harkness said that Guy Lewis came up to some Loyola players after the game and said, "I'm sorry for this."[16]

It struck him as an act of decency standing out in an animal house. Worse for the Ramblers, the city's disgraceful treatment continued after the game, outside of the arena. Players were hungry and they headed to a restaurant for a postgame meal, but the restaurants in Houston were either closed or wouldn't serve them.

The Ramblers found an open eatery, went in, and sat down, but no waiter came. Finally, someone from the establishment approached them and informed the players, several African Americans among them, that they could place an order and take it out, but they couldn't eat their meal there.

The already frazzled Harkness couldn't believe what he was hearing. "What?" he demanded. "I was so mad." Miller said, "You heard the guy. Let's get out of here."[17]

That night Harkness was not in an accommodating mood. He was on the verge of starting trouble, something he would ordinarily never do. "I took offense," Harkness said.[18]

They all did, but the circumstances reminded them they were involved in what seemed to be a never-ending war against discrimination and injustice and that it was not going to be won in that restaurant that night. Harkness was furious at the restaurant, furious at the waiter, ticked off at Miller for his low-key response, and was just teetering on the ragged edge. "I was messed up," Harkness said. "I was just all messed up."[19]

The day had been too long and too much, but the salve was the victory. The Ramblers had won and they could lord it over the Cougars for that reason.

Compared to Houston, Harkness remembers the New Orleans trip as a walk in the park. There things were segregated, but the players were sheltered, housed, and fed by other black people who admired them. In Houston, there was no buffer, only the consolation of winning the game.

"We played well," Harkness said. "We weren't physical or bullies. We never played that way, anyway. But I'll never forget Houston."[20]

The next year Loyola played Houston again, in Chicago, and trounced the Cougars, 98–68. Miller said the day after the game he bumped into Guy Lewis and Lewis said, "I've got to buy you breakfast. You beat our brains out two years in a row."[21]

A certain slyness (and maybe a tiny bit of satisfaction) slipped into Miller's voice as he described that moment. "The next year," Miller said, pausing a beat, "he recruited Elvin Hayes. He saw the light."[22]

Loyola head coach George Ireland (left) and his assistant coach Jerry Lyne, study the game action during the Ramblers' 1962–63 championship season. Courtesy of the Loyola Sports Information Office.

CHAPTER 13

THE BENCH

The bout with mononucleosis ruined Chuck Wood's chances of playing more. He missed eleven games because of the illness, and by the time he recuperated enough to put on the uniform again, with five regular-season games left, coach George Ireland was too set in his ways and too locked in his successful formula to mess around with his lineup.

That was one reason the Ramblers became the iron man five down the stretch. Overshadowed by the quick exile of sixth and seventh men Pablo Robertson and Billy Smith was the departure of Earl Johnson, as well.

Johnson, who came from Cleveland, appeared to be a budding star. He averaged twenty-five points a game for the 1961–62 freshman team, and although his playing time was limited because of the sheer amount of talent on the roster and Ireland's hesitation to rely much on backups, Johnson averaged 3.1 points and 3.5 rebounds a game for the 1962–63 squad.

More than anyone else at the time when Robertson and Smith were cut loose, Johnson seemed poised to benefit with extra playing time. Only within days of their exile for failing to maintain an acceptable grade point average, Johnson withdrew from school and was never part of Loyola basketball again.

Poof! He vanished, gone like the others. The serial departures reduced the roster from twelve to nine able-bodied players, and that's why the Ramblers did not have a full complement of second-string players for practice and why reporter Bill Jauss could make his joke about pulling a passerby off the street to fill out a scrimmage lineup.

So as Loyola embraced the homestretch of the regular season and the approaching opportunity to play in the NCAA tournament, the squad was perpetually shorthanded. It was mid-February, with barely more than a month remaining in the season (if Loyola could advance all of the way to the championship game), before the Ramblers took on the full-fledged traits of the iron man team it later became.

With Robertson and Smith taking the train home to New York there were no longer even hints of a debate about whether someone besides Jerry Harkness, Ron Miller, Johnny Egan, Les Hunter, or Vic Rouse should start, or even if their minutes should be reduced much to conserve their strength during close games.

It was not as if Ireland announced a policy, but he acted one out. He was going to dance with the ones that brung him. He was going to ride the broad shoulders of the starting five as far as they could carry him. If someone should foul out—and God forbid that should happen—then, and maybe only then, would Ireland ask one of his four remaining players to rise up off the bench, strip off the warm-up jacket, and take a few turns running up and down the court.

His choices, if one of the main men got tired (rarely), in foul trouble (almost as rarely), or injured (nobody did), came down to Chuck Wood, Rich Rochelle, Dan Connaughton, or Jim Reardon. Sometimes those guys had to wonder if Ireland even remembered their names. That's how seldom he called them out. The thinking by all of them had to go something like this: Hey, I can play basketball, too. That's why you wanted me to come here, isn't it?

Yes, there were times Robertson and Smith may have believed they should have been starters for the Ramblers during the 1962–63 campaign, but not Rochelle, Wood, Connaughton, or Reardon. Heck, they just wanted to work up a good sweat occasionally. They just wanted to play at all, not to have box scores continually printed without their names even mentioned, as if they didn't exist. Unlike the current habit in professional basketball where the box scores include the names of players who do not appear in the game with the notation "DNP-coach's decision," these guys were bigger ghosts than that. If they didn't play there was no proof they had even been there, except for eyewitness accounts amongst spectators who glanced their way as they sat for most of the game's forty minutes.

Connaughton, from Hamilton, Ohio, on the outskirts of Cincinnati, was a sophomore that season and was a little surprised to be a member of a team that was ranked as high as number two nationally with genuine aspirations to play for a national title. One reason Connaughton chose Loyola, he said, was it seemed like he would get a decent chance for playing time. Unlike Cincinnati, in his backyard, with its Oscar Robertson–driven reputation and its annual cruises to the Final Four during Connaughton's high school years, and Ohio State, a mere one hundred miles away and another perpetual national title contender, Loyola seemed small-time.

"'Oh, Loyola,' I thought," Connaughton said, "'they're kind of a half-assed independent school. I'll get to play a lot.'"[1]

Right. He learned quickly that season, as Rochelle so eloquently and sarcastically put it, that one of the starters practically had to die for Ireland to consider inserting him into a game. It was no different for the others among the quartet on the bench, whose primary role on many game days was to fill out the layup line.

The late Jim Reardon was a six-foot-four forward who played three varsity seasons for the Ramblers after enrolling at Loyola as a freshman in the fall of 1959. He predated the big guns, and during his 1960–61 sophomore season he averaged five points a game. No doubt he figured his turn for more playing time, perhaps to start, was coming, especially since in the second game of his varsity tenure Reardon poured in eighteen points in an easy win over Western Ontario. He surely would not have imagined that the game's point total would stand as his career high. Instead of becoming a bigger factor as the years passed, he mostly acquired blisters on his butt as a junior and senior.

Point guard Johnny Egan called Reardon "the brightest guy on the team" and a guy who would also "give you a truthful answer and an accurate answer" when asked a question.[2] It was not that he was showtime outspoken, but given a forum he said what he thought.

Ireland recruited over Reardon, bringing in better talent that relegated the Chicago Leo High School player to the bench. As a junior, during that 23–4 season, Reardon played in just eight games, averaging 1.9 points per game. During 1962–63 Ireland was hardly more generous to his senior. Reardon showed up in fourteen box scores and averaged 2.2 points a game. Twice that year, in early-season routs of Milwaukee and South Dakota, Reardon contributed eight points in a contest.

All of those highlights occurred in games when Loyola slaughtered the competition. Even the Western Ontario game during the 1960–61 season, when the Ramblers were a comparatively less-overpowering 15–8, was a thorough rout of 104–63. In the two contests when Reardon scored his eight-point seasonal highs in his last year, Loyola trounced Milwaukee by sixty points and South Dakota by forty-seven.

The point is that Reardon got his most meaningful playing time when

Loyola was far ahead, not in close games. The bench guys knew that Ireland didn't really trust them to hold leads in close games. He didn't have to say so; his actions consistently supported those beliefs.

"Every kid sitting on the bench feels he can contribute to the team," Rochelle said. He said one game Ireland cursed him out for scoring too much because his role was supposed to be using his six-ten height to play defense and rebound. He said he was so shocked that if he had been savvier about what it took to transfer, he probably would have left the Ramblers. "Had I known then what I know now," Rochelle said recently, "that probably would have been my last experience at Loyola. I felt a little bit trapped."[3]

Rochelle had good size and had had a good career playing high school ball. He said besides wooing his mother, Beatrice, so successfully, Ireland invited Rochelle to show his stuff at Alumni Gym. The coach said to come down to the school for a workout session with the other guys during the summer. When he showed up, Rochelle said, Clarence Red, one of the stars, and like Rochelle an African American, greeted him.

The offer to Rochelle included a full scholarship, room, board, and fees. Lately, there has been considerable attention given to the idea that the NCAA should pay college basketball players. At other times during NCAA history there have been payments offered for laundry fees and the like, something on the order of fifteen dollars at a time. Not for Rochelle. "As far as having money in your pocket, that wasn't mentioned," he said.[4]

While such schools as Tennessee State and Arkansas State were among those that made overtures to Rochelle, he was not interested, at least partially because he didn't want to attend college in the Deep South. As a youngster, Rochelle lived in Kansas City and said he experienced racism and discrimination that was worse than anything he saw living in the Chicago area, and he did not want a repeat. "We moved to Chicago when I was a freshman in high school," Rochelle said. "I had always been leery after that. I'd been subjected to racism in Kansas City."[5]

He was not at all surprised when the Ramblers were split up in New Orleans or were subjected to the angry sneers of the crowd in Houston. "It's what I knew," Rochelle said. "It was a way of life for me. It is what I expected."[6]

Rochelle's basketball career essentially began when he moved to Evanston. He learned a lot on his own, he said, and at Loyola he felt he had potential, at least because of his impressive size, but he admitted he also still needed coaching. "I had to learn from the ground up," Rochelle said. "I should have been a better rebounder in high school. I didn't learn the fundamentals of blocking out."[7]

It wasn't as if Rochelle was on Ireland's bad side where he was being punished and he didn't play for that reason. It was more like Ireland had a philosophy of counting on his regulars and not wanting to tamper with success. Rochelle felt he could have contributed. Maybe playing defense, maybe blocking a few shots, rebounding, and scoring from the pivot position in the low post. "We worked hard every day in practice, so if our number was called and we could give a break to, or spell another guy, we were ready," Rochelle said.[8]

There were some long waits for those numbers to be called for Rochelle, Wood, Connaughton, and Reardon. It was almost as if Ireland started to dial their numbers sometimes, realized he was calling a wrong number, and hung up.

Everyone on a team believes they belong and can help. It can wear a player down mentally if he never gets a chance. There is always a last man on the team no matter the size of the team in every sport. Rarely does a player find himself on a team where nearly half of the roster hardly plays. Over the decades an uncountable number of athletes have quit their teams because of disputes with coaches over playing time. It's not because they are playing too much.

The athlete who shows up every day, who practices every day, and who never gets the reward of live action must have a certain type of mental resilience. It can be demoralizing, a blow to the ego, almost insulting, to be informed by your coach that you are not really needed for the team to win. Some players can't take that and quit. It takes a true commitment to know going into a game that the odds are you will not see any type of action and to still stick it out. Rochelle, Wood, Reardon, and Connaughton all stuck it out. They also helped each other because each could identify with what the other was enduring. "We were all friendly," Rochelle said. "We got along and supported one another."[9]

Rochelle's season totals were much like Reardon's. He also appeared in fourteen games. He took just twenty-five shots from the floor. He averaged 2.2 points a game, and his game high was six points against South Dakota.

"A lot of good friendships were born during those four years," Rochelle said. "The support system that was formed during some trying times was pretty special."[10]

By the time Ireland noticed Connaughton he had prepared well for becoming a student at Loyola, although it was not planned. He attended a Jesuit high school, St. Xavier in Cincinnati, and while he played football, basketball, and baseball, the demands on the students were serious enough that Connaughton said he was studying every night by 6:30 or 7 p.m. on nongame days.

Connaughton definitely wanted to compete on a sports team in college, but he had to make a harsh assessment of his body. He didn't think he had the thickness and the sturdiness to play college football. "I didn't have the build," said Connaughton, who was listed as six four. "I had skinny legs. I had quick hands. Basketball was kind of my niche."[11]

Memory tells Connaughton that he had inquiring letters or calls from a dozen or so coaches that were interested in him continuing his hoops education. Hometown Xavier, another Jesuit school, wanted him, but he would have had to live at home instead of in a dorm and he didn't want to do that. Loyola happened to be in Cincinnati to play Xavier at the same time Connaughton's team's season-ending banquet took place, and that's where he met Ireland. Ireland invited Connaughton on a recruiting trip to Loyola for a weekend, and if nothing else a getaway to the big city sounded like fun.

"How could you go wrong going to Chicago?" Connaughton said.[12]

To Connaughton Ireland seemed like an energetic, articulate coach who made enough of an impression on him at seventeen to sway his thinking. Chicago wasn't that far from home and he even had a friend living there. He graduated from high school in the spring of 1961 and joined the varsity as a backup sophomore for the 1962–63 season.

"What a year to break in," Connaughton said.[13]

In the very beginning of the season, when Loyola was crushing every other team bold enough to take a jump ball with the Ramblers on the same court, Connaughton was pleased to be deployed. The games were all wipeouts, and briefly Ireland was more generous with playing time than he would be again all season. "Early on I had playing time and I was enjoying it," Connaughton said.[14]

As Loyola mashed North Dakota, Connaughton got in long enough to score six points. Against Milwaukee he scored his season high of eight points. Against South Dakota he added seven points. While certainly his playing time wasn't making the difference between winning and losing, there was every reason to feel proud about how things were going. Then the playing drought followed. Connaughton scored in just three more games all season, although he appeared in seventeen altogether. He became part of the forgotten quartet, especially in close games.

"We could have got more playing time," Connaughton said much later. "I was always having that hope [that he would get into the game]. George Ireland trusted the first five implicitly. After a while he was just going with his iron man five. He was just so confident with this five. Maybe in the back of his mind he kept thinking about us as this mid-major school still having to prove itself and had fears that we might lose."[15]

If Loyola had a reputation at all in college basketball during the 1962–63 season, it was built almost solely on the legs of the 1961–62 team that turned in the consolation-game-winning finish in the NIT. Connaughton had not been a member of the earlier team. As a freshman he was ineligible to play that season. But he watched in wonder in the early going as the Ramblers dismantled foe after foe. He may not have been a college hoops analyst (there weren't any back then) and he may not even have considered himself an expert, but his eyes didn't lie and what he saw as Loyola ripped through team after team told him a lot.

"It was certainly clear and apparent to me early on that we were going to be a very good team," Connaughton said. "We could dominate a lot of teams. It was never in the recesses of my mind, though, that we would be in the Final Four."[16]

Sure Connaughton wanted to play more, but as one of the newer guys on the team and with his recognition of how good the team was, he was perhaps a little more content to watch than he might have been if he was a senior rather than an underclassman. "All year it was just going to class and going to practice and enjoying the run," he said.

Wood might have enjoyed the run more if he hadn't been sick. Anyone who has experienced the illness knows that having mono is no fun. It is an energy-sapping disease that leaves a person with one basic desire—to go to sleep. Wood was shut down for eleven games during the season, and it was a good thing for Loyola that he was out when Robertson and Smith were still around or the shorthandedness may have been an even bigger handicap. Ireland would have been suiting up team managers, Girl Scouts, gymnasts, or anyone who could dribble to fill out the practices.

Wood was an excellent all-around athlete. Growing up in Racine, Wisconsin, which is just a hair too far north to accurately be described as a Chicago suburb, he originally thought he would follow his father LeRoy's path and become a baseball player. Then he fell in love with football. Basketball was OK, but at St. Catherine's, the private school he attended, he had his first disappointment as a young player in football. One game where the team creamed the opposition, every single player on the sideline got into the game except Wood, so he quit the team.

He ran track, doing the high and low hurdles, and the jumps, the high jump and the long jump, both of which fit in with his on-court rebounding capability. "I could dunk as a sophomore," Wood said.[17]

He didn't play enough to be given a varsity letter, however, and that frosted him. Not even his mother, Cecelia, gave him sympathy, though, saying, "Obviously, the coach didn't think you deserved one."[18]

Growing to six three, adding muscle, and gaining maturity, Wood made sure he won his share of varsity letters after that as a punter, safety, and end on the football team and as a forward on the basketball team. He led the conference in scoring, and his teams either won local titles or contended for national Catholic school titles.

Wood's father was a window cleaner and Wood worked for him during school breaks and summer vacation. The idea of being able to get a college education free through sports was a pretty big deal. His ambition was to play football and basketball at the University of Wisconsin, but he noticed that the Badgers' roster was loaded with sophomores. That meant those older, more experienced players would be a roadblock for his entire career. He looked closely at Marquette, but with sixty schools contacting him Wood had many options.

Loyola and Ireland were suitors. As was typical for someone living close, Ireland invited Wood to take a visit to Chicago. He attended a Cubs baseball game at Wrigley Field.

Wood said he chose Loyola because it was close enough for his parents to come to see him play and because Marquette was on the schedule every year, so he would also play in Milwaukee.

As Jerry Harkness discovered when he believed he was going to attend New York University, some colleges require certain entrance examinations. On his first trip to Chicago, Wood took the train from Racine to Evanston, transferred to the L, and waited for the Loyola stop, where he was supposed to meet a friend. The train was speeding right along and the fast-spoken, somewhat muffled public-address announcements Wood heard completely baffled him. It was as if the conductor were speaking a foreign tongue. "I couldn't understand the guy," Wood said. "I finally got off, only it was at DePaul University. Then I got back on, went to the L station in Evanston, and rode the train all of the way home."[19]

He left without taking the exam. Wood's father was incredulous when he relayed the story. "Big shot," he said. "You're going to college and you can't even find the school."[20]

Eventually, Wood and Loyola found one another.

Wood had his share of frustration during the 1962–63 season. First, he was sick and missed out on about a third of the season. When he returned he wasn't all that peppy. In Wood's first game back he was so weak, "I couldn't run down the court."

And then, like Rochelle, Reardon, and Connaughton, he sure wished Ireland would think more fondly of him and put him in the darned game more often. "I felt sorry for myself," Wood said.

Egan, who roomed with Wood part of their time together as teammates, said Wood was hard on himself, disappointed that he wasn't producing as much as he thought he could, but was a great teammate who never complained.

"He was disappointed," Egan said. "He wanted to be a bigger part of the team. He knew he had the talent and he did. He was not sulking or anything like that."[21]

Wood's stats pretty much mirrored the others on the bench. He got into seventeen games, but his points per game average during the 1962–63 season was just 1.9 and again like the others he was not expected to shoot when he got into the games. Wood shot just twenty-eight times all season.

Wood said he used to tease Harkness. "'Hey,'" he would say, "'before I got here you weren't an All-American. When I began covering you in practice, you became an All-American.'"[22]

Even if it was gallows humor, there was a certain pride in the statement, a way for Wood to say he was making a difference on this team. And Harkness, the All-American, did admit "he could guard me really well. I think Chuck got messed up a little bit mentally. He was good, but I think Ireland got in his head. He was screaming at certain guys. I thought Chuck was better than he showed because of that. He was a good athlete. He could shoot. He was good, a quick jumper, and he could come in, but Ireland was on that five-player thing."

Yep, that five-player thing was a staple of Ireland's game plan in the latter stages of the 1962–63 season. At times it seemed like a reckless strategy, but there is no second-guessing winners.

Most assuredly, Ireland could have boxed himself into a difficult situation by so rarely employing Rochelle, Wood, Reardon, and Connaughton, but he went with his gut. Although it never happened where one of the starters fouled out of an important game late in the season, Ireland might have been in a fix if it had. There would have been a bit of flying blind for Loyola. Ireland would have had to rely on a player to whom he had barely given playing time along the way. It would have classified as a storybook success if one of them had come through to win a big game. Certainly, Ireland's commitment to the big five and no one else could have backfired on him, but it didn't.

"Ireland didn't trust the other guys," center Les Hunter said. "And they hadn't played enough to where they could really contribute."[23]

They hadn't had the chance to be eased into the mix at crunch time, so it was only going to be in case of crisis that Ireland would call upon the bench guys when everything was on the line. Since no emergency arose, no one found out if the bench could have made the difference.

CHAPTER 14

GOING AFTER THEM ALL

till undefeated. That was Loyola's status after the journey to Oklahoma City. The next contest was a rematch with Dayton, the school that ended Loyola's season in the NIT the season before. The Ramblers won, 74–69.

Two more victories followed against teams representing places where the African American players on Loyola had been treated rudely the season before. These return matches were in Chicago, however. In the first one, Loyola crushed Marshall, 103–58. There were no reports of anyone on the Marshall team having difficulty being served a hamburger after the game.

Loyola's high scores were misleading to some distant fans, instilling a belief that the Ramblers did not prize defense. Without games on television, only word-of-mouth descriptions of games, and sometimes just the scores, made the circuit of college basketball. But Marshall coach Jule Rivlin knew what hit his team in the forty-five-point loss. "Their press threw us off," Rivlin said. "We didn't keep a chart, but my guess is that we had about 33 turnovers."[1]

Turnovers were not an official statistic in basketball during the early 1960s, but that would be a colossal figure that no team could overcome.

Certainly, the Ramblers recognized what a weapon their full-court pressure could be. "The weaker teams crack under the press," said Loyola forward Jerry Harkness, who held Marshall's top scorer to five points in the game.[2]

The other follow-up win came over Loyola of New Orleans, 88–53, another wipeout of a team from that segregated town.

Ireland, the architect of the masterpiece being developed, was pleased, enjoying every minute of Loyola's thorough triumphs, but also cautious about what lay ahead. Yes, he knew his team belonged near the top of the

George Ireland, coach of the 1963 NCAA champions, holds a trophy late in life. Ireland passed away in 2001. Courtesy of Paul Smulson.

national rankings, but it was a long way from weekly mention in a nationwide poll to a place standing on the podium at the end of a national tournament.

"I'm not thinking about championships," Ireland said in midseason, though he undoubtedly was. He said he was focused on Loyola's upcoming run of games, not the end of the next month when the NCAAs would be decided. "But, of course, everyone is talking about this team and there's a reason: We're different. Sure, we're different. Maybe we're fabulous because we have a group of kids who are thoroughbreds. They don't fold up.

They respond when they're asked, just like thoroughbreds. Now, they say we don't play defense. The heck we don't play defense! Our defense is just something different."[3]

With its dominating fast-break style on offense and its pressure all over the court on defense, a game against Loyola could appear to be helter-skelter, so perhaps that offended purists. But Loyola made good teams look bad. Loyola was disruptive.

Ireland saved letters from other coaches and newspaper clippings where other coaches were quoted after they faced the Ramblers and had their best opportunities stifled, forcing them out of their game plans with the predictable result being a Loyola romp. He came into possession of one article in which Indiana coach Branch McCracken consoled his team following the loss to Loyola with these words: "You boys played a darned good game. That was one fine basketball team you played—the best we've faced this year. You won't find a much better group of individual players outside the pros."

The Ramblers' next game was on the road in nearby Milwaukee. Loyola and Marquette, located less than one hundred miles apart, are both Jesuit universities and, given that commonality of interest and geographic proximity, had been regular opponents on the hardwood. The schools typically played twice a season, which meant that four-year players on the rosters got to know one another better than some might have known their girlfriends. Only with not so much love involved.

Loyola point guard Johnny Egan played fearlessly. He dove for loose balls, always made the scrappy play, routinely ran the guards covering him into picks or screens so they bounced off Loyola big men like Les Hunter and Vic Rouse, and always made a pest of himself. Opposing fans couldn't stand him. Watching him harass their players once was enough for most of them, but to see him over and over again (and the distance from Milwaukee to Chicago was so short that it invited visiting fans to make the trip for road encounters), made them practically break out in a rash.

Egan said he remembers one game at Marquette when all of the starters for Loyola were introduced and received polite applause, except him. When the public-address announcer called his name there were reverberating boos. "I appreciated that," Egan said. Didn't faze him one bit. In fact, Hunter was standing next to him when the boos echoed and said, "They love you up here."[4]

During that period, Marquette, which has had much more success than

Loyola overall, didn't love to see any of the Ramblers coming. The game that season in Milwaukee ended 87–68, Loyola. The victory over Marquette in Milwaukee was the first of a four-game road stretch that the Ramblers swept, defeating Marquette, Western Michigan for the second time that season, Kent State, and Ohio University. Now the Ramblers were 17–0, and that was a pretty good start.

Ireland reflected on his team's strength, an ability to play with a voracious appetite for points and with a demonic desire to keep the other team from scoring. The style required constant hustle, never surrendering an inch, and swiftly taking advantage of every tiny opening spotted.

"We're different because we can keep going," Ireland said. "We play the entire game with the same speed, the same pace. We never let up, even with some of the squad out because of injury or ineligibility."[5]

The first win over Marquette, facing a Warriors team that was 7–3, brought some bonus fame to the Ramblers. Television technology was comparatively primitive to what is possible in the 2000s, and the interest in college basketball had yet to be deemed nearly as widespread. However, after Loyola bested Marquette, an NBC camera crew rode the team bus back from Milwaukee to Chicago to create a half-hour TV special about the team. During the game captain Jerry Harkness, who scored twenty-three points, even better obliged those making the film by setting two school records. He gained the team all-time scoring record for a three-year varsity player and set the record for most career free throws.

"I said it before the season even started and I'm saying it again," said Marquette coach Ed Hickey. "Harkness is definitely All-American timber."[6]

By this point, the ailing Chuck Wood had been ruled out for the rest of the season, but he managed to beat the doctors' predictions and returned to uniform before the season concluded. However, for some of his absence, the Ramblers were depleted by the ineligibilities of Billy Smith and Pablo Robertson. Before Wood made his surprisingly swift recovery, Ireland brazened the situation out with reporters, saying Earl Johnson, a six-foot-four backup, and Dan Connaughton would step in. "Both Johnson and Connaughton will surprise you," he said. "They'll do an adequate job."[7] But Johnson quit school and Ireland hardly ever let Connaughton climb off the bench.

This made Loyola's dependence on and continued execution of the running game and high-pressure defensive approach even more impressive because those were energy-sapping ways to play the game.

After disposing of Ohio, the Ramblers were scheduled to participate in a college doubleheader at Chicago Stadium, patterned after Madison Square Garden's very popular method of showcasing top collegiate teams. Interestingly, the home Chicago team was not in the featured game. That game pitted the University of Illinois, at that moment ranked fourth in the country, against number one–rated Cincinnati. Ireland's Loyola number two–ranked bunch was going up against unranked 9–4 Santa Clara in the early game.

At the time, Ireland felt Loyola was overshadowed by the other game and half-jokingly asked Chicago sportswriters to tell their readers the Ramblers were playing, too. He didn't relish the idea of Loyola being a secret in its own town.

The sportswriters knew how good Loyola was, and one posed the question to Ireland of whether his guys were starting to feel any pressure to maintain their unbeaten mark after the seventeen straight wins.

"They don't feel the pressure," said Ireland, who may have been right and not just saying the acceptable thing. "They take each game as it comes. Afterward, there's no jubilation. They're unemotional. They take their showers and they just want to know one thing—'When do we eat?'"[8]

The Ramblers did react maturely to victory. They had a solid belief in their abilities, had remarkably steady confidence, and felt they were as good as anyone in the country. That made the appearance of Cincinnati, the one team in the United States that other people consistently voted better than the Ramblers, an intriguing night out for spectators at the tournament. The Ramblers stuck around the stadium to watch Cincinnati beat Illinois and filed away their impressions for later, just in case the two teams happened to meet in the NCAA tournament.

There was a recognition that Cincinnati was a good team—it had to be as a two-time defending NCAA champion with several key players returning—but the Ramblers did not walk away awed. They walked away thinking the Bearcats were beatable.

"You can't get behind them early," was Egan's analysis, "not the way they can control the ball. If we got ahead, I think they'd have to run with us. And they couldn't dominate the game on the boards."[9]

It was idle chatter in early February, long before the two teams could possibly meet, but Loyola, which had never been ranked number one for a minute but hovered at number two, logically had to wonder a little bit about what it would be like to face the top team. At the moment the Ramblers remained perfect and that's all a team can do, win every game the schedule puts in front of it. Not every win had been a snap, either.

As easily as Loyola had pasted its season-opening opponents, there had been times in games later on when the squad trailed, and other times when it gave away a lead after seeming to be in control. The Ramblers' record was perfect, but Ireland did not pretend they constituted a perfect team. He reveled in the real challenges and the way his players overcame them.

"When they have to put on the pressure, they put it on," Ireland said. "Against Ohio University . . . we led by 12 in the second half. When Ohio came back to tie us, I called time out and applied the whip like I've never applied it before. Within three minutes we had six baskets to break the game open."[10]

Loyola took care of business against Santa Clara, upping its record to 18–0 with an 82–72 triumph. Not long after the game Ireland received a note from the California school's coach talking about how impressed he was by the Ramblers and how his players made his team play poorly. "I'm sorry we didn't play well in the Stadium," Santa Clara coach Dick Garibaldi wrote. "The reason we didn't play well was because you didn't let us."[11]

In a way, it was the summary of Loyola's season to date.

The defeat of Santa Clara began a stretch of four straight home games following the four straight road games, and Loyola won all of those, too. After Santa Clara, Loyola topped Washington University in St. Louis, Iowa, and Marquette for a second time.

Marquette was the first opponent Loyola faced with its ultrathin bench. In a bold comment, but really the only thing he could say, Ireland said losing Smith and Robertson to grades shouldn't make an impact on the Ramblers seeking to stay unbeaten. He was nearly proven wrong in the first game without them in another doubleheader appearance at Chicago Stadium.

The Ramblers' home of Alumni Gym seated just two thousand fans. Attending a hoops game on campus was an intimate experience, more so than ever as the triumphant team lured crowds of spectators with its lofty ranking and its unbeaten record. Players liked the small arena where their loud fans made the walls vibrate, but they also were glad to at last be playing before a wider Chicago audience that would appreciate them. Chicago Stadium held about twenty thousand fans for basketball and was filled for that doubleheader that had also included the Cincinnati–Illinois game. The crowds were not as thick for other Loyola appearances at Chicago Stadium, against Marquette (8,113) and against Iowa (6,876), though there were far more people present than could have watched at Alumni Gym.

"We have great respect for Loyola, but we're not about to drop over and play dead," said Hickey, the Marquette coach, of his 12–6 team. "We've got the stuff to beat them and I think we can. Of all the fast-break teams I've seen since I've been coaching [over a twenty-four-year period], Loyola rates No. 1 in its ability to get the ball. Loyola can be controlled, slowed down. No one has done it yet, but we might have something to say about it tonight."[12]

Marquette never did slow down Loyola in the rematch, but it nearly pulled off the upset anyway, falling 92–90 in overtime. The Ramblers looked quite rusty after a ten-day game layoff. At one point Ireland moved the six-foot-two Ron Miller, a high school center, back to his old position. As unlikely as it seemed, the strategy worked and he scored a game-high twenty-eight points. "I don't even practice at center," Miller said after the game, "but it all came back to me from high school."[13]

Harkness scored two baskets in the last forty-eight seconds, and the Ramblers' last six points overall, to carry the team to its twenty-first straight win. When the buzzer sounded, Harkness was carried off the court on the shoulders of his teammates and some fans. It was not as if Loyola had captured any kind of title with the triumph, but any win over Marquette was to be savored. Maybe holding off the rival Warriors made for a little bit of a release, too. The win was definitely a great escape.

Being 21–0 and ranked second in the country rather astoundingly did not make Loyola the favorite in its next game. The Ramblers were headed for a rematch against Bowling Green, a team it had handled 81–68 the preceding season.

The Ohio team had a special team of its own during this era. Center Nate Thurmond later became one of the great NBA rebounders of all time with the San Francisco Warriors and despite playing in the shadow of Bill Russell and Wilt Chamberlain had a Hall of Fame career. The six-foot-eleven Thurmond, nicknamed "Nate the Great," became a seven-time pro all-star, and he had a several-inch height advantage over any of the Ramblers. Guard Howie "Butch" Komives was a terrific shooter who led the nation in scoring a year later as a senior and then played for the New York Knicks and other teams over ten years in the pros.

Feeling burned by the loss to Loyola the year before, the Falcons were like a snake in the weeds waiting to ambush the Ramblers on their home court in Bowling Green, Ohio. Wood, who had been proclaimed missing in action for the remainder of the season, must have ingested wonder drugs because he came back much sooner than expected. It was just in time to gaze upon Thurmond's sculpted body in the pivot.

"Holy cow, he was a monster," Wood said of the big man who remains eighth on the NBA's all-time rebounding list.[14]

The arena was packed, the 5,734 fans at Memorial Hall were loud and hungry for a big win over the nationally ranked team, and it was frenetic and noisy even before the game started as the teams ran through their layup lines to loosen up. Chants of "We Want Loyola!" rang out.

"We're gaining national recognition," said Loyola guard Dan Connaughton, "and teams are looking at us as a real feather in their cap if they could knock us off. It was so loud in there, an incredible atmosphere, nonstop cheering. You couldn't hear the guy next to you in warm-ups."[15]

From the opening jump ball Bowling Green played a virtually perfect game. The Falcons had a guard named Wavey Junior. Right away the ball came into his hands and he heaved a jump shot at the hoop from another area code. "He takes two dribbles and lets one fly from twenty-five or twenty-eight feet," Connaughton said. "He banked it in and the crowd just about jumped through the ceiling."[16]

It was Bowling Green's turn and Bowling Green's night. Running up a 9–0 lead after the opening tip, the Falcons maintained a frenzied pace and led by between eleven and seventeen points for most of the game on the way to a thorough 92–75 victory.

"They were waiting for us," said Ron Miller. "It was homecoming. Nate Thurmond, Howie Komives, whom we could not guard. All he needed was about an inch to shoot and then it was a flick of the wrist." Komives, who had twenty-three points by halftime, dropped in thirty-two and Thurmond added twenty-four.[17]

"They just jumped all over us," said Les Hunter, who led Loyola with twenty-four points. "That crowd was on top of us. That was the one game we legitimately deserved to lose that year."[18]

That was the end of Loyola's undefeated season. The Ramblers returned to Chicago 21–1. Bowling Green captured the Mid-American Conference crown and advanced to the NCAA tournament with one of the best teams in school history.

"That night down there, probably nobody could have stopped Bowling

Green," Ireland said. "But we pulled within six points a couple of times, only to let it get away."[19]

Ireland and some of his players said Bowling Green had just been waiting for revenge from a loss the year before and the gym was packed well ahead of tip-off, with fans making noise that could be heard a block away.

Loyola shot just 41 percent from the floor, ran into foul trouble, an especially dangerous circumstance without much of a bench, and saw Vic Rouse turn an ankle, although it was not a serious injury.

The Loyola team that had conquered the adversity of racism faced its first on-court adversity of the season. The Ramblers had been riding high, but they didn't have time to mourn their single loss. They had a quick turnaround game against St. John's. This was a time for the Ramblers to show what they were made of. They could either be sent reeling by another loss or shrug off the Bowling Green encounter and resume their normal level of play to put the defeat behind them. Many times a team in such a situation finds that what comes next is all in the head, mental preparation.

It was still only mid-February, with several regular-season games to go. If Loyola wanted to hang onto its number two national position it had to play at its best once more. As perhaps one incentive for a good showing the St. John's game in New York City was being televised back to Chicago. And there was another interesting development. After the team arrived in New York, Ireland received word that the NCAA was extending an invitation to the Ramblers to play in its postseason tournament.

Unlike the modern method of waiting until the regular season and conference tournaments are completed, during that era the NCAA sometimes issued early invitations to teams like Loyola that were independents. It had to be heartening for the Ramblers to learn that they had already accomplished enough to be welcome in the national championship event.

In Chicago, Loyola's athletics board had previously discussed the topic in a meeting and agreed that if an invitation was extended, the Ramblers should accept. So Ireland promptly did so. Then Loyola went out and stomped St. John's, 70–47, demonstrating that the loss to Bowling Green might not be a fluke, but it wasn't traumatizing either.

The NCAA approval and the dominating win made Ireland feel a little better, though not even a steady diet of chicken soup was going to help his health. Earlier in the season he had coped with a virus. He was always dealing with ulcers and years earlier had had some of his stomach removed in surgery because of them. And right after the St. John's win, tests showed Ireland had internal bleeding. He was hoping his doctors would not require him to enter the hospital. The tests showed that Ireland had kidney stones— one of the most painful conditions known to man besides losing a game by upset—and would need some more postseason scalpel work. He skipped the team flight back to Chicago. That may have been for the best, as the flight was detoured to St. Louis because of fog in the middle of the night. Assistant coach Jerry Lyne had to deal with the aggravation of finding the Ramblers a place to sleep and then discovered the cab driver and limo driver couldn't sort out where that hotel was.

"The limousine driver apparently gave the cab driver the wrong directions," Lyne said, "because he went to another place ten miles away from us and it was another half hour before the second group finally got to the motel."[20]

As if the side trip wasn't enough fun for Loyola, the next road trip was the hellish journey to Houston where the crowd was hateful and the Ramblers barely survived the southwest hospitality for a 62–58 win.

Loyola moved to 24–1 by belting Ohio, 114–94, at Alumni Gym as February concluded. It was a close game during the first half, but the Ramblers pulled away later.

Before the game, Harkness was notified that he had been chosen as a first-team All-American by both the Associated Press and United Press International. He scored thirty-two points that night and wasn't even the Ramblers' high man, with Les Hunter pouring in thirty-four points.

"I really didn't expect to make the first team," Harkness said. "And I never would have made it with another team, even if I scored just as much. A lot depends on these guys. Les and Vic get the boards. Jack and Ron Miller take care of the playmaking. That allows me to use my talent to the best advantage."[21]

Sitting at 24–1 Loyola had one regular-season game remaining before the NCAA playoffs and an official quest to win a national title could begin. Wichita State, a formidable outfit, was ranked eighth in the country. The Shockers did not appear to be the least bit frightened by Loyola's reputation. For one reason: Wichita State had already shocked number one Cincinnati. Dave Stallworth, a six-foot-seven forward, scored forty-six of his team's sixty-five points in the squad's one-point decision that ended Cincinnati's thirty-seven-game winning streak. He was complemented by six-foot-ten center Nate Bowman. Both players later played for the New York Knicks in the NBA.

"We know Loyola has an exceptionally fine offense and likes to press and run," said Shockers coach Ralph Miller before the contest against the Ramblers. "That's the way we like to play the game, too, so this should be a most interesting head-on battle of the same styles."[22]

Loyola's reaction to the suggestion that any team would want to run with it was always the same: bring it on. Wichita State did.

Ireland predicted that Wichita State, in town for another Chicago Stadium doubleheader that also pitted Notre Dame against Bradley, would be the toughest match for Loyola all year, including Bowling Green. He was right. It was far from Loyola's best performance of the season and Wichita State won, 73–72, before 18,778 fans who booed the referees from the Shockers' Missouri Valley Conference. Both Les Hunter and Vic Rouse fouled out, one of the Ramblers' worst-case scenarios. Although Loyola had five double-figure scorers, the Ramblers shot just 39.4 percent from the field.

The result showed that although Loyola was ranked number two in the land and was going to be competing in the NCAA tournament, it was hardly invincible. It was a wrong-time defeat and it pointed out the Ramblers' lack of depth if any of the starters got hurt or into foul trouble.

Loyola completed the regular season 24–2. It was a tremendous accomplishment and marked the best record in school history. The Ramblers had achieved nationwide respect and now it was March; now it was time to show that all of the grief suffered in the South for playing African Americans, all of the hard-fought games battled through, positioned them for greatness.

The very best thing that the Ramblers could do was forget all about Wichita State. From now on any loss represented the final game of the season. Lose and go home for the year. Win and play on. Every year in the NCAA tournament, one college basketball team has its dreams come true. In 1963, Loyola was determined that it would be the one.

Forward Vic Rouse came to Loyola from Nashville, Tennessee, where he was a high school teammate of Les Hunter. The six-foot-seven forward scored the game-winning basket against Cincinnati. Courtesy of the Loyola Sports Information Office.

CHAPTER 15

THE NCAAS BEGIN

I n 1963, the biggest sports news came from Major League Baseball's spring-training camps during March, not from a college basketball tournament that in subsequent decades would have such a firm grip on the American consciousness that it would be labeled "March Madness."

Americans were more likely to be watching *The Fugitive* or *The Patty Duke Show* on television than basketball. In fact, not even the NCAA championship game itself, never mind the early rounds, had reached a position of eminence in the country to demand live prime-time coverage. College basketball was part of the sporting firmament, but it was not a dominating element that could command center stage.

The NCAA championships date back to 1939 when Oregon won the first title in Evanston, Illinois, at Northwestern University's gym. The NIT, which was founded in 1938 and saw its first championship won by Temple, retained a nearly equal level of prestige (although not for long).

In 2013, invitations to the NCAA's postseason tournament were offered to sixty-eight schools. In 1963, as the tournament began on March 9, the field consisted of twenty-five teams. Winners of certain conferences were automatic invitees. As an independent, with no league affiliation, Loyola was a discretionary pick, but the Ramblers made it easy for selectors with their dominating play and 24–2 record. Loyola had known since mid-February that it would compete in the NCAAs, so there was no nail-biting suspense with players sitting around wondering if the season would be extended.

That alone was something to savor, since this marked the first Loyola NCAA appearance in school history.

Loyola had come a long way in barely more than a year. When the 1961–62 season started, hardly any basketball fan around the country had the Ramblers on the brain. The 23–4 finish and the showing in the NIT implanted Loyola in the minds of fans and experts, and Loyola had been on the national radar all season during the 1962–63 campaign.

As much as they could be without national television exposure, the Ramblers were now a known entity. They had national respect in the form of their high national ranking all year. They had a gaudy record. They led the country in scoring. And they were known for their style of play. Anyone who knew anything about Loyola knew that the team's specialty was the fast break and that it was complemented by pressing defense.

It took great athletes, from the explosive Les Hunter and Vic Rouse, to the shifty Jerry Harkness, to the savvy Johnny Egan and Ron Miller, to do what Loyola did, so when George Ireland used a thoroughbred horse analogy to describe his team, those in the know nodded sagely.

What was also apparent to the participants is that what Ireland had promised when he recruited them had come true. They had become part of something special. They had played major roles in putting Loyola on the map in college basketball. When Ireland wooed them in their living rooms and said he was building something in Chicago, he wasn't exaggerating. He made it happen by bringing them all together. They had taken a giant step together during the 23–4 season, and they had improved on that as they continued to grow and mesh.

As a group they weathered every type of basketball challenge, but also unforeseen racist experiences that did nothing except draw them closer together. Ireland led them to the doorstep of opportunity. Now was the time to walk through that open door and seize the moment with two strong hands, or really ten strong hands.

Leading up to the start of the NCAA tournament, the players don't recall Ireland giving them any rah-rah pep talks about being a team of destiny or anything like that. As Harkness said, Ireland had long ago delivered his speech about what they could be. "He said all of that way back when he recruited us," Harkness said.[1]

For all of the success and preparation there were reasons for concern as the tournament approached. The recent trip to Houston rattled the sensibilities of several players and the game had been uncomfortably close. Then the Ramblers lost to Wichita State in their final regular-season game. There was no room for lapses in the NCAA tournament. There was no time for recovery. Every team was going to be a good team and playing poorly could easily result in defeat. A loss would end the season and would spawn a lifetime of regret.

It became apparent, on full display in the Houston and Wichita State games, that despite the initial boasting that the loss of Billy Smith and Pablo Robertson wouldn't matter, it did make some difference. Any type of the mildest injury diminishing the effectiveness of a starter, or any type of foul trouble, exposed Loyola's bench weakness. Certainly, Ireland felt that there was a drop-off in capabilities without Smith and Robertson.

"We don't have depth, that's true," Ireland said. "If Les Hunter gets in trouble, Rouse will move to center and [Chuck] Wood to forward. If Rouse gets in trouble, it's Wood, of course. If both Hunter and Rouse get into trouble at the same time, we're dead."[2]

Enough had been seen of Loyola entering the NCAAs that coaches began offering theories on how to contain a team that could easily score one hundred points. "Loyola will probably see a lot of zones," said Marshall coach Jule Rivlin. "That's the best way to slow them down except that they're so fast they don't give you much chance to get back in time."[3]

After Loyola began the season by plowing under its first four opponents by huge margins, there had been complaints the Ramblers were merely scoring big wins over pushover schools. But the schedule toughened up as the season went on and Loyola deflected almost all comers. Now that didn't really matter. All of the twenty-five schools in the tournament were good. All had either won league championships or, like Loyola, distinguished themselves against top-level foes playing an independent schedule.

Loyola was assigned to the Mideast Regional, which included Tennessee Tech, Notre Dame, Illinois, Mississippi State, and Bowling Green. The Ramblers knew all about Bowling Green firsthand. They had seen Illinois play in Chicago. Nearby Notre Dame, roughly ninety miles east in South Bend, Indiana, was Ireland's old school. Mississippi State had won the Southeastern Conference title, interrupting Kentucky's usual dynastic domination. And Tech, located in Cookeville, Tennessee, shared the Ohio Valley Conference crown with Morehead State. The Golden Eagles were in their second NCAA event after falling to Notre Dame in their debut in 1958.

The other big-gun teams from the regular season were sprinkled around the brackets. Duke, 24–2, was sent to the East Regional. Cincinnati was assigned to the Midwest. Highly regarded Arizona State was in the West, along with Seattle. For Loyola to face Cincinnati or any of the western teams, it would have to reach the championship game. To get that far the Ramblers might have to get past Bowling Green in a rematch, in-state rival Illinois, and possibly Duke. That meant there was plenty to worry about before jumping ahead to a possible showdown with Cincinnati, which is what all of the players wanted.

Loyola started the year 21–0 but was coming into the tournament with two losses in its previous five games. The aura of invincibility was gone. The Wichita State defeat, seemingly coming out of nowhere, still stung, especially since it was the most recent game.

"There's no use crying over spilt milk," Ireland said. "But I feel that if we hadn't lost Billy Smith and Pablo Robertson through ineligibility nobody would have touched us. Their loss sapped our reserve strength and that Smith was a terrific rebounder."[4]

It was not difficult to imagine that a full-strength Loyola could have gone unbeaten at 26–0, but that was not reality. Smith and Robertson weren't coming back, and the long list of winners in the NCAAs was the minefield Loyola had to wade through. It would take five victories to win the championship, but advancing step by step, game by game was how you played it, not thinking too far ahead.

Loyola drew Tennessee Tech as a first-round opponent. The Golden Eagles, at 16–7, had one of the least impressive records in the field and also had a very young roster, but they also had slightly more height than the Ramblers and planned to throw a zone at them.

"Tech is strictly a zone team," Ireland said. ". . . it's hard to tell how well Tech's offense will work against our man-to-man. But they haven't seen us play, so they're at the same disadvantage."[5]

It turned out that nothing Tennessee Tech intended made the slightest difference. What followed was the most overwhelming performance in the history of the NCAA tournament. Loyola so incredibly dominated the first-round game that the final score of 111–42 still stands as the greatest single-game plurality in tournament annals. At the 2012 regional at Louisville's Yum Center the scoreboard even flashed the score as the answer to a trivia question. It is a margin of victory that may never be broken.

"We kind of knew going in that we were going up against a weak sister," said Loyola's Rich Rochelle. "It wasn't going to be much of a challenge."[6]

Johnny Egan was the ringleader in trying psychology on an opponent. Egan said that John Adams, the center for Tennessee Tech, played with him on his high school team at St. Rita in Chicago.

"He was the top field-goal percentage shooter in [Tech's] conference," Egan said. "He was a real quiet guy. I hardly talked to him in high school, but he was a really good student. We're coming into the building [at Northwestern], and he's going to his locker room and I'm going to my locker room. I haven't seen or talked to him since he was a senior in high school. Did you ever have the feeling that when you're crossing paths with someone he's intentionally ignoring you, or looking the other way, but he really sees you and he doesn't want to say hello? I decided, 'That's crazy.' So I turned around went back to him and I said, 'John, you missed me.' He goes, 'Oh, hi, how are you?' He's clearly uncomfortable talking to a member of the enemy and doesn't say anything else. But I walk into his locker room with him.

"He sits down and I keep talking to him. His teammates see my Loyola bag and have got to be thinking, 'What the hell?' They probably think I'm a manager or something. He sits down and I'm standing there talking to him. I think he's trying to ignore me and pretend I'm not even there. He's trying to tell me to get the hell out of there. I put my hand on the back of his head and say, 'John, it'll be over in a little while. Don't you worry about it.'"[7]

When Egan told his teammates what he had done, they were incredulous. They said if they had been part of a team he did that to they would have thrown him out of the locker room in a heartbeat. Egan was right, though. By any definition the game was over pretty fast. The Ramblers led by forty points at the half and still Ireland tried to find something to be irritated about during the intermission in the locker room, presumably to keep the team's mind on the game.

"Now what can he be upset about?" Egan wondered. Halftime refreshment was fresh oranges, which were cold and sweet. Oranges then were dispensed in lieu of Gatorade-type electrolyte replacement drinks. The troublemaker in Egan reared up during the otherwise less-than-tense halftime break. "I liked to think I was close to the guys on the bench, so I have no problem getting them in trouble. Just trying to have fun. So I'm standing by Ireland and I say, 'Where the Christ did all of the oranges go?'"[8]

The idea was that the oranges were for players who worked up a sweat and that some of the backups feasted on the oranges. Since the Ramblers were playing a practically perfect game, Ireland had nothing else to yell about, so he seized on the oranges issue.

"Ireland loves the first string and he seems to hate the second string," Egan said, "so he looks at the second-string guys and goes, 'You orange-eating son of a bitches.'" Egan almost collapsed in laughter.[9]

In the second half Loyola just kept stretching the lead to the unbelievable final margin.

"We pulled that one out," Egan said sardonically.[10]

As the lead ballooned, the situation became more and more unreal to the Ramblers. As good as they believed they were, this was the NCAAs and they had zero expectation of winning a game by as wide a margin. "You never go into a game expecting to win by seventy," Chuck Wood said. "We just played. Our guys did not demean the other team. We didn't laugh at them."[11]

Les Hunter said he recalls a newspaper story leading up to the game that came out of Nashville in which Tennessee Tech coach John Oldham dissected how beatable Loyola was. Decades later, Oldham, in his late eighties, retired, and living in Kentucky, laughed when someone asked him to discuss the 111–42 defeat. "Let's not talk about that," Oldham said as he chuckled.[12]

It was difficult to fathom that the game would become such a wipeout, Oldham admitted. "We led 2–0," he said. "Honestly, their press was more than we could handle. I don't think we crossed the ten-second line for nine minutes."[13]

Stealing the ball repeatedly and converting into layups is just about the only way a team can score so quickly that it could run up such a point differential. When talk turned to that 111–42 plurality remaining the standard for the worst NCAA beating, Oldham said, "At least I hold the record."[14]

Before the game Oldham believed his team might have a shot at upsetting Loyola. After the game he admitted the Ramblers were probably the finest team in the land. "Loyola's the best we've seen this year," he said.[15]

Not everyone connected to Loyola realizes the sixty-nine-point difference is still the all-time record. "It is?" said Dan Connaughton. "I knew it was a huge margin. It's just kind of hard to believe any team could be that outmatched."[16]

And Tech was a team that not only had a winning record but also shared a piece of its conference title. It was impossible to imagine Loyola playing a better game. Ron Miller scored twenty-one points, Jerry Harkness scored nineteen, Egan and Rouse added eighteen each, and Hunter scored seventeen.

Ireland even deigned to give the bench guys some playing time, with Connaughton and Wood collecting six points apiece and Reardon and Rochelle also breaking into the scoring column. Still, in a contest decided almost immediately and with record-breaking point differentials compiled, Rochelle, for one, thought Ireland should have shown a bit more mercy in giving additional rest to the starters so as not to so dramatically humiliate Tennessee Tech.

"I wasn't in favor of humbling another team that way," Rochelle said. "It's demoralizing and unnecessary. He [Ireland] wouldn't call the dogs off."[17]

Hunter said that Tech's strategy seemed to be to bring the ball up slowly and pass it around, but that the Ramblers' overpowering defense simply wouldn't allow Oldham's group to do what it wanted to do. "They wanted to slow it down, but they couldn't because they couldn't get the ball up the court," he said. "They just couldn't keep up with our speed."[18]

Blowouts of that magnitude, especially against teams that are league champs, don't come along very often. Harkness said that was probably as close to a perfect forty-minute game as it could get for the Ramblers.

"We couldn't have played a better game, ever," he said. "I don't care who was out there against us. I know they were beaten before we got them because they were intimidated. The coach thought they could get us. I heard that later on. But that day you can look at any other teams in the NCAA, even after that, even UCLA, I don't care. We blitzed them. We hit long shots. We hit everything. Everything was magic that day. We played good defense. We just knew that day that we were very, very good"[19]

Loyola's smashing win advanced the Ramblers into the next round of the tournament. They were scheduled to face 21–5 Mississippi State in East Lansing, Michigan, on March 15. A shell-shocked Oldham was asked what type of advice he could give to the Bulldogs as they prepared to meet Loyola. "Call your worst enemy and ask him to substitute for you," Oldham said while still processing the massacre.[20]

After Loyola handled Tennessee Tech, the Ramblers glanced at the NCAA bracket to determine what team they played next. They knew little about Mississippi State, and it loomed as just another game, another obstacle to be overcome if they wanted to keep playing and reel in a national title.

Bulldogs coach Babe McCarthy was a firsthand witness to Loyola's destruction of Tennessee Tech, and he was impressed. "They're the best fast-break team I've ever seen," McCarthy said. "You can't stop them with any particular defense."[21]

No one playing for Loyola or Mississippi State had any sense that they were about to be part of a historic basketball game with implications that far transcended the court.

Periodically during their two-year journey together, this group of Loyola basketball players stumbled into circumstances not of their own making that very much reflected the tenor of a raging society outside the doors of their locker room. It happened in New Orleans. It happened in Houston. It was about to happen again in Michigan, but if those first two road trips were more private experiences, more contained-within-the-team-huddle experiences, Loyola's game against Mississippi State was something more, something bigger. The headlines were bigger, the stakes much larger. Everything was magnified because this game wasn't just another in a long series on a regular-season schedule, it was in the national spotlight.

The basketball game between Loyola of Chicago and Mississippi State of Starkville, Mississippi, was nominally about which team would keep playing in pursuit of the 1963 NCAA crown, but it was not all about basketball. It was also about whites and blacks and segregation and change knocking down previously bolted doors.

That is, it would be, if the game actually was played as scheduled. There were some serious doubts about that.

CHAPTER 16

IT'S ON, IT'S OFF

A s soon as Loyola eliminated Tennessee Tech, there was doubt about the Ramblers' next game. Not whether or not they could win and continue their NCAA progress, but whether or not there really would be a game.

From the hindsight of a half century in the future it seems to border on insanity that there was any iffiness swirling around the scheduled second-round game against Mississippi State. But the NCAA basketball tournament was minor league at the time compared to the most popular sports in the United States and easy enough to blow off if a school felt it was not to its advantage to compete. The future payoffs, worth six figures per game, were not then part of the equation.

And in Mississippi, treading water in an environment that sometimes seemed little changed from the Civil War era, adherence to the blind principles of segregation could take precedence over logic. It could even override participation in events that indicated Mississippi was actually a member of the United States.

Across the state, segregation was dug in as deeply as the roots of the magnolia tree, something else emblematic of life in Mississippi. Throughout the reign of Kentucky coach Adolph Rupp (1930–1972), the Wildcats were the dominant college basketball program in the Southeastern Conference. However, beginning in 1959, when the Bulldogs won their first title, Mississippi State caught up for a time. The Bulldogs won the league crown that year and again in 1961 and 1962.

Each time, the championship earned Mississippi State the right to compete for a national championship in the NCAA tournament. However, in each of those seasons Mississippi State declined to enter because state government policy ruled that whites and blacks could not mingle on a sporting field.

Still vivid in some people's minds was the occasion during the 1955–56

Jerry Harkness was the captain and leading scorer for the Loyola University NCAA champions of 1962–63. Harkness was voted an All-American that year, and he later had a brief professional career. Courtesy of the Loyola Sports Information Office.

season when the Bulldogs played a game against an integrated University of Denver team in a tournament in Evansville, Indiana, and then–school president Ben Hilbun ordered the team to come home immediately.

So now the NCAA scenario arose again. Mississippi State, 21–5, the 1963 SEC champ, accepted a bid to the NCAA tournament—as had been promised to players previously shut out. And ironically the foe on the schedule was a team laden with African American players. It was not an *if* that the Bulldogs might be forced into playing a team with a black player; it was a certainty that Mississippi State was going to play against a team dominated by black players.

In Mississippi, diehard segregationists began agitating, seeking to prevent the Bulldogs from competing in the tournament game in East Lansing, Michigan. As Loyola players of the era so often say when thinking back to the 1960s, "remember the times."

The times in Mississippi were crude, mean, unfair, and dangerous for African Americans who were denied the right to vote, held back in every possible way professionally, discriminated against in terms of use of public bathrooms and water fountains, and in educational opportunities from the lowest grades of public schools to admission to the best state universities.

In 1962, wearing a suit and tie, James Meredith became the first Afri-

can American to enroll at the University of Mississippi. He had to be accompanied by US Marshals, the National Guard, and US Army troops, six
thousand protectors in Oxford in all. Meredith, who became a lightning-rod
symbol for hopeful blacks and angry whites alike, said that President John F.
Kennedy's inaugural address inspired him to make the new administration
live up to its ideals and enforce civil rights.

"I went there to fight a war to break the system of racial segregation,"
Meredith said.[1]

At that point Meredith had completed two years of college at historically black Jackson State when he decided to transfer to the all-white school.
When Meredith showed up, a riot broke out. Two people died that day, including a French journalist, and many were injured. And all of that was just
to get Meredith in the door. Meredith's stay on campus was no picnic, either,
though he gained acceptance from many students.

As an offshoot to the unrest when Meredith arrived that first day, the US
government imposed a fine of ten thousand dollars on Mississippi Governor
Ross Barnett and tried to jail him for contempt of court. It was felt that Bar-
nett instigated the riot with a speech the night before when he said, "I love
Mississippi! I love her people. Our customs. I love and respect our heritage."
When Barnett spoke in public, usually the podium was decorated with a
Confederate flag.[2]

Barnett fought the charges in court and won on appeal, but his politics
were no secret.

Barnett served as Mississippi's governor from 1960 to 1964 and was a
staunch segregationist. A successful attorney, Barnett claimed that the Bible
decreed segregation. "The Good Lord was the original segregationist," he
said. "He put the black man in Africa. He made us white because he wanted
us white and He intended that we should stay that way."[3]

Barnett planned to be the sword of that implementation, and when the
first Freedom Riders came to Mississippi in 1961 he saw to it that they were
arrested, sent to the state's toughest prison, and treated harshly while incar-
cerated. The Ku Klux Klan roamed the state in its white sheets shielding
identities, burning crosses in front yards, and threatening to lynch any black
person who offended whites.

Given that backdrop, there was no surprise that when the topic of the
Mississippi State basketball team playing against a team densely populated
with black men broke into the news, Barnett refused to sit quietly on the
sidelines.

Soon after Loyola crushed Tennessee Tech, wire services in Mississippi began reporting that the Bulldogs might not compete in the NCAA tournament after all. The word trickled north and Chicago newspapers began coverage of the situation. Coach George Ireland called his team together for a meeting. He said the Ramblers would prepare as usual and would travel to Michigan as planned. Yet, he added, it was possible that there would be no game—Mississippi State might not show up to play. He did not play up the possibility, but most players recall him at least mentioning it.

It didn't sink in at first. To a group of twenty-year-olds in the middle of the greatest basketball run of their lives playing a game they loved, such a notion seemed preposterous, and not truly comprehending the venom and obstacles in Mississippi, they just assumed that it was all talk. "I don't think I was aware before we left for this game that we might be looking at racial implications," said Loyola's Dan Connaughton. "It became a bigger issue when we got up there. 'Are we gonna play?'"[4]

The tension surrounding the situation mounted during the few days between Loyola's victory over Tennessee Tech and the March 15 scheduled game against the Bulldogs, especially after Loyola arrived in Michigan and Mississippi State wasn't there. "It seemed unfathomable to us," Connaughton said. "It was just so foreign to me not to play a team with black players."[5]

Throughout the South numerous cities and states had laws on the books prohibiting such on-court mingling. No race mixing, not even under the guise of a fairly played sporting event. No game? Ron Miller never believed that Loyola might travel to Michigan not to play and would advance in the tournament by forfeit. "I never even thought about it," he said.[6]

Chuck Wood remembers Ireland giving the Ramblers the lowdown on what was going on in Mississippi and said he had trouble assimilating the information. "Ireland said, 'There's a possibility we might travel and not have a game,'" Wood said. "I thought, 'That can't be happening. A state would stop a team from playing? A governor would stop them?'"[7]

Even though the Loyola players had sampled discrimination, segregation, and even hatred on road trips to New Orleans and Houston, those were transitory experiences. Most of them—with the exception of Les Hunter and Vic Rouse, from Nashville—had been born in and grown up in the North. To them the doings in Mississippi might be something you read about in the national news section of *Time* magazine or saw in film clips on the evening news. To them Mississippi might as well have been South Africa—and for the African Americans who lived there, it pretty much was.

Much to Wood's and the other players' disbelief, a governor and a state government *would* interfere with one of its state university basketball teams competing if that meant taking the floor against black players.

Decades later, Jerry Harkness's son Jerald Harkness spearheaded production of a documentary entitled *Game of Change*, which focused on that single contest between Loyola and Mississippi State, the fears and controversy that roiled the Magnolia State. The film deftly illustrated the amount of courage it took for the Bulldogs to defy their own local government.

Although he nominally had nothing to do with the basketball program, a key individual in the drama as it played out and in determining that Mississippi State would show up to compete was the school's president, D. W. Colvard, Hilbun's successor. The easy path for Colvard would have been to duck the entire matter and stay nonaligned. But he had seen the flames and the violence consume Ole Miss in 1962 when Meredith showed up and he did not want his school consumed by similar hatred. He also believed he could not shirk a responsibility he powerfully felt in order to become an agent of change. "Somehow I found myself not running away from the potential race problem," Colvard said. "It's a major issue of our time."[8]

Until Babe McCarthy, a former Standard Oil employee, showed up in Starkville as the head men's basketball coach in 1955, these types of complications were not an issue at all because Mississippi State wasn't good enough to qualify for the NCAA tournament.

That began to change in the 1958–59 season when the Bulldogs swept to the Southeastern Conference title with a 24–1 record. In the late 1950s, the team was blessed with its greatest player of all time, a forward named Bailey Howell, who would later star for the Detroit Pistons and Boston Celtics in the NBA and be enshrined in the Basketball Hall of Fame. Years later Howell said that his all-white teams lamented being unable to play for national honors because the Bulldogs would have faced black players on the court. They never got to test themselves against the best.

"We were victims," Howell said. The law, he added, denied people opportunities.[9]

And after winning a third straight SEC crown it was going to happen again to the next generation of Mississippi State players, including the so-talented Leland Mitchell, Joe Dan Gold, Red Stroud, Howard Hemphill, and Bobby Shows. Ironically, in a skewed way, they were being punished for being white. Much like Loyola's group, most of them had come up together, recruited by McCarthy, meshed together, and molded into a unit that as the freshman team was also better than the varsity.

Some Mississippi State players may have been backwoods boys, but it wasn't as if they were unaware that African Americans could also make for good ballplayers. "Most of us boys had played with blacks in our backyards," Shows said. "That was no issue for us."[10]

Some fifty years after Mississippi earned the reputation of being one of the worst states in the union for race relations, Shows said, "I'm embarrassed reliving Mississippi's history."[11]

Gold had actually traveled to watch Kentucky (which got to go after the Bulldogs turned down their chance) face Iowa State in an NCAA game the preceding year and soaked up the atmosphere. "So this is what we're missing," he thought.[12]

McCarthy had had enough, too. In a team meeting during the season he informed the Bulldogs that if there was any way possible for the club to compete in the NCAAs he would make sure it happened. Then he went public, and a local newspaper offered the headline, "Babe Wants Playoff Spot." No one could say that Mississippi's higher-ups hadn't been warned by the weather report of a potential storm.

By all accounts, McCarthy, who died from cancer in 1975, was an astute coach. His record at Mississippi State was 169–85, and three times he was the SEC Coach of the Year. He was also a two-time American Basketball Association Coach of the Year during his professional tenure with the New Orleans Buccaneers, Memphis Pros, Dallas Chaparrals, and Kentucky Colonels. As a man he was regarded as principled and witty, with a clever sense of humor.

On the broader stage McCarthy was better known as a professional coach by the time he passed away at age fifty-one on March 18, 1975, close to the twelfth anniversary date of the game against Loyola. His nickname was "Old Magnolia Mouth."

Larry Brown, then a player but later a famed coach, said he loved McCarthy but tired of being called a "pissant" because he was a small guard. Not that Brown should have taken the description too personally; McCarthy used it all the time.

Steve Jones, one of McCarthy's former ABA players, recalled some of his old coach's vintage sayings in the locker room in the book *Loose Balls*, an account of the upstart league's heyday. "In the dressing room, he was hilarious," Jones said. "He'd say, 'Tonight we've got to get after them like a biting sow.' I'd be sitting there, biting my lip so I didn't laugh. Another of his favorite expressions was, 'We're gonna cloud up and rain all over them.'"[13]

Those who knew McCarthy best thought he enjoyed coaching college ball more than the pros because the younger men listened to him when he spoke and the pros just seemed to be counting their money.

At Mississippi State, McCarthy created winners, but he was best remembered for the role he played in making sure the Bulldogs played in the 1963 NCAA championships. There was plenty of room for heroes and villains in the days leading up to the scheduled game against Loyola and both emerged in the drama.

As Colvard mulled over the circumstances, some three hundred students gathered peacefully on the front lawn of his home, signaling a rising interest in the issue on campus. On March 6, Colvard affirmed his belief publicly that the Bulldogs should play and notified McCarthy.

However, Colvard believed his job was on the line over this matter, of particular concern since he and his wife had three children. But he also believed that he must do the right thing, even in the face of other government officials' growing opposition and public threats that poured into his office. Colvard worried about his daughters' safety and the threat by state senators to cut his school's budget.

Governor Barnett chimed in, saying that he believed Mississippi State should not play because it was not in the best interests of the school or the state "or either of the races."

George Ireland offered an irritated comeback for that comment. "How asinine can you get?" he said.[14]

Colvard, who later said "it was a tense period," actually considered resigning the presidency of Mississippi State over the issue. He was buoyed by pockets of support, including letters praising him and a Jackson, Mississippi, TV station's poll that showed a remarkable 85 percent of those asked felt the Bulldogs should play. Then State students marched to his home in support of the decision.

A critical moment came when the State College Board overseeing the university system voted 8–3 in favor of the Bulldogs traveling to Michigan for the game and gave Colvard a 9–2 vote of confidence. One board member introduced a resolution calling on the board to fire Colvard, but it did not come to a vote because there was no second to his motion. Outside of the meeting in the state capital of Jackson, four white students picketing were run off by police officers. Their placards read, "Don't discriminate against whites. Let State play."

While favorable in sentiment, the board's votes did not end the dispute. Word reached Colvard that other government officials were preparing a request for a court injunction that would prevent the players from leaving the state and that the paperwork was headed to the county sheriff for serving.

As game day approached, Colvard, McCarthy, and his assistants hatched a plan to evade any type of injunction that would ground the team. McCarthy was snacking at a hamburger place when he was picked up, driven across town as he hunched down, hiding, in the backseat, and spirited away to Nashville. Colvard informed his wife he was going "to disappear for a while" and didn't even tell her where he was going to avoid being served. His escape-hatch city was Birmingham, Alabama.

The sneak-out-of-town-under-cover-of-darkness tale occasionally gets a little murky because of contingency plans that were later revealed. Accompanied by trainer Dutch Luchsinger, the players departed on a plane from Starkville. Originally, only the backups were scheduled to go on that flight, with the starters driving out of state. Then the two team factions would get back together in another state before traveling to East Lansing. At the last minute, when the coast was clear and no one waited at the airport to stop them, all of the players boarded the single plane for Michigan. Mississippi State captain Joe Dan Gold said, "We kind of cheered when the plane took off."[15]

All of the Bulldogs aboard were relieved.

"That was the first time we really knew we were going," Shows said.[16]

A number of stories made the rounds about Mississippi State's travels, and several Chicago sportswriters referred to the secretive nature of the Bulldogs' embarkation to the tournament as "a cloak-and-dagger junket."[17]

It was wise to take precautions. An injunction *was* prepared and law enforcement officials sought to deliver it at Colvard's house, but it was too late. He could not be found and neither could McCarthy or the players. Mississippi State's all-white basketball team was on its way to Michigan to face a team with a lineup dominated by African Americans.

The details of these goings-on were not immediately revealed to or on the minds of Loyola players, who were just focused on playing basketball and for the most part fully expected Mississippi State to be present and accounted for when it was time for the opening tip. They possessed little knowledge about what the opposing players might be going through just to take the court, and they would not likely have had much sympathy for the troubles of white players at the time.

In retrospect, however, Loyola players grew reflective. "It was a sign of change that it [the game] did take place," Rich Rochelle said. "They [the white players] had been denied before. We didn't know each other. For us every white in Mississippi was a racist and you had to watch your back."[18]

As Harkness said, when he thought of the word *Mississippi* the only thing that came to mind was racism. He was certainly not alone among black people harboring that perception. Good cause had been provided.

Hunter, who grew up in segregated Tennessee, was shocked when a sportswriter from Nashville interviewed him. That's when he figured this game must be something special. "'Boy,'" he said, "'this must be big.' Because prior to that they didn't talk about blacks in the newspaper down there. They sent a man to talk to me and Vic Rouse about that game. I knew it was a big deal then."[19]

Only a few years earlier Hunter had followed the news about the integration of public schools in Little Rock, Arkansas, and the violence that accompanied it. To him Arkansas and Mississippi were the same, equally racist, and that led him to believe Mississippi State just might not show up for the game. "Well, I know they're probably not coming if it's Mississippi," was what Hunter concluded.[20]

Stories about Mississippi State possibly skipping the NCAA tournament game were sent out nationally on the Associated Press and United Press International wire services. That resulted in more awareness about Loyola using four African American players in its starting lineup and in more hate mail being directed to the players' dorms and to Ireland. Many of the incoming letters were vile, and Ireland took steps to intercept letters to players before they reached their mailboxes.

Ireland had been dealing with such cranks for much of the season. He got more nasty phone calls and hate mail the more prominent Loyola became. Once, he said, he got a letter asking "if I wanted my daughter Kathy, who was a cheerleader then, to come home with a black baby. And when people called I killed them with politeness. I'd listen to them and when they'd take a breath I'd thank them for calling and hang up." Another time he heard from someone present that when one such caller hung up the pay phone in a saloon, he threw his drink and broke the mirror behind the bar.[21]

Ireland informed the Ramblers what the mail was bringing, but for the most part he shielded them from it. The players knew it was out there, but only a small percentage of it came directly into the hands of players. Jerry Harkness said "one or two got through."

Summarizing the content years later Harkness said the topics were fairly limited in range. "The 'N' word and all that was there," he said. "People wrote, 'Don't play in this game.'" Yes, they were suggesting Loyola be the team that stayed home. "'Who do you think you are?' That kind of stuff. 'You're not supposed to be playing with white people,' and all that. 'The world is not supposed to be this way.'

"That sort of sucked," Harkness added. "We started to feel it now, where before it didn't play a part, but now it was part of your makeup and you knew how important a game was against a Loyola of New Orleans and those other games. You played hard, but now it [racism] was right out front."[22]

Even if they never saw the letters, the players knew they were out there, that they had become the objects of someone's scorn and hatred. "The dorm was intercepting letters," said Chuck Wood. "I never saw one of them. We heard there were threats from the Ku Klux Klan."[23]

A simple basketball game was turned into a cause, but it was also seized upon as a symbol by the other side, too. "The black community told us, 'You better not lose,'" Harkness said.[24]

Whether because it was part of the overall historical record or because it was part of his own historical record, whether it reminded him of a controversial bygone era when he was on the right side or for other reasons, Ireland always kept the hate mail, the letters and postcards, in a box in his Skokie, Illinois, home in the Chicago suburbs.

Once in a great while he would pull them out, either to remember or to share (though only very briefly and only with a limited number). Maybe he kept them because as time went on it became more and more unbelievable that such a thing happened, that just because a team had black players on it, it was vilified by the ignorant and small-minded. Who would believe American society was in such a place?

CHAPTER 17

SHOWDOWN WITH
MISSISSIPPI STATE

The moment it struck home for the Loyola basketball players that their confrontation with Mississippi State in this NCAA game might be more than a game came moments prior to the opening tip on the evening of March 15, 1963, at Jenison Fieldhouse.

Everyone talks about the flashbulbs, the bright lights from spectators' cameras illuminating the Michigan State arena as fans snapped pictures for what ordinarily is a routine, fairly dull ritual: the captains of the opposing teams shaking hands at center court.

By then, anyone who was paying attention to the matchup knew a certain number of particulars. Mississippi State's roster was filled with all white players. Loyola started four black players. The Bulldogs had to sneak out of town to evade the clutches of government officials who didn't even want them to show up for this game in order to preserve an outmoded, nasty way of life built around separation of the races that was disintegrating around them.

Sometimes, with all of the off-court stuff going on, it was good when someone reminded the participants and observers that a basketball game was scheduled. It was a big basketball game, too, with national implications, and at stake was the ability to continue competing for an NCAA crown.

"It sounds crazy," Loyola guard Ron Miller said, recalling the outside issues. "I remember hearing the stories about them sneaking out [of Mississippi]. That has always fascinated me. It was clearly an amazing thing. It was just a ball game."[1]

The event finally became just a ball game after that handshake between Loyola's Jerry Harkness and Mississippi State's Joe Dan Gold ignited what seemed to be enough brightness to power television sets throughout the Midwest.

Frank Perez was part of the New York connection, one of the players steered by amateur coach Walter November to Loyola's George Ireland so he could escape the city and get an education while playing college ball. Courtesy of the Loyola Sports Information Office.

Jerry Harkness (left) and Ron Miller, in December of 2012, point to a newspaper story heralding their return to Chicago for a special game between their alma mater, Loyola, and Mississippi State, fifty years after the so-called Game of Change. Courtesy of Paul Smulson.

Harkness was aware that black residents of Chicago considered this game as much crusade as sporting endeavor. During the course of the last two seasons the Ramblers had become representatives of more than just Loyola. They made fans in the black community at large in Chicago. If white basketball fans could hold their skin color against them, then they could also be embraced because of their skin color, just as when they had been when parceled out to private homes in New Orleans. The "you guys gotta win this" faction grew louder the nearer to Loyola's departure for Michigan. "We didn't realize the significance of the thing. We got that 'you have to win this' message. 'This is more than a game. You've got to win this.'"[2]

Although Harkness was either unaware of it or wasn't thinking about it, many of those vociferous communiqués to Loyola from the South Side of Chicago came from African Americans who had been part of the Great Migration north for work in the preceding decades, blacks who had abandoned the hostility of Mississippi for a new life in Chicago. No wonder they felt connected to the Ramblers: "You've got to win this." Mississippi State represented the bad old days for them.

Game time. Harkness walked to midcourt to represent the Ramblers. Gold walked to midcourt to represent the Bulldogs.

"There were so many lightbulbs, pop, pop, pop," Harkness recalled. "I was a little bit shocked. Yes, this is more than a game. We had just won big over Tennessee Tech and I was confident, but somehow I knew we were not going to win big this time. It kind of reminded me of the Houston game all of a sudden, with all of that pressure and all of the people yelling things. I wanted to play well. I knew mentally that this was more than a game, this was about life."[3]

Loyola, which had been swapping positions in the top five of the national rankings all year, hovering around number two or number three most of the time, was considered the favorite with its 25–2 record. Mississippi State, also a top ten team, was 21–5 and the vanquisher, once again, of mighty Kentucky, winning its fourth Southeastern Conference title. When the final Associated Press and United Press International polls were released before the tournament, Loyola was number three in both. Mississippi State was number six in the AP rankings and number seven in the UPI poll.

There was a sort of breathless approach to the game because of the flap with government officials in Mississippi, and many wondered if the game would really proceed as scheduled. The more details leaked out about Mississippi State's team efforts to escape from its home state and dodge the authorities, the more admiration grew for the Bulldogs' character.

"It was this very idea of this team, these white guys who wanted to run away from their own state and their own state troopers and sneak out of the state to go play a predominantly black team," Chicago journalist Bill Jauss said. "I mean, that was revolutionary at the time. There wasn't a redneck on that team, and when they went out to shake hands at the start for the center jump—and this of course is just my perception—they looked one another in the eye and there was respect on both sides."[4]

When Ireland shrewdly drummed up support for the game as Mississippi churned, he pretty much stuck to basketball, with only a periodic swerve into the civil rights lane.

"Babe McCarthy, the Mississippi State coach, is a wonderful man," Ireland said, "and since his kids won the Southeastern Conference championship I feel they have a right to go to the NCAA no matter what the segregationists say. They may be the best in the country and if they are they have a right to prove it."[5]

This was one occasion involving a basketball game when there was a court and there was court. The sport was going to be played out on a court housed in an arena. For it to take place, the Mississippi State basketball team had to elude the reach of its state court. Two days before the game the Mississippi State Supreme Court granted a temporary injunction at the behest of state senators to stop the Bulldogs from playing. A day later, after the players and coaches made a clean getaway from the state, the court rescinded the restraining order. At the least, even if many were unhappy, that prevented the Bulldogs' game against Loyola from being declared illegal in Mississippi.

Right up until almost game time, forces massed against the Bulldogs' participation. The *Jackson Daily News* editorialized against Mississippi State playing Loyola and ran a picture of the Loyola starters, with its four black members, to emphasize its point. The photograph ran five columns wide in the newspaper and was accompanied by commentary urging readers to clip it out and send to "the board of trustees of the institutions of higher learning." Although the newspaper was published a thousand miles away, details of its contents made their way to the Loyola players.

Speaking to reporters, Harkness said of the campaign, "I expected that. I'm getting a little immune to it. They called us names when we played in Houston, called Jack Egan names, too. The players are alright, believe me [only fans derided them, he added]. Sure, I think the players want to play us. If they don't, they'll never know how good they are."[6]

That was a sharp-edged comment from Harkness, more powerful because of the truth of it. Most people did seem to know how good Loyola was. The Ramblers had become a national measuring standard. March 14, after the Mississippi State team arrived, Ireland and Bulldogs coach Babe McCarthy held a press conference. They implored fans to view their game simply as a basketball contest and not as either a Supreme Court case on race relations or a renewal of the Civil War.

A *Chicago Daily News* story by reporter Jauss said that before leaving Chicago, Les Hunter and Harkness had received "fan mail" from the Ku Klux Klan that in part urged the black Loyola players to "bring along their shoeshine kits" and "come down here and pick cotton."[7]

Point guard Egan said Ireland let the players know the tone of the mail crossing his desk. "His position was, 'I'm getting all this damned hate mail,'" Egan recalled. "He didn't have to say too much about it because we knew what the hate mail was about. He'd say, 'You guys aren't seeing half the stuff I see. These are morons out there.' The moral was that we couldn't react to any of that stuff because we were above it. Just go down there and kick their asses."[8]

While the political landscape roiled in Mississippi, the Ramblers acted maturely in public and sought to remain removed from the controversy. "There'll be no problem," Ireland said prior to the game. "The players are always fine, wherever we go, North or South. It's the fans who cause trouble and I'm sure they don't have that type of fan in East Lansing."[9]

When Ireland said he didn't foresee any problems, he was talking about issues in the grandstands, not on the court. He recognized that Mississippi State was a good team and could present some difficulties for the Ramblers. He knew very well that the Bulldogs would not be a sixty-nine-point pushover as Tennessee Tech turned out to be. "To become champion of the Southeastern Conference, Mississippi State had to be very good," Ireland said, "and they won't be as soft a touch as Tennessee Tech."[10]

Despite the exhausting preamble swirling around the will-they-or-will-they-not-come issue, there was no indication Mississippi State thought it couldn't beat Loyola. The Bulldogs were weaned on a steady diet of tough SEC schools, so they felt they were playing top teams all of the time. Loyola didn't have the pedigree of a Kentucky, so what was there to fear?

Once present in the Michigan gym, Bulldogs players were heartened to hear another school's band playing their fight song as a gesture of generosity so they wouldn't feel so alone. They knew it wasn't their band, left behind in Mississippi, and the players never discovered which school's musicians performed on their behalf.

After the flashbulbs ceased exploding in the players' faces and the teams lined up for the center jump, basketball followed. It was not the basketball that the Ramblers envisioned playing, either. Respectful of Loyola's explosiveness and speed, Mississippi State set out to do what many other foes tried—put the brakes on the running game.

In the beginning, the Bulldogs were successful, using a half-court patterned offense to take a 7–0 lead. The Bulldogs relied on a careful, well-thought-out offense that took time off the clock by making numerous passes before a shot rose up. Unlike so many other teams that Loyola faced during the 1962–63 season, Mississippi State was good enough to stick to its preferred tempo.

"They slowed it down," Harkness said. "We kind of adjusted to their pattern and the rest is history. It was a well-played game, a good game, not a high-scoring game. Not many mistakes. We had to play their way, which we hated, but we did that."[11]

Backup Dan Connaughton, who was never put in the game by Ireland, said Loyola did not play at its peak when the game began. "There was a lot of obvious nervousness," Connaughton said. "The guys were just a little bit off. I don't think we remotely played one of our better games."[12]

Despite falling behind early, Loyola regrouped quickly and led 26–19 at the half. For a team used to flirting with one hundred points in a game, that was low-scoring indeed, but the Ramblers were still on the right side of the score.

While Loyola's first NCAA game was played in Evanston, this second-round game against Mississippi State was just far enough away from campus to make it a challenge for students to attend if they didn't own their own cars. That was a rarer on-campus luxury then than it is now. Not even members of the freshman team were able to tag along in an official bus. If those players wanted to see the Loyola–Mississippi State game they had to make their own way the 220 miles north and find tickets on their own, too.

One freshman player who did so, and got to East Lansing the hard way, was Frank Perez. Joined by "civilian" friends, non-basketball-playing acquaintances, Perez and other freshmen hitchhiked to Michigan. When they got there, accommodations were at a premium, as well. "I had to sleep in a bathtub," Perez said.[13]

He didn't even hang out with the varsity players, who had an assignment on their plate, but did bump into Les Hunter and was able to wish some of the Ramblers good luck. Years later Perez couldn't remember how he got into the arena without buying a ticket, but he was sure his group formulated some scheme to sneak past the ushers and watch the game. As soon as it ended, however, he and his friends rushed back to Chicago.

"I was only at one game," Perez said. "I had to get back to school."[14]

Being absent without leave from class may be more understandable in the 2000s if a school is advancing through NCAA play, but there were no free passes for skipping school in 1963.

There was no free pass against Mississippi State, either. The Bulldogs played solid defense and prevented the Ramblers from running wild on them. Despite all of the tension leading up to the contest, as Ireland had predicted, there was not a hint of animosity between the players on either side. It was a hard-fought but clean game.

"The common bond is athletics," said Bulldogs guard Doug Hutton. "We were just out there competing."[15] White and black together. White and black against one another.

Jauss, who covered the game for the *Chicago Daily News*, said the "play was fierce and strong and clean and it was just ten guys going at it like ten buddies. It may not have been recognized as quite so important a game at the time as it's been magnified to be in time, but we recognized the impact of it, certainly."[16]

On this day Loyola was ten points better, winning 61–51 to advance and play another day in the NCAA tournament. Mississippi State had to go home and deal with the fallout from its commitment to play and try to win a national championship. To the Bulldogs' surprise, there was none, really. A long road to equality lay ahead, with some demoralizing setbacks, including the infamous murder of civil rights workers in Philadelphia, Mississippi, in 1964, but the path to desegregation was laid and would be followed. "It was a loss, but it was a victory," said Bulldogs player Bobby Shows.[17]

Harkness, who was so concerned about the atmosphere affecting his play, was the leading scorer with twenty points. Vic Rouse, the rugged forward who never let any situation faze him, scored sixteen. Les Hunter added twelve points and Ron Miller eleven. Egan scored just two points. The only other Rambler Ireland played was Chuck Wood, who did not score.

"There wasn't a peep either way," Wood said, dispelling any thought of the type of trash talking between players that became more common in sporting events a generation into the future. "If someone got knocked down, the other team put out a hand to help them up. Those guys couldn't have been nicer."[18]

That was just the natural personalities of the players on both teams, white or black, Shows said.

"There was no animosity between us," Shows said.[19]

Maybe that's what all of the naysayers feared—that once white and black players got together they would discover there weren't many, if any, differences between them, and they might want to do it again and again. "They say athletics can break down barriers and that game did," Wood said. "That game had social implications on the South and the state of Mississippi. In talking with the guys from Mississippi State, they said it was all ridiculous. Everyone's attitude that night was 'Bring 'em on, black, green, white, polka dot.'"[20]

All ills were not cured overnight. The South was not a Disney movie. But as each year passed more African American students enrolled at Mississippi State and it became an everyday thing. African American basketball players enrolled at Mississippi State, too, and as time passed they became more than curiosities and instead mainstays of the team.

The segregationists, above all, those who wanted to maintain the status quo, those who wanted to keep the white basketball team locked within the confines of the state's borders, learned that when the dike springs a leak, a flood follows. You can't put the genie back in the bottle or the toothpaste back in the tube. The adults in supervisory positions in Mississippi grasped that, of course. That's why they fought so hard to prevent the game. Mississippi State basketball players just wanted to be part of the NCAA tournament and play against whatever team came up on the schedule. Ditto Loyola.

"All those guys from Mississippi State didn't know the impact they made," Wood said. "We all thought it was just a game then, but it was more than that."[21]

For players like Harkness and Hunter (keenly aware of the hate mail that came into Loyola and Ireland) as well as Rouse, there was a very deep-seated hunger to defeat the Bulldogs. Hunter and Rouse were from Tennessee, and except for the drawing of a state border, that meant they were from a place not so different. They wanted this win badly, for their own pride and their own NCAA achievement, but also because of the racist face that Mississippi showed to the United States.

"It meant a lot to me to win that game," Hunter said, "especially to me and Vic. I don't know whether it had as much significance for Ron and Jerry, but for me and Vic it was everything. We had both played ball in the South and knew what happened, knew what was at stake. That game probably took on more of a racial aspect to us than any other game."[22]

Hunter absolutely wanted to prove a point about African American ballplayers' talents compared to white players as the eyes of the nation focused on the game. What was unexpected, what caught Hunter a bit by surprise, was the personality of the Bulldogs team, the attitudes of the white players. "Those guys were just perfect gentlemen," he said, "the nicest guys."[23]

The funny thing was, in an appropriate mirror comment, right after the game, Bulldogs captain Joe Dan Gold said exactly the same thing about the Ramblers. "They were perfect gentlemen—just like any other team," he said.[24]

It was a simple statement that in later times would probably be shrugged off as a cliché, but in this context what Gold said was meaningful. It was also telling that he added the phrase "just like any other team."

As he had done since the start of the brouhaha leading up to the contest, Mississippi State coach Babe McCarthy chose to focus on basketball in his postgame remarks.

"Let's talk about the way they played basketball, not their color," McCarthy said. "They're one of the greatest teams in the country and they beat us even though we played a pretty good game. We'd have to be near-perfect to beat Loyola."[25]

Given the intensity of the emotions spilling over from the people in Mississippi, some fans and sportswriters were on the lookout to see if the game might degenerate into a particularly rough one. That didn't happen, either. The total number of fouls whistled during the forty minutes was thirty-one. That was a routine number. While it was a grind-it-out game, there was nothing extreme about the physicality of the event. Everyone said Loyola's rebounding strength was a decisive aspect of the game.

"There was no punching, shoving, or bickering out there to show that they have boys as good as we do," Ireland said. "Babe wouldn't allow his boys to do it any more than I would."[26]

No one was pleased more by the milestone victory than Loyola's six-foot-seven forward Vic Rouse. The win came on his twentieth birthday. "I didn't think it would be too nice of a birthday gift to lose," Rouse said.[27]

Rouse admitted to what few players do, though it was easier to do so after a triumph. Yes, he said, he was tight, nervous for the start of this big game, and the Bulldogs' very methodical approach did keep Loyola out of its preferred high-speed style. But Rouse and his teammates adjusted and pulled away. Rouse shot 6-for-11 from the field, all of them big baskets in the ten-point win.

"It was one of my biggest games," Rouse said at the time, "in that it was one we had to win. It was one we couldn't lose—for the tournament's sake, for Loyola's sake, and for me. We had to beat those guys. The players themselves had nothing to do with my feelings.

"As for playing against white ballplayers, we didn't even think of that. There was no malice involved, as far as we were concerned. It was just the idea behind it. This was Mississippi State and so many things have happened to colored people in that state."[28]

The Ramblers were spoiling for a rematch with Bowling Green in the next round, but the Falcons were bested by Illinois. In those days a third-place game was still played in each region, and Mississippi State topped Bowling Green. Bowling Green was another school with three African Americans in its lineup.

Chicago American columnist Bill Gleason, a legendary figure in Chicago journalism, was a witness at the tournament. He instantly comprehended the significance of Mississippi State's involvement and mingling with such black-populated teams as Loyola and Bowling Green with the most eventful consequences being tightly played basketball games.

"I am convinced this tournament played on the campus of Michigan State University in East Lansing is the most important thing that has happened in American sports since Jackie Robinson came into Major League Baseball," Gleason wrote.[29]

Far-thinking in his analysis, Gleason said the Bulldogs showed courage in playing and that by doing so they would eventually lead to the integration of basketball in the Southeastern Conference. "The day when Negro boys will play on teams in that conference is closer than Governor Ross Barnett may think. Tremendous progress was made in only 24 hours."[30]

Gleason was right, and he probably didn't even know about the reception the team received when it returned to Starkville and the school. Thousands of people came out to cheer for the team and welcome it home. The Bulldogs received such rousing support, with fans lining the streets from the airport to campus, that it seemed like a victory celebration, as if they had won the NCAA title, not merely played two games in the tournament.

"The KKK boys were a nasty, ugly minority," said player Bobby Shows. "Most people weren't like that. And even though we lost we came home as winners. All of us did."[31]

In the big picture of the civil rights movement at the time, the game was overshadowed by protest marches in the streets, by snarling sheriffs clubbing innocent people, by Dr. Martin Luther King, Jr., in Washington, DC, speaking of having a dream. But later, as historians brought their ink to the story, the significance of a simple basketball game took on special meaning and was acknowledged as a milestone event in a grand fight for right.

A commemorative ball from Loyola's 1963 NCAA men's basketball championship in Louisville, Kentucky. Courtesy of Paul Smulson.

CHAPTER 18

THE LIGHTS GROW BRIGHTER

If all Loyola did was best Mississippi State it would have been significant, an important contribution to desegregation through sport. But it also would have been anticlimactic if the Ramblers promptly went out and lost the next game. That would have been especially galling considering the next opponent.

There is little time to revel in victory, no matter how big it is, in the middle of a tournament, and the Ramblers had a quick turnaround game looming against the University of Illinois, the Big Ten champions from downstate. The Illini eliminated Bowling Green and eliminated the desired rematch.

If it had been a typical Saturday night during the middle of winter, in the featured game of a doubleheader at Chicago Stadium, a Loyola–Illinois confrontation would have been a big deal. Now it was a bigger deal, on a neutral court in Michigan, but almost incidental to the real goal of capturing the NCAA crown. For Loyola, in-state supremacy was nice but mostly irrelevant. As much as they could be, the Illini represented just another opponent in the way. As Dr. Martin Luther King, Jr., said about the long-term pursuit of civil rights in America, it could be said of Loyola in the NCAA tournament: Eyes on the prize.

However, the Chicago newspapers did give the game the appropriate attention. Headlines on stories about the game appeared in skyscraper-sized type, such as "Illinois–Loyola Showdown in Mideast Cage Final!" And yes, that was complete with an exclamation point, a punctuation mark almost never used in headlines.

Loyola may have been higher ranked than Illinois, but in public perception Illinois was the big school, with the bigger reputation. "I remember going to the game and everyone expected them to win because they were Illinois University," said Ron Miller. "It never crossed my mind that we could lose, but I remember thinking it could be a tough game."[1]

The Illini were 20–5 and league titlists. They also liked to run more than some of Loyola's other foes, though not as much as the Ramblers did, who believed in the style as a way of life.

"We truly respected them," Rich Rochelle said. "They were a good basketball team. But when we looked at them on paper we felt we had a distinct advantage."[2]

Although Illinois had plenty of height, including six-foot-eleven center Skip Thoren, the Ramblers feared no one on the boards because of Les Hunter and Vic Rouse. The advantage, though, came from team speed. Unless a team suited up five Jesse Owenses, Loyola was going to be faster.

In the end, speed killed, as it often does in sports. It was a day when Jerry Harkness really showed why he was a first-team All-American. Harkness was not a drop-dead accurate outside shooter, but usually got his twenty points a game on midrange jumpers and after slithering past defenders to gain access to the hoop. But Illinois had no one capable of covering the six-foot-three Harkness at all, so this became his night. Harkness pumped in thirty-three points and it seemed like a million.

"I was never a guy who got a real lot of points in a game," Harkness said. "I wasn't greedy. It was easy to get twenty points for me. I could hit a couple of jump shots, hit a couple of breakaways, and make six or seven foul shots."[3]

It was a glum night for Illinois fans. If they hoped to deflate Loyola's balloon and demonstrate who was boss in the state, the Illini failed miserably. Loyola won handily, 79–64, after leading by twenty points with nine minutes left. Hunter, whose nickname was "Big Game" for his tendency to come through when needed most, had a big game with twelve points and fifteen rebounds.

The win advanced Loyola to the Final Four, beginning March 22. The Ramblers were one of only four teams remaining in the hunt for the national crown.

For Hunter, the victory was just another step along the way to a championship, an accomplishment he had quietly predicted was within Loyola's grasp after the Ramblers began the season 20–0. At the time, Hunter's girlfriend (and later his wife) was still living in Nashville, and he wrote her a letter informing her that the Ramblers were going to win the national title. "I actually sensed that we would win it all during the regular season," Hunter said later.[4]

Perhaps because there had been some critics early on in the season who suggested Loyola didn't play defense, George Ireland stressed how superb the Ramblers' defense was in this game. "We played man-to-man tonight," he said after the Illinois thumping, "because it makes us more aggressive and is an equalizing factor. I think boarding was the big factor. Illinois is explosive, but I think we defensed them well."[5]

Miller scored fifteen points and Johnny Egan added thirteen. Rouse had nineteen rebounds. Except for a brief appearance by Chuck Wood, Ireland stuck with his starters for the entire forty minutes.

By this point in the season, Loyola's bandwagon was so large that it was tough to obtain tickets for the ride. It was more important that Loyola win than beat Illinois, but since they came as a package deal it was delectable. If only the coaches, the players, and a coterie of fans were enamored of Loyola at the beginning of the season, there was evidence that all of Chicago was caught up in the Sheridan Road excitement now. One way to measure such interest was how the local newspapers covered the phenomenon. The size of headline type grew on each subsequent game story. Also, the *Chicago American* wrote a feature story on Ireland's family.

In 1963 a sports figure had to be doing something pretty special for writers to express interest in his home life. Ireland was married to Gertrude and they had three children, one boy, Mike, and two girls, Judy and Kathy. Mike was already twenty-five and Judy twenty-four. Only Kathy was young enough to live at home. Over the years, the kids attended home games. In March of that year, however, Mike was in Atlanta on a job-training assignment. Until that point, though, Mike Ireland had been an official scorer at Loyola games. Judy, a Loyola nursing school graduate, was living in California with her doctor husband. Before her move she attended the games and sat with the family behind the Loyola bench.

Judy Van Dyck was both a frantic and frenzied Loyola fan that March. Until she moved West she was a loud supporter, got to know the players, and was a rabid rooter for her dad's club. She was a self-described gym rat who loved the game. Between computer access and twenty-four-hour sports television on cable, it is easy to keep up with the accomplishments of just about any team in the country now. Not so in 1963. Whenever Loyola played during the regular season, Van Dyck had to go through considerable gyrations in Northern California to find out the final score. She developed the habit of telephoning the sports department of the closest major newspaper to her home and requesting that someone scour the wires for Loyola results.

"I got to know all the guys at the *San Jose Mercury*," she said.[6]

When she still lived at home it was easy to tell how Loyola had fared when Ireland returned from a road trip. He was very quiet. "We knew if he lost," Van Dyck said.[7]

During Loyola's glorious March of 1963, she talked to her father on the telephone often. He expressed amazement that there were people in the world who would write the kind of hate mail he received about his black players. "He would say, 'The world's crazy,'" she said. "He would say, 'Why would anyone do that?'"[8]

Dealing with a newborn at home and a news blackout on game nights, Judy Van Dyck burned up those telephone lines that month trying to keep up with Loyola. It was not clear how fast one piece of news traveled that Loyola wanted capped. After the Ramblers beat Illinois, Egan went out drinking and got nabbed by the police. Ireland was furious. The Ramblers had come too far to jeopardize their chances and Ireland didn't have the personnel to bench Egan as punishment, so he resorted to the silent treatment. He did not speak to his point guard at all until after the season ended. They communicated through assistant coach Jerry Lyne.

One by one the opponents fell. One by one the contenders in the other brackets fell. The last four teams standing in the NCAAs were Cincinnati, Loyola, Oregon State, and Duke, the Ramblers' next opponent. They were in the Final Four, headed to Louisville's Freedom Hall (somehow the name of the stadium seemed apt) to play in the national semifinals.

On paper, Duke was quite formidable. This was the Blue Devils long before the tenure of Mike Krzyzewski. The coach was Vic Bubas, who led Duke to its first real moments of glory on the national stage. Duke was ranked number two in the final wire service polls, and the Blue Devils' strength was their potent scoring behind guard Jeff Mullins, who went on to a long career in the NBA, and Art Heyman. Heyman, a six-foot-five swingman, was more heralded at the time, like Loyola's Harkness a first-team All-American.

"Art Heyman, he was one of the top four or five players in the country," said Rich Rochelle. "Heyman could play forward, guard, or center and play effectively. He was a ballplayer and obviously Mullins was a ballplayer. They just didn't have the speed to contend with us. We were organized mayhem. I had so much respect for Duke coming in. I had my concerns about Duke. But every time I looked at a team I thought we could beat them."[9]

Nothing about Heyman's game was a mystery to Harkness. One summer they played on the same team in a league in New York. And unusual for the time, Ireland secured a film of one of Duke's games from a friend to use for scouting.

The Blue Devils were the kings of the Atlantic Coast Conference and Heyman's career college scoring average was 25.1 points per game (before averaging 13 points per game in the NBA and ABA). Duke bested St. Joseph's to reach the Final Four.

Wood remembers Duke staying at the same hotel as Loyola in Louisville. One day he was waiting for the elevator with Hunter and Rouse. When the elevator stopped and the doors opened, Heyman was the only one in it and he said, "It's full." Wood said the Loyola players muttered, "We'll see you on the court."[10]

Egan had been recruited by Duke because of his good marks in school, though he said the Duke of today, with its recent basketball history, would never recruit him now. "Duke was not what it is," he said.[11]

On game night, before 19,153 spectators, Duke, 26–2, was not really what a lot of people thought Duke was then, either. "They attempted to run with us and that's what happened," Egan said.[12] What happened is that Loyola managed the challenge early and blew out the Blue Devils late for a 94–75 victory after Duke closed to within three points in the second half. Heyman finished with twenty-seven points.

"They have fine balance," Bubas said. "Harkness, all of them. They're a great group of runners and tremendous jumpers."[13]

Hunter had a huge game with twenty-nine points, eighteen rebounds, and an unofficial seven blocked shots. "Big Game" Hunter indeed. Harkness, who didn't feel he was sharp, still scored twenty. Miller had eighteen, Egan fourteen, and Rouse thirteen. Any team that merely glanced at a scouting report knew where Loyola's points—and for that matter, minutes—were coming from. Although the final margin was impressive, Ireland never bothered with his bench until the game was clearly decided. Jim Reardon, Rochelle, Wood, and Dan Connaughton all appeared in the box score, though none of them scored.

Connaughton, who laughed, said he didn't recall the final score but knew Loyola won by a lot. "It must have been big," he said. "I got in to play."[14]

The NCAA tournament resembled the Agatha Christie classic mystery *And Then There Were None*: each of the twenty-five teams entered in the tournament were knocked off one by one until there was just one left—the champion. On March 24, 1963, then there were two: 28–2 Loyola and 26–1 Cincinnati, conqueror of Oregon State by a smashing score of 80–46.

The game had been season-long in the making. It was to be the upstart Ramblers against the two-time defending NCAA champion Bearcats, now in their fifth straight Final Four.

Marquette coach Ed Hickey, who saw plenty of Loyola during the regular season, said of the match, "If anybody can beat Cincinnati, it's Loyola."[15]

Acknowledging that Loyola might be the highest-scoring team in the nation, Cincinnati's esteemed coach Ed Jucker said this game would be all about defense, the specialty in which his team ranked number one. "We don't talk about how many points we scored," Jucker said. "The important thing is—'Did you take care of your man?' We're not interested in taking the ball away by lunging or grabbing for it. We're interested in creating bad passes . . . by harassment."[16]

Unlike the present setup where there is a day off between the semifinals and finals, there was no break in the schedule for the NCAAs in 1963. The semifinals were played on Friday night and the championship game was played on Saturday. The Ramblers had less than twenty-four hours to celebrate the Duke win and prepare for Cincinnati between the late-evening game finish on March 22 and the tip-off March 23.

The adrenaline was flowing and it was hard to calm down, never mind sleep. The Ramblers retreated to their hotel rooms trying to get some rest, though at first they didn't try too hard. One activity some players recall indulging in was a non-predetermined time filler.

"We did silly things as a tension releaser, like a pillow fight," Rochelle said.[17]

A pillow fight? Sounds like a teenage sleepover. The great journey was nearing an end, it was about to culminate with the biggest challenge of the season, and the Ramblers were holed up in their digs having a pillow fight.

The players were nineteen, twenty, twenty-one, some were old enough to drink, but no one was partying this night with booze. In Wood's recollection it all seemed like one big giggle. He remembers Hunter running around in his jockey shorts, Hunter and Rouse and the others acting like five-year-olds. "You wouldn't believe it," Wood said. "The guys were up until 4 a.m. having a pillow fight. We were so excited that we were playing for the national championship. We were like kids in a candy store enjoying the moment."[18]

In between the swats with the puffy pillows intruded a few moments of serious introspection. Rouse, who came from a religious family, quoted from sermons. Harkness alternately laughed about the pillow fight and let his thoughts turn to Cincinnati. And then just about everyone was doing it, batting one another with the pillows and chanting, "We've got to win!" in rhythm with the swings.

It was a strange scene, a peculiar way to psyche each other up for the next night, but the mission was clear: "We've got to win!"

After Loyola defeated number one–ranked Cincinnati for the 1963 NCAA crown, the team was met at O'Hare Airport by two thousand fans, including Mayor Richard J. Daley (arms crossed). Captain Jerry Harkness cradles the championship trophy and is flanked by fellow starters Les Hunter, Ron Miller, and Vic Rouse. Courtesy of the Loyola Sports Information Office.

CHAPTER 19

TOE TO TOE WITH CINCINNATI

The locker room at halftime was quiet. The Ramblers knew they had not played up to their capabilities against Cincinnati in the first half. Here they were in Freedom Hall, nearly twenty thousand people roaring, sharing the court with their dream opponent and just a tantalizing twenty basketball minutes away from pulling off one of the great college basketball feats of all time, and they couldn't do anything right.

Loyola was playing Cincinnati's game, Cincinnati's tempo. The Ramblers' press was not producing dividends. The Ramblers' running game was getting tangled up in their own feet. Shots weren't falling. It felt as if they were trying to sprint in quicksand.

It was all on Jerry Harkness, Les Hunter, Vic Rouse, Johnny Egan, and Ron Miller. Coach George Ireland barely looked at his bench guys of Chuck Wood, Dan Connaughton, Rich Rochelle, and Jim Reardon. If they broke a sweat this night it was going to be because the temperature rose in Freedom Hall, not from any exercise on the court. The best that could be said for them was that they had a good view.

"I had the best seat in the house to watch the game," Connaughton said. "My usual seat three down from Ireland."[1]

It wasn't as if Loyola was getting clobbered. They trailed by that 29–21 deficit at the half with plenty of time to make it up. Everyone felt things were going to be all right in the second half. Even Ireland did not treat them so harshly. It was a funny thing, but sometimes he blasted the Ramblers at halftime when things were going well, maybe so they wouldn't lose interest and hence lose a lead. When things were not going so smoothly he tended to ease up on them rather than yell, a gesture of confidence and recognition that this team could handle anything and would eventually come around.

Well, things were not coming around. Cincinnati's lead expanded to

Greeting fans in front of the championship banner of 1963 are (left to right) Jerry Harkness, Rich Rochelle, and a waving Les Hunter on a visit back to campus decades after the title run. Courtesy of the Loyola Sports Information Office.

39–27 and radio commentator Red Rush told the fans at home, "This is a rough game."[2]

With the score at 39–30, Rush predicted that the Bearcats would go into stall mode. In the early 1960s there was no thirty-five-second clock requiring teams to shoot on a possession. Teams could dribble and pass the ball around for minutes at a time if they wished, frustrating the defense.

Ron Bonham, the slick-shooting guard, nailed a jumper about seven and a half minutes into the second half to give Cincinnati a 45–30 lead. The fifteen-point margin was the Bearcats' biggest lead and prompted Rush to exclaim, "You wouldn't believe it unless you were here." The fans who were there apparently didn't believe it when Cincinnati went into a slowdown game with slightly more than thirteen minutes to play. "It is called keep away," Rush said. "Come on and get me if you can."[3]

"We played a terrible game," Ron Miller said. "The exact tempo they wanted. I've never been able to figure out why. Maybe we were nervous.

When I see the film, we're not running our plays. All the shots were off. Everything is tight. There was no flow."[4]

Ireland stuck with his iron man crew of five, though periodically he started to insert Wood in the game. Wood would run up to the scorer's table to check in, and Ireland invariably called out for him to return to the bench. "C'mon back, c'mon back," Ireland said.[5]

Oh, the Ramblers were frustrated. Egan thought maybe they were trying too hard.

"I think maybe sometimes you want something so much you don't play as well," Egan said in retrospect, "instead of sitting back and letting it happen. They rebounded well, so we weren't getting a lot of decent shots. We weren't getting layups. I was thinking to myself, 'Even if we don't win this game, let's show them something. Can we walk out of this place playing this way?' So it was a matter of not getting disgraced. It was terrible and the worst thing was, you know, I can handle getting beat. I can handle that, I really can. I want to win, but if you play well and lose, you think, 'Gosh, I wish we would have beat them, but we didn't.' But to come there and stink up the place . . ."[6]

When Cincinnati's lead reached fifteen points with just about a quarter of the game left, Loyola had to send up an emergency flare. Compared to the current style of play, two factors mitigated strongly against Loyola's making a comeback. With no shot clock Cincinnati could waste time, and the three-point shot didn't exist yet, so points couldn't accumulate as quickly.

"You're turning to your darkest thoughts," Connaughton said of when the score was 45–30. "There was no shot clock. There was no three-pointer. It was improbable to come back. It was beyond bleak."[7]

Because in theory it should have worked against Loyola, Cincinnati did move into a semistall. Some key players had picked up their third foul (and ultimately their fourth), and Coach Ed Jucker made the critical decision to back off so that nobody earned a game-disqualifying fifth foul. However, the change of style appeared to hinder the Bearcats. They lost their aggressiveness. They stopped attacking the basket and just passed the ball around. And finally, Loyola began to make some shots. For all of that it was still 48–37 Cincinnati with seven minutes, thirty-eight seconds to play.

A critical Rouse fallaway jumper helped and then Harkness made his first basket of the game. The game turned. The quick strike was Loyola's specialty, and steals helped the Ramblers cut the lead. When Harkness stole the ball, made a layup, was fouled, and made a free throw, the lead was trimmed to 48–45 with 4:24 to go.

"A control team theoretically can slow a faster team down more than a faster team can force a slow team to play its game," said Tay Baker, who was then the Cincinnati assistant coach. "We were criticized for holding the ball too much, but we picked up our third personal foul on three key guys."[8]

Loyola had been in tight games before and one of the team's signatures was its ability to throw in big spurts, bend other teams to its will for short intervals that resulted in piling up points fast. They were blitz stretches. Hunter said that's what he was waiting for against Cincinnati, and it finally occurred after the Ramblers were at their nadir with that fifteen-point deficit.

"I remember thinking we always had a spurt in which we would throw down three or four baskets in a row and just throw together lightning-quick baskets on teams," Hunter said. "We hadn't done that yet and every single game that had happened. I was expecting it. We were also in much better shape and much quicker than a lot of teams. We were much quicker than Cincinnati."[9]

Loyola rolled like an unstoppable tidal wave. About three minutes remained when Harkness canned a five-foot jump shot from the baseline to pull Loyola within two, 50–48. "He scores! He scores! He scores!" Rush shouted into his microphone.[10] You could practically hear the applause and cheers up and down Sheridan Road as fans listened to his voice in their apartments.

Still, Cincinnati had possession of the ball and Loyola's only recourse was to foul and hope the Bearcats missed free throws. That was the situation with 1:38 left when Harkness fouled Cincinnati guard Tony Yates. Yates made one shot and missed another: 51–48. Loyola got a bucket on a Cincinnati goal-tending call to close to 51–50.

As the suspense graduated to the superintense level in Freedom Hall, Bearcats guard Tom Thacker, a future NBA player, made a layup. Hunter tapped in a missed Loyola shot with nineteen seconds left to pull within one, 53–52. The Ramblers fouled Cincinnati's Larry Shingleton, and he sank his first free throw for a 54–52 lead. If the left-handed Shingleton made his second shot, Loyola was almost surely finished.

"I just so vividly remember Larry Shingleton's shots with about eleven seconds left in the ballgame and he just nailed the first one," Connaughton said. "In my innermost thoughts I thought we were probably screwed. The first one was the pressure one. I just believed in my heart of hearts he was going to make the second one."[11]

But he didn't. The second shot bounced off the rim on the left side of the basket and into Hunter's hands. Loyola's cheerleaders jumped and clapped. Fans roared. With two seconds left, Hunter made the familiar outlet pass to Miller, approaching half-court, the play the Ramblers had completed so many times before. Miller fed Harkness, and Harkness finished the play at the buzzer, dropping the ball through the hoop from about twelve feet away to send the game into overtime at 54 all.

Forevermore this has been a controversial play. Bearcats dispute not the clock running out or the legality of Harkness's shot, but they say Miller should have been whistled for traveling. Yet no violation was called.

"When they got the shot at the end the referee just got the whistle stuck in his mouth," said Cincinnati center George Wilson, a future pro. "We were up twelve points and the next thing you know, it's tied."[12]

Film of the Loyola–Cincinnati game—the first NCAA game to be shown nationally, although it was on taped delay—does exist. However, it was not recorded with the bells and whistles and technology of the current era. A limited number of cameras followed the action, and there was no instant re-play, so definitive proof of whether or not Miller took too many steps when passing to Harkness remains elusive.

Connaughton said he thinks Miller did take an extra step, routinely re-ferring to the play with the phrase, "Ronnie, who traveled a little bit . . ."[13]

About fifty years later a candid impression of what he thinks transpired can be wrung from Miller. "I took the extra step," he said. "Don't tell anyone from Cincinnati that. I could see Jerry breaking. He was going to be one-on-one. I'm at half-court when Les gets the ball to me. It was textbook, Jerry scoring."[14]

It was about as loud in Freedom Hall as it would have been standing on a runway at the nearby Louisville airport. Loyola had completed its unlikely comeback and pushed mighty Cincinnati into a five-minute overtime peri-od. From dead in the water, Loyola had resurrected its chances of winning the title.

"We had it won," Thacker said. "We just had a few mistakes. We still should have won the game. We changed styles. You lose your momentum."[15]

Momentum is an intangible and it can swing more swiftly than a calibrated pendulum, but because of the way Loyola charged back and tied the game before the clock ran out, most would say momentum was on Loyola's side at the beginning of overtime.

The Ramblers, behind Harkness, scored the first basket of OT to take a 56–54 lead. That forced Cincinnati to play. No more holding the ball. Wilson got the ball in the low post and made a shot: 56–56.

"Win, lose, or draw, this is a great one," said Loyola broadcaster Rush.[16]

Miller hit an outside shot to put Loyola up, 58–56. But Shingleton, making up for his free-throw miss, made a huge shot to tie things at 58. The situation was set up for heroics. Loyola passed the ball in with one minute, forty-six seconds to go. With the game knotted and no clock pressure to shoot, Loyola could play for the last shot. It was the only strategy that made sense. That way if the Ramblers missed, then at the least they would go on to a second overtime.

Loyola passed the ball around the perimeter, not even looking at the basket. Everyone assumed that when the time came to take a run at the hoop it would be the All-American Harkness lined up for the shot. The only problem with stall ball, although Ireland had no sensible alternative, was that the up-tempo Ramblers never played in that manner.

"We're going to hold the ball for one shot," Miller said, "and we had never even practiced holding the ball. It was set for Jerry to take the last shot."[17]

As the clock ticked down Harkness had the ball in his hands. He was going to drive to the hoop as his teammates cleared out and hope he could beat the Cincinnati defense. But the Bearcats, from Ron Bonham to George Wilson trying to clog the middle, cut off his lanes. Very aware that time was running out, Harkness had to try something. He was about twelve feet out when he went up in the air to shoot, but out of the corner of his eye he saw Hunter open a little bit closer to the hoop inside the lane.

"When I went up, I just didn't feel it," Harkness said. So instead of following through with the jumper he dropped the ball off to Hunter, who was positioning himself for a possible rebound.[18]

"I'm not thinking, 'Hey, give me the ball,'" Hunter said. "I'm thinking rebound. I was thinking, 'He's going to shoot it' and 'Man, I'm going to follow this ball up.' So when he threw it to me, my momentum was going forward and I put it up."[19]

Loyola's other players were among the most caught-off-guard people in the stadium. "I was surprised he passed," Wood said.[20]

Hunter's shot was short, and the ball bounded off the rim. Opportunistic as always, and neglected when it came to blocking out, Rouse skied into the air, grabbed the ball on the right side, and laid it in as time ran out. "Your heart stops for a second," Wood said. "The ball misses and Rouse is right there."[21]

Bang, bang, Rouse's shot goes through the hoop, the buzzer sounds, Loyola is the NCAA champion.

"We won! We won! We won the ball game!" Rush was almost in hysterics on the radio.[22]

Yes, they did. The Ramblers beat number one–ranked Cincinnati, 60–58, with a surreal comeback and an amazing overtime finish, with an iron man five playing all forty-five minutes. Because of its four black starting players the team had endured more hassles and adversity than any other championship team in college basketball history. Loyola overcame horrible shooting of 29 percent with its trademark defensive pressure and an unflagging will.

The moment was sudden and electrifying. The Ramblers on the court hugged. The Ramblers on the bench bounded into the air. It was bedlam at Freedom Hall.

"They [Cincinnati] wanted anyone other than Jerry Harkness to take a jump shot," Rochelle said. "We ended up with Les shooting because Jerry wasn't open. They got what they wanted."[23] But not what they really wanted. The big prize belonged to Loyola.

"I jumped up off the bench," Rochelle said. "I didn't know what to do or where to go. I wanted to hug my friends. I was acting a little crazy. It took about two minutes for it to sink in that I was on a national championship team."[24]

Emotions exploded like lava streaming from a volcanic eruption. Players were mad with joy. "I just leapt about eight feet off the ground and ran around hugging people," Connaughton said. "I basically lost my mind, as we all did."[25]

Hunter was Loyola's high scorer with sixteen points. Harkness ended up with fourteen despite his slow start. Egan had nine and Miller six. Rouse scored fifteen points, none larger in his life than the two that clinched the game.

"I never thought we'd lose it," said Rouse, who was proclaimed the savior of the hour. "We came too far to lose it. I've played with Les for a long time, so I was able to get into position. I didn't have any trouble getting to the spot."[26]

Rouse might have been the only one in the building who didn't realize at the moment his shot fell through the hoop that it had won the game. He had lost track of time and was about to retreat on defense thinking some seconds remained. So he was a split second late in celebrating.

When the ball dropped through the hoop for the 60–58 final with the buzzer sounding almost simultaneously, Ireland jumped off the bench and shouted, "It's unbelievable! It's unbelievable!"[27]

The first thing Hunter did was grab Rouse in a bear hug. Appropriately, the two longest-term pals on the team shared the first moment of being champions together.

It might have been expected that Walter November, who had ties to several Loyola players, would have been in the stands at Freedom Hall, but he had stayed in New York. "My ulcer really acted up when Jerry [Harkness] played so badly in the first half," November said. "But he finally scored when it counted."[28]

Cincinnati players were stunned. They were so used to winning they didn't believe they could be beaten. A half century later when discussing the Bearcats' three straight visits to the championship game with two titles, Thacker said, "We should have won three."[29]

At his Cincinnati home, a nine-year-old boy named Kent Stephens, who grew up to become curator of the College Football Hall of Fame, was more shocked than the Bearcats. In his youth he lived and died with Cincinnati's fortunes, which to that point in his experience had always been good.

"It was the worst night of my life," Stephens said decades later. "The only thing I knew in life was that the sun rose in the east and the Bearcats won the national championship. I was so devastated that I had to sleep with my parents that night. If I die tomorrow [said in 2011] that night in March of 1963 will still be the worst day of my life."[30]

Loyola players boogied on the floor like dancers performing on *American Bandstand*. Fans screamed in the stands. In Chicago, where the televised version of the game was shown on tape delay, those around the Loyola campus erupted from their dorms and apartments and jammed Sheridan Road. Frank Perez, the member of the freshman team, was one of them.

"The whole dormitory just went outside hollering and screaming," Perez said. "We hit the streets." Hundreds flooded those streets peacefully, happily, shouting, "We did it! We did it!"[31]

Somehow, in an achievement worthy of the occasion given that it was an era before cell phones, Judy Van Dyck reached her father on the telephone to congratulate him while he was still in the locker room at Freedom Hall. "I had to talk to him that night," said Van Dyck, who said she was crying tears of joy. When Ireland heard her weeping, he said, "It's OK, honey, we won."[32]

The Ramblers spent the final night of their triumphant season in their hotel, wearing a glow of satisfaction that has never really worn off. From a window Harkness watched Loyola supporters reveling in the streets, rocking vehicles. The players couldn't stop smiling, but they felt a little dazed, a feeling that didn't wear off for some time.

The next day the team returned to Chicago and was greeted by a crowd of about two thousand chanting fans at O'Hare Airport's Butler terminal, a throng that included Mayor Richard J. Daley.

"We're Loyola! We're number one!" is how the chant went. "We made mince out of Cince!" It was no longer wishful thinking, it was accurate. They posed for a picture in front of a sign reading, "Welcome Home Champs."

The Ramblers then boarded buses for a police-escorted motorcade to the student center on campus where another four thousand people waited to fête them. Wild applause greeted Ireland, Harkness, and the others, who took turns holding aloft the tall championship trophy.

Eventually, the party slowed and then stopped, but the Loyola Ramblers who made a months-long magnificent run to an NCAA basketball title in 1963 learned as the years passed that some things last forever. Life continues, the pages turn on the calendar, but once in a great while something you accomplish remains frozen in time, an experience turned into a picture in the mind and framed. And no one can ever take it away from you.

Current Loyola coach Porter Moser hopes his teams can be inspired by the accomplishments of the 1962–63 season. Courtesy of the Loyola Sports Information Office.

EPILOGUE

n 1963, the player reward for NCAA champions was a watch. On the plane on the way back to Chicago some of the Ramblers realized they had been presented with the wrong watches. Instead of reading "NCAA Basketball Champions" they read "NCAA Basketball Finalists."

"Three or four of us got them," said Dan Connaughton. "What the hell?" That meant some Cincinnati players received the other watches. It took about a month and a half to conclude a swap, Connaughton said.[1]

The only starting senior on the title team was Jerry Harkness. Harkness's college basketball career ended with the Cincinnati game, but his high-profile play and his three seasons of averaging more than twenty points a game earned him a shot in professional basketball. He was drafted by the NBA's New York Knicks and played in a handful of games for the 1963–64 squad before being cut. There was a few-year gap, during which he thought he was finished with basketball, but in 1967 he joined the Indiana Pacers of the ABA for two more seasons. Harkness holds the distinction of making the longest shot in professional basketball history. During a 1967 game he sank a ninety-two-foot shot with time running out that won a game for the Pacers.

After his playing days, Harkness, who settled in Indianapolis, became a sportscaster and immersed himself in civil rights causes. Among the prominent leaders he either met or later worked with were Dr. Martin Luther King, Jr., the Reverend Ralph Abernathy, and the Reverend Jesse Jackson.

Once they had captured the NCAA crown—the first, and to this day, still the only school from Illinois to do so—Loyola was on the map of college basketball. The Ramblers were expected to do very well again in the 1963–64 season and they did, finishing 22–6. Again invited to the NCAA tournament, Loyola defeated Murray State in the first round, but then lost, 84–80, to Michigan State. The Ramblers won a regional consolation game over Kentucky to complete the year.

That was the final season for Les Hunter, Vic Rouse, John Egan, and Ron Miller. Hunter had a spectacular senior season, averaging 21.4 points and

Athletic director Grace Calhoun recognizes the strong link to the past and the tremendous accomplishment of the 1962–63 men's basketball players. She would love to see history repeated. Courtesy of the Loyola Sports Information Office.

15.3 rebounds a game. Rouse also played terrifically, averaging 15.6 points and 12.5 rebounds a game. Miller, who had trouble breaking into the starting lineup because of his skin color as a sophomore, averaged 21.9 points a game as a senior, and sterling for a guard, also 9.3 rebounds per game. Egan's numbers also improved and he averaged 18.5 points per game. That group of four players led Loyola to a three-year varsity record of 74–12.

Hunter, like Harkness, became a professional basketball player. He was a power forward in the pros, first with the NBA's Baltimore Bullets and then with five teams in the ABA through the end of the 1973 season. Hunter was a two-time ABA All-Star and an educator after leaving basketball, and he now lives in Overland Park, Kansas.

Rouse, who died in 1999, was the most scholarly player on the team. After he earned a degree from Loyola, he continued his college education almost nonstop, earning several master's degrees.

As he had aspired to from the start of his college career, Egan became a lawyer. He is a criminal defense attorney in Chicago and has been teased by former teammates with the joke, "Now you're playing defense." Two of Egan's children attended Loyola.

Sensing the time was ripe for opportunities for young black men with all of the attention on the civil rights movement, Miller came right out of college at twenty-two and became a production line supervisor at Campbell's Soup in Chicago. After two years in that position he worked for US Steel and then Container Corporation of America.

"Businesses needed minorities," Miller said. "They were under pressure to hire blacks."[2]

After about two decades of working in Chicago, Miller settled in California, where he still lives. Miller has five children and ten grandchildren. "I have good memories of that whole period of time," Miller said of his college basketball career. "It's an experience I would not trade."[3]

Reardon, a six-four forward, was the other senior on the championship team. His career scoring average was 3.1 points per game and he has passed away.

Rochelle never got the playing time he felt he deserved, even the next year, when he got into just nine games and averaged 1.6 points a game. A retired educator still living in the Chicago area, through a quirk of life he was brought together at a family party with Cincinnati's George Wilson decades after the game. Rochelle's brother-in-law is Wilson's cousin. Sure enough, when Wilson learned Rochelle was on the Loyola team that beat the Bearcats for the title, he began talking about how Cincinnati was robbed because Miller traveled.

"He was angry and animated about the game," Rochelle said. "I said, 'George, that team beat you with our All-American having his worst game of the year. George, that game was fifty years ago.' He said if we played it a hundred times we wouldn't beat them. I said, 'George, we played it once and you lost. It's not life and death.'"[4]

Connaughton did not see much more action as a junior, but he played a bit more as a senior and averaged 4.1 points a game. He became an attorney and practiced law in his home area near Cincinnati. "I just happened to be there at a serendipitous time," Connaughton said of his years at Loyola. "I was there at the right time."[5]

Playing forward, Perez, who was on the periphery of the championship team as a freshman player, began to shine as a junior during the 1964–65 season when he averaged 12.9 points a game. He then averaged 8.9 points a game as a senior. During a later road trip to Memphis, Perez recalled, the Ramblers once again had a housing problem at a hotel because of the black players on the team. Perez went into the army, leaving Loyola twelve credits short of graduation. He said Ireland "was very gracious," offering to pay for tuition and books so he could complete his degree, but when Perez married he went back to school at Michigan State instead.[6]

Wood played in twenty-five games as a senior, but despite scoring twenty points in a game early in the 1963–64 campaign, he averaged just three. Wood still lives in Racine, Wisconsin, where he is athletic director at his old high school. A couple of years ago when venerable Freedom Hall was closed for basketball in favor of a new arena opening in Louisville, Wood's wife, JoAnne, surprised him with a keepsake harkening back to the 1963 championship. She bought him a piece of the floor. "It was nice," he said. "I didn't expect it."[7]

John Crnokrak, the backup forward on the varsity while most of the future champion Ramblers players were freshmen, shared the title win vicariously. Later in life he wrote self-help books. One is titled *How to Be Fast, Daring, Different: 33 Ways to Achieve Personal and Professional Success*. Some might say that also described the 1962–63 season.

Pablo Robertson, who showed so much promise in his seventeen Loyola games, found happiness with the Harlem Globetrotters. He became one of the famed team's most popular players and when the world-traveling outfit signed a deal for a cartoon series, Robertson was one of the players portrayed.

Governor Vaughn, the executive director of the Globetrotters, said that Robertson, who passed away in 1990 at age fifty-six, was an instant hit as a little-guy dribbler when he joined the team in 1967. Robertson's real name was Paul, but he received the nickname Pablo early in life. The Globetrotters visited many Spanish-speaking countries and the fans there figured Robertson was one of them. He eventually learned to speak some Spanish.

One of Robertson's Globetrotters teammates was Hall of Fame baseball pitcher Ferguson Jenkins of the Cubs and Phillies, who moonlighted for the basketball team for a couple of years during his off-seasons.

"He was a great dribbler," Jenkins said of Robertson. "He was just an all-around athlete. He was one of the mainstays in a couple of the skits. He was quite agile. He did a lot of the dribbling, behind his back, through his legs. He did a lot of the things that now are commonplace."[8]

For some at Loyola, the biggest surprise was the return of Billy Smith to the school. Smith went to a junior college, got his grades up, and came back to play for the Ramblers. Some players said he showed great courage in doing so. The six-foot-five Smith matured in every way and was the team's biggest star in 1964–65 when he averaged 24.5 points and 12.7 rebounds a contest. During the 1965–66 season he averaged 18.8 points and 13.3 rebounds.

Smith blamed himself for not doing the work to keep up his grades and later did not sound bitter about missing out on an NCAA championship.

"I was happy for them," Smith said of his ex-teammates. "Sometimes you must accept the consequences for what you did. They're your people. I played a half a year with them. I wish I would have been able to stay. But you can't mull over what has passed."[9]

Smith came close to finishing, but did not earn his degree. He was sixty-eight as he talked of still trying to pull it off. Since he completed his college basketball career, Smith said he tried to live "off the grid." He said he worked at bars, at strip clubs, for the New York transit system, but also said he had been arrested forty-two times without serving any prison time. He tried to keep to himself and out of sight most of the time. Smith said he read a lot of philosophy, books by Kahil Gibran, and cited "The Prince" by Machiavelli as another read.

"I don't hear about Loyola," Smith said, referring to the school's basketball team. "I haven't heard about Loyola in such a long time."[10]

When sportswriter Bill Jauss retired after more than fifty years in journalism he rated the greatest events he had covered. Although Loyola's NCAA victory was some forty-five years in the past, the Ramblers' championship earned his number one ranking. However, because what Smith said was true, more recent Loyola basketball accomplishments did not clutter his list. Jauss died in late 2012 at age eighty-one.

Old age has claimed some of the Ramblers, the coach included, but at least one symbol of their achievement remains on perpetual display. For decades, a bold, colorful banner announcing the accomplishment hung on a wall in the old gym that was their home court, a glittering and proud piece of history on view to every fan who ever visited campus to watch successive generations of Ramblers. Then, in 2011, when a replacement gym opened with spanking new seats and all the amenities of a modern basketball palace, the banner of pride was the first decoration hung on the new wall.

Winning the 1963 NCAA men's basketball title is by far the grandest achievement by any Loyola sports team. Ireland continued coaching at the school through the 1974–75 season, but his clubs never again attained anything close to the level of performance that particular group did. He was having heart problems when he stepped down from coaching, but he was unhappy when he was pushed out of the athletics department in 1977. Ireland was succeeded by longtime assistant Jerry Lyne, whose best of five seasons at the helm was 19–11 in 1979–80.

In the early 1980s, Gene Sullivan built what seemed to be a solid foundation for a revived program, and his 1984–85 team went 27–6 and won two games in the NCAA tournament. It was not until the 2006–07 season that the Ramblers, under Jim Whitesell, won twenty games again, finishing 21–11 that year. Loyola before and after suffered through a long list of losing seasons.

Current Loyola coach Porter Moser said when he moved into his office after getting the job in 2011, he found a picture in the closet of the parade celebrating Loyola's title and he framed it and put it on his desk. He has met many of the surviving Ramblers and said the accomplishment is something the school should not only be proud of at all times but also work to emulate.

"We're talking about the only NCAA title in Illinois history," Moser said. "I know it was a long time ago, but it has happened here. I show recruits that. It's a reminder to me, too." The championship is imbedded in the DNA of the program. "There's not many places where something that happened fifty years ago is talked about as much as this. It's amazing how often it comes up."[11]

Not only at Loyola and not only in Chicago, but in his travels, Moser hears comments about being a representative of a school that won it all. In an era when college basketball has become a big-money sport with huge receipts from television, Loyola is what is called a mid-major, meaning the school is Division I in the NCAA but is at a disadvantage competing against the superpowers of the biggest leagues that spend millions of dollars a year on their programs.

Over the past couple of years, Loyola has thoroughly renovated its home gym, revamped the press room, and decorated its walls with scenes from the 1963 title run. New athletic director Grace Calhoun wants not only to celebrate the accomplishment but also to use it as an inspiration to lift the athletic program to greater success.

"It is part of our history," Calhoun said of the 1963 basketball championship. "It will always be a source of pride for the university. It is part of our living history. This provides a representation that it can be done and so it can be done again. You can be the small school with the little budget and assemble the pieces."[12]

In addition to the banner bragging about the 1963 championship, hung high in the rafters were retired jersey numbers of the stalwart iron man stars, all of whom are in the school's athletic hall of fame. In 2010, Loyola opened the hall of fame's doors to the bench guys, too.

"They put us scrubs in the hall of fame," Connaughton said, sounding disbelieving well over a year after it happened.[13]

Ireland retired with a 321–225 record, and in his later years he spent time coaching mentally challenged youngsters at a neighborhood center. He said it was the only time in his career he called practice beautiful. Ireland was eighty-eight when he died in 2001. He was called on more than once to reflect on the glory road of 1963, and he always talked about what fine students and men his recruits turned out to be.

"We had a 98 percent graduation rate when I coached," Ireland said. "A lot of my kids came up the hard way and they were marginal students. But we tutored them [after 1963] and worked with them. Now they are doctors and lawyers and dentists. We need more of those than pro basketball players."[14]

In his eulogy at St. Lambert Church in the Chicago suburb of Skokie,

Rev. Matt Creighton said, "George influenced thousands of people. Some were famous, others quite ordinary. He loved them all."[15]

On various anniversaries of Loyola's great triumph, Ireland reminisced with reporters. He still couldn't believe what kind of racist behavior the Ramblers faced in New Orleans, in Houston, and prior to playing Mississippi State. When he died, Ireland, who had saved it all, left the hate mail from the period to daughter Judy, who said that the baby boy she had at the time of the championship almost was named "NCAA." Van Dyck is not sure why Ireland left the distasteful letters to her, but she still has them and almost never shows them to anyone. "There are enough to know it happened," she said recently.[16]

Since there are revisionists who actually deny that the Holocaust occurred, she is probably wise to hold onto proof of the disgraceful behavior lest later on people deny it. That has become less likely, however, as in some ways Loyola's game against Mississippi State has on occasion drawn more attention than the actual championship victory over Cincinnati.

Harkness's son Jerald made the documentary *Game of Change*, which first appeared at a film festival in 2008. In 2009, participants in that game were invited to the NCAA Final Four in Detroit at Ford Field and were honored for their courage. The younger Harkness's film was shown to the group.

"It was quite moving," Wood said. "You sat there and you'd say to yourself, 'Did that really exist?' The way the governor of Mississippi is talking about blacks. You couldn't believe it."[17]

At times, Ron Miller said, he has wondered what Loyola's journey of a half century ago means. Then something happens to remind him how special it was. He received a letter from a Loyola alum in his fifties who wrote just to tell him that his father had died, but "how much that championship meant to him." "It was very nice to have touched other people," said Miller.[18]

When asked about the circumstances surrounding the Mississippi State game, upon reflection, Miller said he has come to believe that the Loyola African American players were part of the civil rights movement when every little step of progress mattered.

"It's very hard when you think of those things," Miller said of the hate mail and other acts of prejudice. "How could it have been like that? It almost doesn't seem real. How could it have been that bad?"[19]

The world is a very different place in the second decade of the 2000s than it was in the 1960s. For some in Mississippi it was unthinkable that blacks and whites would play a straightforward game of college basketball together. By doing so, the men who competed in that game became forever linked. Producer and director Jerald Harkness brought some of them together again when he made his documentary, and the NCAA did, as well.

On the night of the game so long ago, Jerry Harkness, captain of the Ramblers, shook hands with Joe Dan Gold, captain of the Bulldogs, and no fireworks display was brighter than the thousands of cameras in the Freedom Hall stands going off with their flashes. Drawing from that shared moment, Harkness and Gold became friends.

In April of 2011, when Gold died of cancer at sixty-eight, Harkness felt he should be at his funeral, which was held in Kentucky, not a long drive from his Indiana home. It was a scene that would have been almost unimaginable a half century ago. Harkness was the only black mourner, but he was received by Gold's immediate family as if he were one of them, with hugs and tears.

Harkness was crying and the relatives were crying. Gold's wife, uncles, aunts, son, and other close relatives cajoled Harkness into posing for a photo with them next to the casket. Harkness was asked if he would serve as part of a secondary honor group, as well—not an official pallbearer, but take his place with Gold's Mississippi State teammates, and he did. He thought, "You know, I'm with the team that's sending him to heaven. I felt part of Mississippi State's team."[20]

Coming full circle, the object of so much hatred so long ago simply because he was black, Jerry Harkness was adopted into the all-white team that taught the world a lesson about integration. He was there with Joe Dan Gold once more and the flashbulbs popped again.

Fifty years after the Loyola iron men defeated Mississippi State in the NCAA tournament, members of both teams reunited in Chicago. Here, (left to right) former Loyola players John Egan, Ron Miller, Jerry Harkness, Rich Rochelle, and Dan Connaughton greet 2012–13 Loyola player Nick Osborne before the December 2012 game against the Bulldogs. Courtesy of Paul Smulson.

POSTSCRIPT

As the 2012–13 college basketball season approached, Porter Moser had an idea. It had been fifty years since Loyola won the NCAA championship and it had been fifty years since Loyola had played against Mississippi State.

The current Loyola coach sought out his coaching counterpart, Rick Ray, in Starkville, Mississippi, and persuaded him to schedule a nonconference, regular-season game for December of 2012. The two schools had never crossed paths on the basketball court again after the Game of Change, and Moser thought it would be an appropriate meeting on a major anniversary of the special contest.

A game between then–Horizon League member Loyola and Southeastern Conference member Mississippi State was scheduled for December 15, 2012, in Chicago. But the event expanded into more than a game. It became a weekend-long celebration of the 1963 NCAA contest, bringing together living members of both squads that took the floor in East Lansing, Michigan, on March 15, 1963.

In addition, a special showing of the *Game of Change* documentary was scheduled on campus with the former players, in their seventies, invited back for a panel discussion about the events surrounding their historic game. That turned the event into a Friday-Saturday Loyola–Mississippi State basketball affair.

Approximately three hundred people attended the film showing at the Sullivan Center. Among them were members of the all-white Mississippi State team of 1962–63 and black and white members of the Loyola championship team. Although they were aware that their game was of national implications and import a half century ago, they have had considerable time to reflect upon the fact that the worlds of then and now are dramatically different.

"It was history," said Jerry Harkness, the captain of that old Loyola team, who came to that conclusion after many years.[1]

The jump ball at the Loyola–Mississippi game of December 15, 2012. This was a
regular-season game held to commemorate the Game of Change from the season
of fifty years earlier. Courtesy of Paul Smulson.

For the most part players on both sides were only concerned with race
at the time because others were, from state officials in Mississippi to the
journalists covering the issue of whether or not there would be a game held
at all. Primarily, they were in Michigan to play basketball, to try to advance
in the tournament.

"We were playing in the NCAAs," said former Bulldogs player Stan
Brinker. That experience had been denied to former Southeastern Conference champs from the school. "Later, it came out to be all of that and more."[2]

Doug Hutton, a guard on that Mississippi State team, said that Coach
Babe McCarthy scared the players when he gave them the lowdown on
highly rated Loyola.

"You should have heard the scouting report," Hutton said. "They had us
afraid to dribble the ball. Those guys were supermen."[3]

Not quite, but the Ramblers were good enough to win the game, 61–51.
In recent years the two teams have shared the spotlight at a few commemorative events and the old players, most of them now retired, have gotten
to know one another as people more than players. They concluded fairly
quickly that they were all just regular guys and they like one another.

The rematch of the 1963 game turned out to resemble the original. Loyola won, 59–51. With one more made basket—and Loyola had the ball with sufficient time to take a last shot, but killed the clock instead—the Ramblers would have won by the identical score. There were bigger differences on this occasion than in 1963. Mississippi State's Coach Ray is African American. So was the Bulldogs' entire starting lineup.

At halftime, Pat Quinn, the governor of Illinois, read a proclamation that declared it Game of Change Day in the state.

The spotlight on the Loyola–Mississippi State game of 1963 has only grown brighter in recent years, but Ramblers guard John Egan made a point about that entire run to the NCAA crown. If Loyola had not kept winning, besting Illinois, Duke, and Cincinnati, too, just how would the Game of Change have been remembered?

"There wouldn't be any meetings like this if we hadn't won it all," Egan said.[4]

But because the Ramblers did win that title, not only has the focus been so strong on the Game of Change, but 2013 became the year of honors for a team with its grandest accomplishment fifty years in the past.

In March it was announced that come November Loyola was to become the first team inducted into the College Basketball Hall of Fame in Kansas City. Then it was announced that the Loyola team would be inducted into the Chicagoland Sports Hall of Fame in September.

All of it was more reason for celebration. It was also a bit of vindication for a local oral surgeon named Paul Smulson, who led the lobbying effort to convince selectors in Kansas City to recognize Loyola. Smulson, sixty, grew up down the block from Coach Ireland, and in Ireland's later years Smulson drove him to many events and became friends with the retired team leader.

Smulson prepared the supporting documentation that suggested Loyola was a very special team, not only because of its victory in the NCAAs but because of its role in cutting through racial barriers as well.

"I'm very happy they got into the College Basketball Hall of Fame," Smulson said. "It was great. Three years of work."[5]

In February the players were tipped off by Loyola officials that an announcement was imminent, but they were sworn to secrecy until the public was alerted. They were surprised at the notification.

"It came totally out of left field," said Ron Miller. "I was surprised. I didn't know they did teams. I'm very proud of that."[6]

Current Loyola University men's basketball coach Porter Moser led the Ramblers into a new league, the Missouri Valley Conference, for the 2013–14 season. Courtesy Loyola Sports Information Office.

Les Hunter, who lives about twenty minutes from the college hall of fame, said that while happy for this burst of honors bestowed on Loyola he thought the team should have been singled out before.

"I thought it was long overdue because of the social significance," Hunter said. "The Chicagoland Hall of Fame, that's the one I really wanted."[7]

In May, Egan, Chuck Wood, and Rich Rochelle were invited to Wrigley Field to throw out the first pitch at a Chicago Cubs game and then lead fans in the singing of "Take Me Out to the Ball Game" during the seventh-inning stretch. They were allowed to bring numerous friends and relatives to inhabit a box, too. There was a potential problem with three former athletes and only one pitch, but Egan said the others didn't want to do it, so he was elected.

Egan disdained the idea of throwing from in front of the mound, so he tossed the pitch to home plate from the full distance of sixty feet, six inches.

"I'm old, but I can still throw," Egan said.[8]

All of these enjoyable perks and experiences played out against a backdrop of some sad developments. Coach Ireland, Vic Rouse, Pablo Robertson, and Jim Rearden had previously passed away. Then in the midst of the good-news stretch, word spread to the surviving players that Frank Perez had died of cancer in Atlanta and that Billy Smith had died of cancer in New York. Perez had just passed his sixty-ninth birthday and Smith was six months shy of his seventieth birthday.

Les Hunter, who maintained the closest contact with Perez over the years, said Perez was initially diagnosed with cancer of the prostate, which spread to the colon, and then with an infection, which also spread. Miller, who roomed with Perez at school one year, said he had kept up with Perez on Facebook, had spoken to him periodically over the years, and knew he was suffering from a variety of ailments.

Smith was fading from cancer for a number of months before his May death. Harkness said several old teammates called Smith and had lengthy telephone conversations with him. "We all took it hard," Harkness said.[9]

Over the last weeks of Smith's life, Egan and Smith, who had not gotten along well as undergraduates, reconnected and conducted long telephone conversations of the type they never shared when playing together.

"I called him when I heard that he had two months to live," Egan said. "He said, 'This pain is excruciating.'" Egan said Smith asked him to send a Loyola basketball keepsake, and Egan sent a team picture and copies of some clippings his father had kept in a scrapbook. Egan also wrote a long letter in which he said, "You know, I always respected you as a player." They also talked through the differences of their youth. "We laughed about those things," Egan said.[10]

Even with the dwindling number of survivors of the dramatic events of a half century ago, the gratification of being remembered for the accomplishments of 1963 has never been sweeter.

In still another surprising honor, all seven of the living members from the 1963 Loyola championship squad, as well as some university officials, were invited to the White House to visit with and be recognized by President Barack Obama, who is not only from Chicago but has a well-publicized interest in college basketball.

The July 11, 2013, visit to the Oval Office left the Ramblers players agog.

"It was really, really nice," Harkness said. "It was awesome. It was the thrill of a lifetime. It was really the highlight of a lifetime."[11]

The fifteen-minute visit included Rambler Les Hunter presenting the president with a Loyola No. 44 jersey and plaque. Harkness, who is left-handed like the president, who has been known to exercise by playing pickup basketball, discussed the challenge of dribbling to the right.

"He said he goes left," Harkness said.[12]

On the same trip to Washington, DC, the players visited the Capitol, met with Illinois congressmen, were honored by Rev. Jesse Jackson's Rainbow Coalition, and were treated to luncheons and dinners by Loyola alumni from the area.

John Egan said the players had about three weeks' notice for the event but were ordered to keep it under wraps until after the meeting took place.

"It's an honor to see any president, but with this president being from Chicago and interested in basketball," Egan said, "I actually feel closer to him."[13]

Despite Obama's enthusiasm for the sport, however, no one-on-one games broke out in the Oval Office.

"No basketball was played," Egan said.[14]

Meeting with President Obama was a thrill hard to top, but the Loyola players could still look forward to another great distinction when as a group they would all be inducted into the College Basketball Hall of Fame.

When Harkness was informed that Loyola was to be the first team chosen for the college hall, he was incredulous.

"I thought, 'Oh, my goodness,'" he said. "Are you kidding me? It's great. We said, 'Wow!' It's really, really nice."[15]

After the news broke, TV stations tracked Harkness down in Indiana, the *New York Times* called, and media outlets on other fronts contacted him.

"It's so much attention," Harkness said. "We're getting more publicity now than we did when we won the championship."[16]

The Loyola Ramblers are being immortalized in ways that ensure what they achieved will always be remembered.

NOTES

Chapter 1

1. Ron Miller, interview by the author, February 2012.
2. Ibid.
3. Ibid.
4. Rich Rochelle, interview by the author, March 2012.
5. Red Rush, radio broadcast, Loyola vs. Cincinnati, March 23, 1963.
6. Ibid.
7. Ibid.
8. Ibid.
9. John Egan, interview by the author, January 2012.
10. Ibid.
11. Ibid.

Chapter 2

1. John Husar, "Ireland's Loyola Champions Triumphed over Racism," *Chicago Tribune*, March 25, 1979.
2. "Greatest College Basketball Teams: Spotlight 1963 Loyola Ramblers Basketball Team," Stellar College Basketball, http://www.stellarcollegebballgame.com/1963Loyola.html.
3. Miller, interview, February 2012.
4. Clarence E. Gaines and Clint Johnson, *They Call Me Big House* (Winston-Salem, NC: John F. Blair, 2004), 33.
5. Ibid., 125.
6. Associated Press, *Sarasota Herald-Tribune*, February 5, 1963.
7. Miller, interview, February 2012.
8. Ibid.
9. Ibid.
10. Jerry Harkness, interview by the author, January 2012.

11. Ibid.

12. Ibid.

13. Ibid.

14. Miller, interview, February 2012.

15. Ibid.

16. Judy Ireland Van Dyck, interview by the author, March 2012.

17. Ibid.

18. Harkness, interview, January 2012.

19. Ibid.

20. Emmette Bryant, interview by the author, August 2012.

21. Paul Kuharsky, "Loyola Pioneered Integrated Basketball," *Tennessean*, April 6, 2003.

22. Associated Press, *Sarasota Herald-Tribune*, February 5, 1963.

23. Bryant, interview, August 2012.

24. Miller, interview, February 2012.

25. Harkness, interview, January 2012.

26. Ibid.

27. Ibid.

28. Van Dyck, interview, March 2012.

29. Harkness, interview, January 2012.

Chapter 3

1. Jerry Harkness, interview, January 2012.

2. Ibid.

3. Ibid.

4. Ibid.

5. Ibid.

6. Ibid.

7. Ibid.

8. Ibid.

9. Ibid.

10. Ibid.

11. Bill Jauss, "Loyola Rates As Team to Beat Next Year," *Chicago Daily News*, March 25, 1963.

12. Harkness, interview, January 2012.

13. Ibid.

14. Ibid.

15. Ibid.

16. Ibid.

17. Ibid.

18. Ibid.

19. Ibid.

20. Ibid.

21. Jerry Harkness, interview by the author, August 2012.

22. Ibid.

Chapter 4

1. Ron Miller, interview, February 2012.

2. Ibid.

3. Ibid.

4. Gaines and Johnson, *They Call Me Big House*, 161.

5. Ibid., 218.

6. Bill Gleason, "Among Loyola Stars . . . Stout-Hearted Egan," *Chicago American*, March 25, 1963.

7. Billy Smith, interview by the author, March 2012.

8. "Greatest College Basketball Teams: Spotlight 1963 Loyola Ramblers Basketball Team."

9. Ibid.

10. Ibid.

11. Ibid.

12. Les Hunter, interview by the author, February, 2012.

Chapter 5

1. Associated Press, *Sarasota Herald-Tribune*, February 5, 1963.

2. Ibid.

3. Les Hunter, interview, February 2012.

4. Ibid.

5. Ibid.

6. Ibid.

7. Ibid.

8. Ibid.

9. George Altman, interview by the author, December 2011.

10. Hunter, interview, February 2012.

11. Ibid.

12. Ibid.

13. Ibid.

14. Ibid.

15. Ibid.

16. Harkness, interview, January 2012.

17. Ibid.

18. Ibid.

19. Ibid.

20. Ibid.

21. Hunter, interview, February 2012.

22. Miller, interview, February 2012.

23. Bill Jauss, "Loyola Legend Rouse Dies," *Chicago Tribune*, June 2, 1999.

24. Miller, interview, February 2012.

25. "Greatest College Basketball Teams: Spotlight 1963 Loyola Ramblers Basketball Team."

26. Hunter, interview, February 2012.

27. Ibid.

28. Ibid.

Chapter 6

1. Harkness, interview, January 2012.

2. Ibid.

3. Ibid.

4. Ibid.

5. Ibid.

6. Ibid.

7. Ibid.

8. Miller, interview, February 2012.

9. Hunter, interview, February 2012.

10. Ed Stone, "Freshmen Brighten Loyola Cage Future," *Chicago American*, January 31, 1961.

11. Ibid.

12. Ibid.

13. Miller, interview, February 2012.

14. Ibid.

15. John Crnokrak, interview by the author, February 2012.

16. Ibid.

17. Ibid.

18. Ibid.

19. Ibid.

20. Chuck Wood, interview by the author, February 2012.

21. Egan, interview, January 2012.

22. Ibid.

Chapter 7

1. Jim Enright, "Height Brightens Loyola Cage Bid," *Chicago American*, November 28, 1961.
2. Hunter, interview, February 2012.
3. Egan, interview, January 2012.
4. Ibid.
5. Ibid.
6. Ibid.
7. Crnokrak, interview, February 2012.
8. Ibid.
9. Ibid.
10. Ibid.
11. Ibid.
12. Harkness, interview, January 2012.
13. Rochelle, interview, March 2012.
14. Ibid.
15. Ibid.
16. Harkness, interview, January 2012.
17. Hunter, interview, February 2012.
18. Ibid.
19. Miller, interview, February 2012.
20. Ibid.
21. Ibid.

Chapter 8

1. Harkness, interview, January, 2012.
2. Ibid.
3. Harkness, interview, January 2012.
4. Ibid.
5. Rochelle, interview, March 2012.
6. Ibid.
7. Miller, interview, February 2012.
8. Harkness, interview, January 2012.
9. Miller, interview, February 2012.
10. Ibid.
11. Hunter, interview, February 2012.
12. Wood, interview, February 2012.
13. Jim Enright, "Loyola Faces New Orleans Bias," *Chicago American*, January 23, 1962.

14. Egan, interview, January 2012.

15. Ibid.

16. Crnokrak, interview, February 2012.

17. Ibid.

18. Ibid.

19. Harkness, interview, January 2012.

20. Ibid.

21. Ibid.

22. Ibid.

23. Ibid.

24. Miller, interview, February 2012.

25. Harkness, interview, January 2012.

26. Rochelle, interview, March 2012.

27. Ibid.

28. "Racial Peace Prevails; Loyola Wins," *Chicago American*, January 24, 1962.

29. Harkness, interview, January 2012.

30. Hunter, interview, February 2012.

31. Crnokrak, interview, February 2012.

32. Hunter, interview, February 2012.

33. Wood, interview, February 2012.

34. Ibid.

35. Harkness, interview, January 2012.

36. Hunter, interview, February 2012.

37. Ibid.

38. Harkness, interview, January 2012.

Chapter 9

1. Jack Clarke, "North Dakota Tests Loyola," *Chicago Sun-Times*, December 3, 1962.

2. Jack Clarke, "Unbeaten Loyola Seeks Third in Row," *Chicago Sun-Times*, December 10, 1962.

3. Miller, interview, February 2012.

4. Harkness, interview, January 2012.

5. Ibid.

6. Marsh Schiewe, "Strategy for Seattle: Loyola May Slow Up," *Chicago Sun-Times*, December 21, 1963.

7. Ibid.

8. Jack Clarke, "Loyola Hits Tourney Trail," *Chicago Sun-Times*, December 26, 1962.

9. "Ireland Sees Arkansas As Threat to Win Skein," *Chicago American*, December 27, 1963.

10. Schiewe, "Strategy for Seattle."

11. Ibid.

12. Miller, interview, February 2012.

13. Ibid.

14. Rochelle, interview, March 2012.

15. Frank Perez, interview by the author, March 2012.

16. Rochelle, interview, March 2012.

Chapter 10

1. Rochelle, interview, March 2012.

2. Hunter, interview, February 2012.

3. Miller, interview, February 2012.

4. Hunter, interview, February 2012.

5. Miller, interview, February 2012.

6. Harkness, interview, January 2012.

7. Miller, interview, February 2012.

8. Harkness, interview, January 2012.

9. Ibid.

10. Miller, interview, February 2012.

11. Ibid.

12. Smith, interview, March 2012.

13. Ibid.

Chapter 11

1. Rochelle, interview, March 2012.

2. Ibid.

3. Perez, interview, March 2012.

4. Ibid.

5. Smith, interview, March 2012.

6. Ibid.

7. Dan Connaughton, interview by the author, March 2012.

8. Ibid.

9. Ibid.

10. Ibid.

11. Egan, interview, January 2012.

12. Harkness, interview, January 2012.

13. Egan, interview, January 2012.

14. Ibid.

15. Smith, interview, March 2012.

16. Ibid.

17. Ibid.

18. Ibid.

19. Ibid.

20. Harkness, interview, January 2012.

21. Perez, interview, March 2012.

22. Rochelle, interview, March 2012.

23. Egan, interview, January 2012.

24. Ibid.

25. Smith, interview, March 2012.

26. Hunter, interview, February 2012.

27. Ibid.

28. Bill Jauss, interview by the author, January 2010.

29. Egan, interview, January 2012.

30. Perez, interview, March 2012.

31. Crnokrak, interview, February 2012.

32. Smith, interview, March 2012.

33. Ibid.

34. Ibid.

35. Ibid.

Chapter 12

1. Miller, interview, February 2012.

2. Ibid.

3. Ibid.

4. Connaughton, interview, March 2012.

5. Ibid.

6. Bryant, interview, August 2012.

7. "Greatest College Basketball Teams: Spotlight 1968 Houston," Stellar College Basketball, http://www.stellarcollegebballgame.com/1968.

8. Chris Duncan, "Guy Lewis Still Waiting for Call from Hall," Associated Press, March 30, 2012.

9. Miller, interview, February 2012.

10. Egan, interview, January 2012.

11. Ibid.

12. Ibid.

13. Harkness, interview, January 2012.

14. Ibid.

15. Ibid.

16. Ibid.

17. Ibid.

18. Ibid.

19. Ibid.

20. Ibid.

21. Miller, interview, February 2012.

22. Ibid.

Chapter 13

1. Connaughton, interview, March 2012.

2. Egan, interview, January 2012.

3. Rochelle, interview, March 2012.

4. Ibid.

5. Ibid.

6. Ibid.

7. Ibid.

8. Ibid.

9. Ibid.

10. Ibid.

11. Connaughton, interview, March 2012.

12. Ibid.

13. Ibid.

14. Ibid.

15. Ibid.

16. Ibid.

17. Wood, interview, February 2012.

18. Ibid.

19. Ibid.

20. Ibid.

21. Egan, interview, January 2012.

22. Wood, interview, February 2012.

23. Hunter, interview, February 2012.

Chapter 14

1. Ed Stone, "Loyola Win Streak to 12, Marshall Thrown Off by Defense," *Chicago American*, January 4, 1963.

2. Harkness, interview, January 2012.

3. David Condon, "In the Wake of the News," *Chicago Tribune*, February 6, 1953.

4. Egan, interview, January 2012.

5. Condon, "In the Wake of the News."

6. Jim Enright, "14-Carat Smiles to Loyola," *Chicago American*, January 9, 1963.

7. Ed Stone, "'Johansson' to Loyola Cagers," *Chicago American*, date missing on clip.

8. Ed Stone, "Loyola Relaxed: Team Doesn't Feel Pressure: Ireland," *Chicago American*, January 23, 1963.

9. Ed Stone, "Marquette Next, but Loyola Looks Toward Cincy," *Chicago American*, February 8, 1963.

10. Stone, "Loyola Relaxed."

11. Condon, "In the Wake of the News."

12. Ed Stone, "Marquette Seeks Revenge, Battles Loyola Tonight," *Chicago American*, February 12, 1963.

13. Richard Dozer, "Ramblers to 2 in 1st Overtime: Jerry Harkness Gets Winning Basket," *Chicago Tribune*, February 13, 1963.

14. Wood, interview, February 2012.

15. Connaughton, interview, March 2012.

16. Ibid.

17. Miller, interview, February 2012.

18. Hunter, interview, February 2012.

19. Jack Clarke, "Loyola Swifties Shrug at Duke's Speed," *Chicago Sun-Times*, March 20, 1963.

20. Richard Dozer, "Plane with Team Forced to St. Louis," *Chicago Tribune*, February 20, 1963.

21. Ed Stone, "Loyola Rally Whips Ohio U. for 24th Win," *Chicago American*, February 28, 1963.

22. "Loyola Seeks 24th Win Tonight," *Chicago American*, February 27, 1963.

Chapter 15

1. Harkness, interview, January 2012.

2. Jack Clarke, "Loyola, Wichita Round It Up," *Chicago Sun-Times*, March 2, 1963.

3. Ed Stone, "Loyola Win Streak to 12, Marshall Thrown Off by Defense," *Chicago American*, January 4, 1963.

4. "Loyola Begins Preparing for NCAA Tournament," *Chicago American*, March 5, 1963.

5. Ed Stone, "NCAA Tests: Ramblers Battle Tennessee Tech Zone Defense," *Chicago American*, March 11, 1963.

6. Rochelle, interview, March 2012.

7. Egan, interview, January 2012.

8. Ibid.

9. Ibid.

10. Ibid.

11. Wood, interview, February 2012.

12. John Oldham, interview by the author, January 2012.

13. Ibid.

14. Ibid.

15. Ibid.

16. Connaughton, interview, March 2012.

17. Rochelle, interview, March 2012.

18. Hunter, interview, February 2012.

19. Harkness, interview, January 2012.

20. Oldham, interview, January 2012.

21. Ed Stone, "'Next Game's a 'Must,' Says Harkness, Ramblers Set Record in NCAA Win," *Chicago American*, March 12, 1963.

Chapter 16

1. "Mississippi and Meredith Remember," CNN broadcast, September 29, 2002.

2. Nick Bryant, "Black Man Who Was Crazy Enough to Apply to Ole Miss," *The Journal of Blacks in Higher Education* (2006).

3. Associated Press, "Ross Barnett, Segregationist, Dies; Governor of Mississippi in 1960s," *New York Times*, November 7, 1987.

4. Connaughton, interview, March 2012.

5. Ibid.

6. Miller, interview, February 2012.

7. Wood, interview, February 2012.

8. *Game of Change*, directed by Jerald Harkness (Team Marketing, 2008).

9. Ibid.

10. Ibid.

11. Bobby Shows, interview by the author, December, 2012.

12. *Game of Change*.

13. Terry Pluto, *Loose Balls: The Short, Wild Life of the American Basketball Association* (New York: Simon & Shuster, 1990), 106.

14. "Loyola Calm at Dixie Fuss," *Chicago Sun-Times*, March 8, 1963.

15. *Game of Change*.

16. Shows, interview, December 2012.

17. Jack Clarke, "Miss. State U. Escapes Dixie, Faces Loyola," *Chicago Sun-Times*, March 15, 1963.

18. Rochelle, interview, March 2012.

19. Hunter, interview, February 2012.

20. Ibid.

21. John Husar, "Ireland's Loyola Championed over Racism," *Chicago Tribune*, March 25, 1979.

22. Harkness, interview, January 2012.

23. Wood, interview, February 2012.

24. Harkness, interview, January 2012.

Chapter 17

1. Miller, interview, February 2012.

2. Harkness, interview, January 2012.

3. Ibid.

4. Jauss, interview, January 2010.

5. "Loyola Calm at Dixie Fuss," *Chicago Sun-Times*.

6. "Loyola Calm in Mississippi Furor," *Chicago Daily News*, March 7, 1963.

7. Bill Jauss, "The Issue: Loyola vs. Miss. State: Bulldogs Set for NCAA Tilt," *Chicago Daily News*, March 15, 1963.

8. Egan, interview, January 2012.

9. "Loyola Calm at Dixie Fuss," *Chicago Sun-Times*.

10. Jack Clarke, "No 'Soft Touch' at East Lansing, Loyola Warned," *Chicago Sun-Times*, March 13, 1963.

11. Harkness, interview, January 2012.

12. Connaughton, interview, March 2012.

13. Perez, interview, March 2012.

14. Ibid.

15. *Game of Change*.

16. Jauss, interview, January 2012.

17. *Game of Change*.

18. Wood, interview, February 2012.

19. Shows, interview, December 2012.

20. Wood, interview, February 2012.

21. Ibid.

22. Les Hunter, interview, February 2012.

23. Ibid.

24. Associated Press, "Miss. State, Loyola Trade High Esteem," *Chicago American*, March 16, 1963.

25. Ibid.

26. Ibid.

27. Bill Gleason, "Rambler Victory Best Birthday Gift for Rouse," *Chicago American*, March 16, 1963.

28. Ibid.

29. Bill Gleason, "What a Difference a Day Makes to Mississippi State Players," *Chicago American*, March 18, 1963.

30. Ibid.

31. *Game of Change*.

Chapter 18

1. Miller, interview, February 2012.

2. Rochelle, interview, March 2012.

3. Harkness, interview, January 2012.

4. Hunter, interview, February 2012.

5. "We Won on Backboards, Says Ireland," March 17, 1963.

6. Van Dyck, interview, March 2012.

7. Ibid.

8. Ibid.

9. Rochelle, interview, March 2012.

10. Wood, interview, February 2012.

11. Egan, interview, January 2012.

12. Ibid.

13. Robert Markus, "Harkness and Bubas Agree," *Chicago Tribune*, March 23, 1963.

14. Connaughton, interview, March 2012.

15. Stone, "'Johansson' to Loyola Cagers."

16. Stone, "Loyola Relaxed."

17. Rochelle, interview, March 2012.

18. Wood, interview, February 2012.

Chapter 19

1. Connaughton, interview, March 2012.

2. Red Rush, Loyola vs. Cincinnati radio broadcast, March 23, 1963.

3. Ibid.

4. Miller, interview, February 2012.

5. Wood, interview, February 2012.

6. Egan, interview, January 2012.

7. Connaughton, interview, March 2012.

8. Tay Baker, interview by the author, October 2011.

9. Hunter, interview, February 2012.

10. Red Rush, Loyola vs. Cincinnati radio broadcast, March 23, 1963.

11. Connaughton, interview, March 2012.

12. George Wilson, interview by the author, October 2011.

13. Connaughton, interview, March 2012.

14. Miller, interview, February 2012.

15. Tom Thacker, interview by the author, October 2011.

16. Red Rush, Loyola vs. Cincinnati radio broadcast, March 23, 1963.

17. Miller, interview, February 2012.

18. Harkness, interview, January 2012.

19. Hunter, interview, February 2012.

20. Wood, interview, February 2012.

21. Ibid.

22. Red Rush, Loyola vs. Cincinnati radio broadcast, March 23, 1963.

23. Rochelle, interview, March 2012.

24. Ibid.

25. Connaughton, interview, March 2012.

26. Jauss, "Loyola Legend Rouse Dies."

27. "'Unbelievable!' Cries Ireland," *Chicago Sun-Times*, March 24, 1963.

28. Jauss, "Loyola Rates as Team to Beat Next Year."

29. Thacker, interview, October 2012.

30. Kent Stephens, interview by the author, October 2011.

31. Perez, interview, March 2012.

32. Van Dyck, interview, March 2012.

Epilogue

1. Connaughton, interview, March 2012.

2. Miller, interview, February 2012.

3. Ibid.

4. Rochelle, interview, March 2012.

5. Connaughton, interview, March 2012.

6. Perez, interview, March 2012.

7. Wood, interview, February 2012.

8. Ferguson Jenkins, interview by the author, April 2012.

9. Smith, interview, March 2012.

10. Ibid.

11. Porter Moser, interview by the author, January 2012.

12. Grace Calhoun, interview by the author, January 2012.

13. Connaughton, interview, March 2012.

14. Fred Mitchell, "Loyola's Ireland Recalls How Times Have Changed Since 1963," *Chicago Tribune*, March 26, 1996.

15. Bill Jauss, "George Ireland, 88, Loyola Legend Remembered, Coach of 1963 NCAA Champs Influenced Many," *Chicago Tribune*, September 19, 2001.

16. Van Dyck, interview, March 2010.

17. Wood, interview, March 2012.

18. Miller, interview, February 2012

19. Ibid.

20. Harkness, interview, January 2012.

Postscript

1. "Game of Change" Symposium, December 2012.

2. Ibid.

3. Ibid.

4. John Egan, interview by the author, December 2012.

5. Paul Smulson, interview by the author, May 2013.

6. Ron Miller, interview by the author, May 2013.

7. Les Hunter, interview by the author, May 2013.

8. Egan, interview, December 2012.

9. Jerry Harkness, interview by the author, May 2013.

10. Egan, interview, December 2012.

11. Jerry Harkness, interview by the author, July 2013.

12. Ibid.

13. John Egan, interview by the author, July 2013.

14. Ibid.

15. Harkness, interview, May 2013.

16. Ibid.

A NOTE ON THE SOURCES

The vast majority of quotations for this project were gathered through interviews, either in person or via telephone, with all of the individuals listed in the notes.

However, in some cases, some important people connected to the Loyola championship story of 1963 were deceased at the time of this writing. Most important, head coach George Ireland, who recruited, assembled, and meshed the talent on the Ramblers, had passed away. Also, his assistant coach Johnny Lyne, as well as Vic Rouse, one of the starting players and stars of the team; Jim Rearden, a backup on the club; and Pablo Robertson, who was a player who was with the team for the first half of the season, had passed away.

Former Loyola players such as Billy Smith and Frank Perez (who have since passed away), along with Pablo Robertson, who played for the Ramblers but were not part of the NCAA tournament, added background about the times and the team. So did John Crnokrak, who played with the Loyola team the year before the championship and witnessed firsthand some of the racism the squad experienced on the road.

This was also true of some Mississippi State players and Cincinnati head coach Ed Jucker. Comments from other Mississippi State players were available, although head coach Babe McCarthy had also passed away. Cincinnati assistant coach Tay Baker was interviewed, and information on McCarthy was gleaned from books that covered his tenure as a head coach in the old American Basketball Association.

Governor Vaughn is one of the chief officials of the Harlem Globetrotters and provided information on Robertson, as did Hall of Fame pitcher Ferguson Jenkins, who played briefly for the Globetrotters with Robertson.

Hall of Fame coach Clarence Gaines, who had many insights to offer about the racial climate in the college basketball world of the period, had also passed away, but he left behind a detailed autobiography.

David Garrow's book examining the impact of the Reverend Martin Luther King, Jr., and the Southern Christian Leadership Conference on the civil rights era, helped explain the background of the racism the Loyola basketball players encountered.

During the 1962–63 season, four Chicago daily newspapers covered the Loyola basketball team during its home games (though not their regular-season road games) and provided contemporary accounts of games and developments involving the team, paying particular attention to the events leading up to Loyola's contest against Mississippi State in the NCAA tournament competition that became known as the Game of Change. The Chicago newspapers also followed the Ramblers through the five games they played in the NCAA tournament, providing box scores from each of the five games.

The Associated Press and United Press International reported on Loyola's regular-season away games, and many of the two wire services' accounts were available to review.

Two videos were used for research in the preparation of this book. The inspiring documentary *Game of Change* was conceived, directed, and produced by Jerald Harkness, son of Loyola captain and star Jerry Harkness, and does an extraordinary job of explaining the significance of that game. The other video was an edited tape of the Loyola–Cincinnati championship game. Unlike current-day NCAA championship games, the contest was not shown on prime-time television. It was the first NCAA title game shown on national television at all, albeit on tape delay. This video had the commentary by the TV broadcasters eliminated and replaced by the Chicago radio call. All of the time-outs were also eliminated, and there are no instant replays, just the continuous action.

Statistics and basic information on Ramblers players, such as their scoring averages, was obtained from Loyola sports information director Bill Behrns, who was also responsible for the preparation of the team's media guide.

Websites were consulted as a resource to double-check Loyola game dates and statistics.

Sports Illustrated and the *NCAA News* were each consulted for single articles that referred to the Ramblers. The author previously wrote pieces revolving around Loyola's NCAA title team for *Basketball Times*.

SELECTED BIBLIOGRAPHY

Full citation information provided in the notes.

Newspapers and Wire Services

Chicago American, Chicago Daily News, Chicago Sun-Times, Chicago Tribune, Racine (Wisconsin) Journal-Times, Associated Press, and United Press International.

Books

How to Be Fast, Daring, Different: 33 Ways to Achieve Personal and Professional Success by John Crnokrak; *They Call Me Big House* by Clarence E. Gaines and Clint Johnson; *Bearing the Cross: Martin Luther King, Jr. and the Southern Christian Leadership Conference* by David J. Garrow; *Loose Balls: The Short, Wild Life of the American Basketball Association* by Terry Pluto; and *Kentucky Colonels of the American Basketball Association* by Gary P. West and Lloyd Gardner.

Videos

Game of Change (documentary) and Loyola vs. Cincinnati, NCAA championship game, aired March 23, 1963.

Media Guides

Loyola Men's Basketball, 2006–07, 2011–12.

Websites

www.ramblermedia.com, www.collegehoopsnet.com, and www.stellarcollegebasketballgame.com.

Magazines

Basketball Times, NCAA News, and *Sports Illustrated.*

INDEX

Page numbers in italic refer to images.